THE
RELATION OF MOLIÈRE
TO
RESTORATION COMEDY

THE
RELATION OF MOLIÈRE
TO
RESTORATION COMEDY

By John Wilcox

BENJAMIN BLOM
New York

Printed in U.S.A. by
NOBLE OFFSET PRINTERS, INC.
NEW YORK 3, N. Y.

To N. K. W.

PREFACE

MY ATTENTION was first drawn to the subject of this volume when I observed the collision of opinion in two studies that appeared at almost the same time: namely, D. H. Miles's *The Influence of Molière on Restoration Comedy* (1910), and John Palmer's *The Comedy of Manners* (1913). My subsequent survey of earlier opinions revealed the fact that the conflict had gradually developed during the last hundred years. By the end of the nineteenth century, students of sources had found so many parallels that their labors culminated in the assertion that Restoration comedy was essentially a child of France. But all this evidence did not disturb the adherents of a contrary opinion, which has been reappearing ever since Dryden asserted it, that what Restoration comedy got from abroad lost all Gallic accent when it appeared on the English stage. Meanwhile, disgusted with the standards of Wycherley and Congreve, a third group declared that their comedy must surely have come from the French, because it is so immoral. Yet a fourth group insisted that this cannot be true, because the English plays are so indecent. Challenged by this confusion, I undertook the hazardous task of maintaining a sound and consistent judgment in a field where the evidence had already produced a large body of contradictory conclusions.

Obviously the same evidence could not lead different people to opposite conclusions except by faulty logic. Perhaps there would be more chance of reaching the truth if I gave consideration to an a priori logic of sources and influences. What constitutes proof that one author has borrowed from another? How could I set a standard sufficiently objective to keep me from merely selecting as fact what I found agreeable to believe? What is a literary influence? How can it be recognized? If influences vary in significance, how can these variations be determined, compared, contrasted? Conceding the intangibility of the basic facts and the subjectivity of the conclusions, I nevertheless tried to develop a system for guiding my judgments. This method, which I have described in Chapter II, is not exactly my invention; it is rather my attempt to make usefully explicit the processes that I think are instinctive with the best thinkers and implicit in sound scholarship.

The book has been developed by applying this method to the study of the primary materials. In it I undertake to find which Restoration plays contain borrowings from Molière, to tell the nature and the extent of these borrowings, and then to arrive at a just estimate of his influence on Restoration writers individually and on their comedy as a type.

To eliminate vexing irregularities in the exact form of Restoration play titles, I have modernized them, except in Appendix B. There I have followed the "Handlist of Restoration Plays" found in the latest edition of *A History of Restoration Drama, 1660-1700,* by Allardyce Nicoll, who reproduces original spelling, punctuation, and capitalization. The dates I have attached to Restoration plays, giving the time of first acting as nearly as it can be ascertained, are derived from the same authoritative compilation.

I am under obligation to several persons for assistance with details of form and style, most notably my wife. I wish to thank Professors Oscar James Campbell of Columbia University, Robert W. Babcock of Wayne University, and J. Paul Stoakes of Marshall College for their useful suggestions. Finally I am glad to declare my gratitude to Professor Paul Mueschke of the University of Michigan. From the time this study was first contemplated, he has aided me at every turn. With endless patience he has read and discussed outlines, preliminary drafts, and tentative conclusions. My debt to him is incalculable.

JOHN WILCOX

WAYNE UNIVERSITY
DETROIT
February 1, 1938

CONTENTS

I: THE BACKGROUND

DURING the first five years of the Parisian career of Jean-Baptiste Poquelin, *dit* Molière, the English began to borrow from his wealth of dramatic substance to deck their newly lighted stages.[1] After John Dryden scored his first success with *Sir Martin Mar-All, or the Feigned Innocence* (August, 1667), for which he had taken essential elements from the sensational French actor-playwright,[2] Molière was plundered on every hand. Fifteen authors were mentioned during their own age as borrowers from him: Aphra Behn, Thomas Betterton, John Caryl, John Crowne, William D'Avenant, John Dryden, Richard Flecknoe, John Lacy, Matthew Medbourne, Thomas Otway, Thomas Rawlins, Edward Ravenscroft, Charles Sedley, Thomas Shadwell, and William Wycherley. When Gerard Langbaine, "the great detector of plagiarism,"[3] wrote his handbook in 1691, he reported use of material from Molière in twenty-five plays of the period.[4]

[1] The reader will recall that Molière's Parisian period began late in 1658. Everyone agrees that Sir William D'Avenant's unimportant *The Playhouse to Be Let* (c. August, 1663) is the first Restoration play to employ material from him.

[2] Discussion of this borrowing is found below in Chap. III.

[3] Samuel Johnson's phrase. "Otway," in *Lives of the English Poets*, ed. by Hill, I, 242.

[4] *Account of the English Dramatick Poets*. Langbaine pointed out the following plagiarisms:

Mrs. Behn's *The False Count: Les Précieuses ridicules* (p. 20);

———— *Sir Patient Fancy: Le Malade imaginaire* (p. 21).

Betterton's [*The Amorous Widow*]: *Les Précieuses ridicules* (p. 445).

Caryl's *Sir Salomon, or the Cautious Coxcomb: L'École des femmes* (p. 549).

Crowne's *The Country Wit: Le Sicilien ou l'amour peintre* (p. 94);

———— *Sir Courtly Nice: Les Précieuses ridicules* (p. 97).

D'Avenant's *The Playhouse to Be Let: Le Cocu imaginaire* (p. 110).

Dryden's *Amphitryon: Amphitryon* (second page of Appendix);

———— *An Evening's Love, or the Mock Astrologer: Le Dépit amoureux* and *Les Précieuses ridicules* (p. 131 and p. 163);

———— *Sir Martin Mar-All: L'Étourdi* (p. 170).

The authors who made these "thefts" took various attitudes. Some acknowledged the debt openly; for example, in the epilogue to John Caryl's *Sir Salomon, or the Cautious Coxcomb,* which was probably staged in 1669 and certainly printed in 1671, one reads:

> What we have brought before you, was not meant
> For a new Play, but a new President;
> For we with Modesty our Theft avow,
> (There is some Conscience shewn in stealing too)
> And openly declare, that if our Cheer
> Does hit your Pallats, you must thank *Molliere:*
> *Molliere,* the famous *Shakespear* of this Age,
> Both when he Writes, and when he treads the Stage.[5]

Some made slight attempts to conceal their borrowings. Some offered explanations: Aphra Behn pleaded haste;[6] Shadwell, laziness;[7] Dryden, that he worked his borrowed matter over so thoroughly that it was really his own;[8] and Wycherley merely ridiculed those authors who had an "Itch of being thought Origi-

---

Flecknoe's *The Damoiselles à la Mode: Les Précieuses ridicules, L'École des femmes,* and *L'École des maris* (p. 201).
Lacy's *The Dumb Lady: Le Médecin malgré lui* (p. 318).
Medbourne's *Tartuffe: Le Tartuffe* (p. 367).
Otway's *The Cheats of Scapin:* "from a *French* Comedy of *Molliere*" [i.e., *Les Fourberies de Scapin*] (p. 397).
Ravenscroft's *The Careless Lovers: M. de Pourceaugnac* (p. 419);
———— *The London Cuckolds: L'École des femmes* (p. 421);
———— *Mamamouchi: M. de Pourceaugnac* and *Le Bourgeois Gentilhomme* (p. 422);
———— *Scaramouch: Le Bourgeois Gentilhomme* and *Le Mariage forcé* (p. 423).
Rawlins' *Tom Essence: Le Cocu imaginaire* (p. 552).
Sedley's *The Mulberry Garden: L'École des maris* (p. 487). [Merely notes resemblance.]
Shadwell's *Bury Fair: Les Précieuses ridicules* (p. 445);
———— *The Libertine:* "*L'Athée Foudroyé*" [i.e., *Don Juan*] (p. 448);
———— *The Miser: L'Avare* (p. 449);
———— *The Sullen Lovers: Les Fâcheux* (p. 451).
Wycherley's *The Plain Dealer: Le Misanthrope* (p. 515).
In all he cites eighteen plays of Molière, five of them more than once.
[5] [John Caryl], *Sir Salomon, or the Cautious Coxcomb* (London, 1671), p. [102].
[6] Langbaine, *op. cit.,* p. 18.
[7] See the preface to *The Miser,* in *Works of Shadwell* (1720), Vol. III.
[8] *Dramatic Works of Dryden,* ed. by Scott-Saintsbury, III, 249-53.

nals." [9] Langbaine generally defended the English authors whose plagiarisms he so diligently traced, because he thought they improved what they took; the only exception of importance was Dryden, whom he attacked with evident gusto.[10] Some forty years later, when Voltaire visited England, he sent back the contrary opinion, "Les Anglais ont pris, ont déguisé, ont gaté la plupart des pièces de Molière." [11] But the idea that Molière's influence and example was an important contribution to Restoration comedy was not voiced before 1835.[12]

[9] *Posthumous Works of William Wycherley* (1728), Part I, p. 3.

[10] *Op. cit.*, pp. 130-77.

[11] "Sur la comédie," *Lettres sur les Anglais*, 1734, in *Oeuvres Complètes de Voltaire*, V, 34.

[12] As in Langbaine, in the histories of the English stage down to John Genest, *Some Account of the English Stage* (1832), references to Molière are made as separate incidental notes on specific plays, free from conclusions about French influence or impressions that it was preëminent. Langbaine was the chief observer of likenesses between Molière and Restoration plays. The rest were generally content to repeat his discoveries with modifications, some of which are intelligent additions, others apparently careless omissions.

[Charles Gildon], *Lives and Characters of the English Dramatick Poets* (1699), softens the asperities of Langbaine's remarks.

[Giles Jacob], *Poetical Register* (1723), II, 292-95, writes a note on Molière and tabulates his plays. After each play he lists the titles of English dramas which have borrowed from it. This matter is essentially a repetition of Langbaine's findings brought down to date. For the Restoration period he makes three additions to Langbaine; viz.: Ravenscroft's *Wrangling Lovers: Le Dépit amoureux;* Betterton's *The Amorous Widow: George Dandin;* and Wright's *Female Vertuosoes: Les Femmes savantes.* He also ascribes Carlel's [i.e., Caryl's] *Sir Salomon* to *L'École des maris,* but this is surely a misprint for *L'École des femmes,* which was mentioned by Langbaine. Jacob shows a livelier interest in the evidence than any of the others between Langbaine and Genest.

Lives of the Poets by "Mr. [Theophilus] Cibber and other Hands" (1753) suppresses and softens some of Langbaine's "plagiarisms," but does not add any.

David [Erskine] Baker, *Companion to the Playhouse* (1764) repeats the information in Jacob, adding the fact that Wycherley's *The Country Wife* is based on *L'École des femmes,* which had been noted earlier by Voltaire in "Sur la comédie," *op. cit.,* V, 34.

Mr. [Charles] Dibdin, *Complete History of the English Stage* [1800], does not retain all the earlier citations; for example, he dismisses Ravenscroft with such contempt, IV, 204, that Molière is not mentioned.

Genest seems to have added the unimportant Penkethman's *Love without Interest* as derived from *Le Mariage forcé, op. cit.,* II, 164. But he drops several, Mrs. Behn's *The False Count,* Flecknoe's *Damoiselles à la Mode,* and Ravenscroft's *London Cuckolds.* He is the first one after Langbaine to discuss any of the similarities between English plays and Molière with enough detail to suggest that he had made the comparisons himself. For example, compare Langbaine, *op. cit.,* p. 419, with Genest, *op. cit.,* I, 125-27.

Critics of the Romantic period and their early Victorian successors seemed to find the contrasts between Restoration comedy and Molière more significant than the resemblances. Often they saw no reason to mention Molière when they were discussing plays in which they knew there were elements borrowed from him. In his *Life of Dryden* (1806), Sir Walter Scott admitted French influence in Restoration comedy except in its "scenes of coarse and naked indelicacy" and except in its structure, which he found more like Spanish drama. A few years later he specifically denied French influence on comic form.[13] William Hazlitt spoke discriminatingly about the borrowings of Wycherley and Vanbrugh from Molière, without ascribing very much to the source.[14] Henry Hallam agreed with Scott that the "French theatre...guided the criticism of Charles's court," although he ascribed the coarse tone of the comedies to "the state of society itself."[15] Leigh Hunt was obviously aware of French material in some of the plays he edited, but he never suggested French sources as a major factor in the comic art of the Restoration.[16] T. B. Macaulay said, when speaking of the tone of the plays written during the Restoration:

In these changes it is impossible not to recognize the influence of French precept and of French example....It would have been well if our writers had also copied the decorum [of the French]....Our theatre was indebted in that age for many plots and characters to Spain, to

[13] See Scott-Saintsbury edition of *Dramatic Works of Dryden,* I, 62-63. In his "Essay on the Drama," first published in the supplement to the *Encyclopedia Britannica,* 1819, Scott mentions Molière only once, and then in reference to a single Restoration play. He says unequivocally, "[The comic poets of the Restoration made] great improvement...in point of art....They did not, however, so far surrender the liberties and immunities of their predecessors, as to receive laws from the French critics." The essay is reprinted in *Prose Works of Sir Walter Scott,* VI, 364.

[14] "Wycherley, Congreve, Vanbrugh, and Farquhar," *Lectures on the English Comic Writers* (1819), Lecture IV, pp. 133-76.

[15] *Introduction to the Literature of Europe* (1837-39), IV, 481-96.

[16] Hunt, ed., *Dramatic Works of Wycherley, Congreve, Vanbrugh, and Farquhar* (1840).

France, and to the old English masters: but whatever our dramatists touched they tainted.[17]

By the middle of the nineteenth century Restoration comedies had long since disappeared from the English stage, and most Victorians seem to have followed Macaulay's advice not to read them. In the absence of information, false generalizations are likely to pass unchallenged; often they develop into assumptions that plague later scholarship. For example, Thackeray gave a most striking expression to the traditional tendency to blame the French for anything of questionable morality. In this case he ignored the evidence completely, but who knew the plays well enough to denounce the judgment? In writing about Congreve, he said:

How can I introduce to you that merry and shameless Comic Muse who won him such a reputation? Nell Gwynn's servant fought the other footmen for having called his mistress bad names; and in like manner, and with pretty like epithets, Jeremy Collier attacked that godless, reckless Jezebel, the English comedy of this time, and called her what Nell Gwynn's man's fellow-servants called Nell Gwynn's man's mistress—the servants of the theatre, Dryden, Congreve, and others, defended themselves with the same success, and for the same cause which set Nell's lackey fighting. She was a disreputable, daring, laughing, painted French baggage, that Comic Muse. She came over from the continent with Charles (who chose many more of his female friends there) at the Restoration—a wild, dishevelled Lais, with eyes bright with wit and wine—a saucy court-favourite that sate at the King's knees, and laughed in his face, and when she showed her bold cheeks at her chariot-window, had some of the noblest and most famous people of the land bowing round her wheel. She was kind and popular enough, that daring Comedy, that audacious poor Nell—she was gay and generous, kind, frank, as such people can afford to be: and the men who lived with her and laughed with her, took her pay and drank her wine, turned out when the Puritans hooted her, to fight and de-

[17] *History of England* (1849), I, 370-74.

fend her. But the jade was indefensible, and it is pretty certain her servants knew it.[18]

The reader of Thackeray's time would accept this statement and associate it with a host of other evidences of French influence on Restoration England. He knew that Charles the Second's mother was French, that he spent much of his exile within Gallic borders, and that he even drew a pension from Louis XIV. He was told that Charles derived his manners, his fashions, his levity, and his immorality from France. It was generally known that, as the Golden Age of Louis XIV developed, the English did bring from France literary doctrines, models, and materials. The plays of Corneille and Racine had enjoyed an extensive vogue on the English stage during the period of the Restoration, and were known to have exerted great force in the development of English neoclassic tragedy. French romance—d'Urfé's *L'Astrée,* de la Calprenède's *Cléopâtre, Cassandre,* and *Pharamond,* de Scudéry's *Le Grand Cyrus, Clélie,* and *Almahide,* to mention the examples most heard of—had left indelible imprint on the substance and style of heroic drama, almost concealing the possibility that it could be descended from Jacobean dramatic styles. So the time was ripe for the sweeping dictum that Molière was the most significant influence on English comedy during the Restoration. This opinion was given by the manuals,[19] from which one could read, for example, that "With the Restoration of Charles II, begins the period of French influence upon English literature,—an influence that was not effectually broken until the time of the French Revolution,"[20] a general statement, which may be vaguely true, but which certainly leads to an unproved assumption when ap-

---

[18] "Congreve and Addison," in *English Humourists* (1853), pp. 57-58.

[19] Conventional literary opinions may be advantageously sought in manuals and textbooks for, in their efforts at brevity and simplicity, such works lack the discriminations and qualifications that characterize those of broader scope and of more original character.

[20] Morley, *Manual of English Literature,* rev. by Taylor (1879), p. 399.

plied to the comic drama. Another textbook made the application with the specific declaration that during the Restoration "In comedy...a new school arose, of which the tone and form may certainly be traced to the unrivalled genius of Molière."[21] Thus during the very time when most critics were too little interested in Restoration comedy to read it, the assumption developed and grew into a literary commonplace.

Encouraged perhaps by the desire to praise Molière, scholarly studies began to marshall specific evidence with which to support and expand the common view. The first important publication of this latter sort came in 1875. Henri Van Laun, a schoolmaster of French at Edinburgh and the translator of Taine, published a translation of Molière with references to English "plagiarisms" in extensive appendices.[22] He brought Congreve and Farquhar into the discussion for the first time, added seven new plays to the list, and alleged twenty-one new borrowings.[23] The introduction of Congreve's name among the imitators of Molière is especially significant.[24] Hitherto the lists of borrowers

[21] Arnold, *Manual of English Literature,* American ed. rev. (1876), p. 199.

[22] *Dramatic Works of Molière Rendered into English.* The citations are repeated in "Les Plagiaires des Molière," *Le Moliériste,* II (1880-81), 143-49, 235-40, 303-7, and III (1881-82), 52-62, 137-46.

[23] These figures are based upon the Langbaine list, as it was modified by critics from his time until Genest's (see notes 4 and 12 above). Van Laun's additions are as follows:
Mrs. Behn's *Sir Patient Fancy: L'Amour médecin.*
Congreve's *Love for Love: Don Juan, Le Misanthrope, L'Avare;*
────── *The Way of the World: Le Misanthrope.*
Crowne's *Country Wit: Amphitryon, La Comtesse d'Escarbagnas, M. de Pourceaugnac.*
Farquhar's *Love and a Bottle: Le Bourgeois Gentilhomme.*
Flecknoe's *Damoiselles à la Mode: Le Cocu imaginaire.*
Otway's *The Soldier's Fortune: Le Cocu imaginaire, L'École des maris, L'École des femmes, Les Précieuses ridicules.*
Ravenscroft's *Canterbury Quests* [*sic,* i.e., *Guests*]: *M. de Pourceaugnac;*
────── *Scaramouch: Les Fourberies de Scapin.*
Shadwell's *Sullen Lovers: Le Misanthrope, Le Mariage forcé.*
Wycherley's *The Gentleman Dancing Master: l'École des maris;*
────── *The Plain Dealer: La Critique de l'école des femmes.*

[24] I do not undertake to settle the minor issue of exactly which scholar brought the name of Congreve into this question for the first time, but I have not found any clear mention very much prior to Van Laun. For example, Claas Humbert, who

had included none of those who had written the finest comedies of manners except Wycherley. A little later Sir Edmund Gosse advanced Sir George Etherege as the first author of a comedy in the manner that culminated in Congreve and as the first Restoration author to understand and imitate Molière.[25] A German dissertation soon amplified Wycherley's generally admitted use of him.[26] Another dissertation then said Dryden had borrowed from him in five plays in addition to the three originally named by Langbaine.[27] The general relation of Molière to Restoration comedy was more conservatively outlined, however, in Hartmann's statement:

had staunchly defended Molière as a comic dramatist from what he considered disparagement by Shakespeare idolators (see *Molière, Shakespeare, und die deutsche Kritik,* 1869), in 1874 wrote (*Molière in England,* p. 8): "Aus dem 17. Jahrhundert sind mir keine englischen Urtheile über Molière bekannt geworden, aus dem achtzehnten nur zwei. Wie sehr er aber gerade damals in England bewundert wurde, zeigen die vielen Bearbeitungen und Uebersetzungen Molièrischer Stücke, sowie der Einfluss, welchen er auf die englische Comödie ausübte. Die grössten Lustspieldichter und komischen Schriftsteller jener Zeit suchten eine Ehre darin, vollständige Werke von ihm oder Bruchstücke aus denselben auf ihre Bühne zu verpflanzen. Später wird von den einzelnen Comödien insbesondere die Rede sein, und da mögen jene Uebersetzungen, Bearbeitungen und Nachahmungen eine Stelle finden. Hier genüge die Bemerkung, dass Männer, wie Dryden, Otway, Wicherley, Congreve, Vanbrugh, Cibber, Foote, und vor Allem der grosse Fielding und Sheridan unter diesen Schülern."

[25] "Sir George Etheredge. A Neglected Chapter of English Literature," *The Cornhill Magazine,* XLIII (1881). Reprinted in his *Seventeenth Century Studies* (1883). Gosse found Etherege's specific borrowings to be as follows:
    The Comical Revenge: L'Étourdi, Le Dépit amoureux, and *Les Précieuses ridicules; She Would If She Could: Tartuffe.*
    He dallies with the idea that *The Man of Mode* might have borrowed from *Les Précieuses ridicules,* but does not assert it clearly.

[26] Klette, *William Wycherley's Leben und dramatische Werke* (1883), added to previous allegations of borrowings the following:
    Love in a Wood: L'École des maris, and *L'École des femmes; The Gentleman Dancing Master: L'École des femmes; The Country Wife: L'École des maris, Le Tartuffe,* and *L'Impromptu de Versailles.*

[27] Hartmann, *Einfluss Molière's auf Dryden's komisch-dramatische Dichtungen* (1885). His list of borrowings adds the following to Langbaine's (see note 4 above):
    An Evening's Love: L'École des maris; The Assignation: L'Étourdi, Tartuffe; Limberham: Les Fâcheux, Tartuffe; Love Triumphant (tragicomedy): *M. de Pourceaugnac; Marriage à la Mode* (tragicomedy): *Les Précieuses ridicules, L'École des maris, Le Bourgeois Gentilhomme; The Spanish Friar* (tragicomedy): *Le Cocu imaginaire.*

Dieser tiefere Gehalt, der dem französischen Lustspiel und vorzüg-
lich dem Molière's erst die rechte Weihe verlieh, ging bei der Nachah-
mung seitens der englischen Dichter durchaus nicht mit in das
englische Lustspiel über. Man wandte sich zu den Franzosen und
speciell zu Molière, nicht weil man die eigne Bühne auf eine höhere
Stufe der Kunst zu bringen bestrebt war, sondern weil die Werke der
französischen Dichter einen reichen Schatz neuen Stoffes boten, um
den man in dieser Zeit der Schnell- und Massenproduktion, welche die
Bühne forderte, oft verlegen war.[28]

When Gosse wrote his *Life of William Congreve*,[29] he ignored
Van Laun's findings on *Love for Love,* but added some others
for himself.[30] He turned up a few vague parallels which he advanced as foundation for an asserted influence. He resisted any
temptation to believe, as his thesis would urge him to do, that
all the resemblances were specific borrowings; but someone is
always ready to perform that doubtful service: simultaneously
and independently, Dr. Alexander Bennewitz produced a dissertation with plenty of such assertions. Congreve, he said, had
simply adopted Molière's characters and plots wholesale.[31] In
The Old Bachelor, which Gosse said offered "no positive evidence of the study of Molière," Bennewitz found that twelve of
Molière's plays had been used! In *The Double Dealer,* he found
four to add to Gosse's three. In *Love for Love* and *The Way of
the World,* where Gosse found no precise parallels, Bennewitz
cited borrowings from fourteen plays of Molière's, from some
of the plays many times.[32] Another dissertation added Wycher-

---

[28] *Ibid.,* p. 6.

[29] In English Men of Letters Series, 1888, rev., 1924.

[30] *The Double Dealer* "has some vague analogy with *Tartuffe*" (*ibid.,* p. 53).
Le Misanthrope and *Les Femmes savantes* are also named as sources for elements of
the play (*ibid.,* pp. 54-55). None of these judgments are altered in the revised edition
of 1924. See pp. 42-43 of the later edition.

[31] *Molière's Einfluss auf Congreve* (1889), p. 13: "... unserer Behauptung—Molière
ist Quelle für Congreve."

[32] Bennewitz's list of alleged borrowings follows:
*The Old Batchelor: Le Mariage forcé, Don Juan, Le Misanthrope, L'École des
maris, L'École des femmes, M. de Pourceaugnac, George Dandin, Les Fourberies de*

ley's *The Country Wife* and Congreve's *The Double Dealer* to the list of plays influenced by *Le Misanthrope*.[33] Still another brought Shadwell's *Bury Fair* under the influence of *Les Femmes savantes*.[34] Thus specialists in source studies kept reporting more and more parallels between Molière and Restoration comedy, many of which are doubtless "like the geometrical sort, in that though followed back to infinity they never meet." [35]

During this very time a few critics and scholars steadily reiterated the essential independence of Restoration comedy. In his histroy of English literature (1864), Hippolyte Taine took the position outlined previously by Macaulay. "Ce théâtre [la comédie de la Restauration]...se forme en même temps que celui de Molière...et d'après lui." [36] Despite French influences, the brutal [37] Englishman cannot keep up with the taste of the refined French:

La comédie française devient un modèle, comme la politesse française. On les copie l'une et l'autre en les altérant, sans les égaler.... L'Angleterre la [France] suit dans cette voie...mais à distance, et tirée de côté par ses inclinations nationales.[38]

He borrows only to degrade:

Scapin, Les Précieuses ridicules, Les Femmes savantes, Le Dépit amoureux, L'Étourdi, La Princesse d'Élide (ibid., pp. 23-24).

The Double Dealer: Tartuffe, Les Femmes savantes, Les Précieuses ridicules, Les Fourberies de Scapin, M. de Pourceaugnac, George Dandin, L'École des femmes (ibid., pp. 26-44).

Love for Love: L'Avare, Le Misanthrope, Les Amants magnifiques, Les Fâcheux, L'École des femmes, L'École des maris, Don Juan, M. de Pourceaugnac, Le Malade imaginaire, Tartuffe, Le Misanthrope, L'Étourdi, Les Fourberies de Scapin (ibid., p. 76).

The Way of the World: L'École des femmes, M. de Pourceaugnac, Le Misanthrope, La Comtesse d'Escarbagnas, Le Malade imaginaire (ibid., pp. 79-88).

Incidentally, this was all competently deflated less than ten years later by Schmidt (*William Congreve, sein Leben und seine Lustspiele*).

[33] Ferchlandt, *Molière's Misanthrop und seine englischen Nachahmungen* (1907).

[34] Heinemann, *Shadwell-Studien* (1907), pp. 71-105. It had been previously assigned to the influence of *Les Précieuses ridicules* only.

[35] I borrow the quip from Lucas, *Seneca and Elizabethan Tragedy*, p. 118.

[36] *Histoire de la littérature anglaise*, III, 99.

[37] "Si on gratte la morale qui sert d'enveloppe [en Angleterre], la brute apparaît dans sa violence et sa laideur" (*ibid.*, III, 13).

[38] *Ibid.*, III, pp. 97-98.

Si Wycherley emprunte à quelque écrivain un personnage, c'est pour le violenter ou le dégrader jusqu'au niveau des siens. . . . S'il invente une fille presque honnête, Hippolyta, il commence par lui mettre dans la bouche des parolles telles qu'on n'en peut rien transcrire.[39]

To the earlier critical opinion of Scott, Leigh Hunt, Macaulay, and Taine that French influence did not go very far in explaining why Restoration comedy was what it was, Alexandre Beljame, A. W. Ward, and Louis Charlanne gave essential assent. All these readily conceded the extensive use of material from Molière, but when reading him in comparison with Restoration comedy, they found such differences that they did not see how the borrowings could account for what the English authors wrote.[40] There remained, in short, a conflict between myopic specialists in source studies and the broader-viewed readers like Ward and Charlanne.

The need of a comprehensive study of the problem as a whole was evident, and several works appeared as though in answer to this need. The first two of these have won almost no other notice than a casual mention in bibliographies.[41] They have made no significant addition to our knowledge of the problem and do not solve the critical difficulties.[42] In 1910 however Dudley H.

[39] *Ibid.,* III, 53-54.

[40] Beljame, *Le Public et les hommes de lettres en Angleterre au dix-huitième siècle* (1883), describes Restoration comedy (pp. 48-56), without reference to Molière, "car tout se modelait sur leurs goûts."
Ward, *English Dramatic Literature* (1875, II, 477), says, "Molière was copied by our English dramatists more unscrupulously than probably any other writer has been copied before or since; but neither his spirit nor his manner descended to his copyists." Writing simultaneously with Van Laun, he assembled the evidence of borrowing substantially in accord with Langbaine and Genest. His critical interpretation and the list of borrowings were repeated in the revised edition of 1899 (III, 315 n, 318), with a slight verbal shift and the addition of two or three borrowings.
Charlanne, *L'Influence française en Angleterre au xviie siècle* (1906) almost copies Ward's words in his summary (p. 372): "En somme, il ne passe presque rien de l'esprit et de la manière de Molière chez les comiques anglais."

[41] Harvey-Jellie, *Les Sources du théâtre anglais à l'époque de la restauration* (1906); Kerby, *Molière and the Restoration Comedy in England* (1907).

[42] I concur fully in this judgment of Miles, *Influence of Molière on Restoration Comedy* (p. 224), and of Gillet, *Molière en Angleterre* (pp. 9-10).

Miles published *The Influence of Molière on Restoration Comedy*. The peculiar distinction of the English comedy of manners, he said, came from plays of the type that Molière developed, a comedy of manners that realistically mirrors the fads and follies of society without criticizing them.[43] When Etherege wrote his initial comedy, we learn, he sought to surpass current English plays by imitating Molière's success in bringing recognizable portraits of contemporary people to the stage.[44] Wycherley also adopted this method in making a "close transcript from contemporary social life," being inspired probably by Etherege's example.[45] The same influences brought Dryden to social comedy. By all these, we are assured, Molière was transplanted to England. Miles found, however, that the lesser dramatists were not influenced, although they delved in the same mine: they took only his materials; the leading playwrights, except Wycherley, caught his spirit.[46] Molière's employment of comic scenes which have little bearing on the plot was imitated with avidity and became a pervasive influence on the vast majority of Restoration playwrights; otherwise his plot structure influenced the English only in minor ways.[47] It seems that he taught the devices of irony, repetition, and staccato thrusts to Etherege, Crowne, and Congreve, but not the prevailing tone of Restoration dialogue, which was really a continuation of the European tendency toward preciosity, against which Molière had launched a satire.[48] The Frenchman taught the dramatic device of overdrawing characters to provide emphasis, but his English borrowers seldom kept the spirit of the original figures. Those who really learned the spirit were important playwrights who "adopted Molière's conception of comedy." [49] By attaching a detailed appendix of alleged borrowings, Miles completed the general impression that almost all Restoration comedy was deeply indebted to Molière. Retaining

[43] *Op. cit.*, p. 33.
[44] *Ibid.*, pp. 61-68.
[45] *Ibid.*, pp. 68-75.
[46] *Ibid.*, pp. 79-99.
[47] *Ibid.*, pp. 109-32.
[48] *Ibid.*, pp. 162-89.
[49] *Ibid.*, pp. 133-60.

most of the parallels accumulated before his day, he made many increases, chiefly in connection with Crowne, Dryden, Ravenscroft, and Shadwell. With Van Laun's total of thirty-four plays raised to fifty-seven, he made the number of specific citations very impressive.[50]

Heralding a revival of interest in Restoration comedy as artistic literature, came the book of John Palmer, in which one finds no evidence of faith in any influence at all from Molière. Palmer joined issue squarely with Miles when he explained Restoration comedy as "an independent growth springing spontaneously from

---

[50] Miles's additions to previous lists are given below. His refusals to accept previous findings are not indicated; these may be compiled by comparing Miles (*ibid.*, pp. 223-41), with footnotes 4, 12, 23, 25, 26, 27, 30, and 32 above.
Mrs. Behn's *Sir Patient Fancy: M. de Pourceaugnac.*
Crowne's *The Country Wit: Le Tartuffe, Les Femmes savantes;*
——— *The English Friar: Le Tartuffe, La Comtesse d'Escarbagnas, L'Avare;*
——— *The Married Beau: Les Précieuses ridicules;*
——— *Sir Courtly Nice: Le Tartuffe, Les Femmes savantes.*
Dryden's *Amphitryon: Le Mariage forcé;*
——— *Love Triumphant: L'Étourdi;*
——— *The Spanish Friar: L'École des femmes, La Médecin malgré lui.*
Etherege's *The Man of Mode: Les Précieuses ridicules.*
Farquhar's *Love and a Bottle: M. de Pourceaugnac.*
Lacy's *The Dumb Lady: Les Fourberies de Scapin, L'Amour médecin.*
Otway's *The Atheist: L'École des femmes, Les Fâcheux.*
Ravenscroft's *The Canterbury Guests: Le Mariage forcé, Le Bourgeois Gentilhomme;*
——— *The Careless Lovers: Les Précieuses ridicules, Le Bourgeois Gentilhomme, Le Médecin malgré lui.*
Shadwell's *The Amorous Bigot: L'Avare, Les Précieuses ridicules, L'École des maris, Les Femmes savantes;*
——— *Bury Fair: Le Misanthrope, Le Bourgeois Gentilhomme, La Comtesse d'Escarbagnas;*
——— *Epsom Wells: Le Médecin malgré lui, Le Misanthrope;*
——— *The Humorists: Le Misanthrope;*
——— *The Scowrers: L'École des maris;*
——— *The Squire of Alsatia: L'École des maris;*
——— *The Woman Captain: L'Avare, L'École des maris;*
——— *The Virtuoso: L'École des maris, Le Misanthrope;*
——— *The Volunteers: Les Précieuses ridicules, L'École des maris.*
Vanbrugh's *The Relapse: Le Bourgeois Gentilhomme, L'École des maris.*
Wright's *The Female Vertuosoes: M. de Pourceaugnac, Le Malade imaginaire, Le Mariage forcé, Les Fourberies de Scapin.*
Gillet (*op. cit.*) centered his attention on the first ten years of the Restoration. He asserts the existence of a profound influence from Molière on twelve plays of the decade, citing thirty-three borrowings in his tabulation (pp. 144-47).

the impulse of English Restoration Society to view itself in re-
flexion upon the stage."[51] Scholars have since developed many
details of the growing opinion that, despite foreign borrowings,
these plays are English in most essential respects[52] and that
much of the "subject-matter which characterizes Restoration
comedy is to be found in the Elizabethan plays down to the
closing of the theatres (1642)."[53] Miss Lynch presented a large
amount of evidence of the continuity of Jacobean social attitudes
in Restoration successes.[54] John H. Wilson showed that the late
seventeenth century was greatly influenced by Beaumont and
Fletcher, to whom he traced the vogue for plays having "as their
foundation the combat between the sexes, which may result in
marriage, fornication or adultery."[55] Numerous stock situations
and stock plots of Restoration comedies, Wilson found, resemble
Beaumont and Fletcher; for example, the bringing of a woman
hater to his knees, a lover's counterfeiting ailments to induce a
mistress to relent, women's bold actions in men's dress, and trick
substitution in the marriage at the denouement. In discussing resemblances of tone, Wilson mentioned cynical gaiety, "disbelief
in the virtue of women and the honesty of men," frankness in
matters of sex, and obscene wit. Both groups of plays treat marriage as the "last resort of the worn out or impoverished rake,"
a "prison for gentlemen," or "an opportunity for women to be
promiscuous" with impunity. In both there are regularly mixtures
of high life with low, of romance with comedy, of satire with
realism, and of intrigue farce with tragicomedy.[56]

[51] *Comedy of Manners* (1913), p. 66.
[52] Nicoll, *Restoration Drama* (1923), pp. 168-81.
[53] Dobrée, *Restoration Comedy* (1924), p. 39.
[54] *Social Mode of Restoration Comedy* (1926).
[55] *Influence of Beaumont and Fletcher on Restoration Drama* (1928), p. 80.
[56] *Ibid.*, pp. 80-90. Wilson summarizes (pp. 116-17) as follows: "The two groups
of dramas [i.e. Beaumont and Fletcher's comedies and Restoration comedies] have
many traits in common. Both expressed a cynical attitude toward marriage and sex;
both dealt in veiled or outright obscenity and in personal, pointed wit.... Both groups
of dramas made use of certain stock situations of intrigue and adventure; they handled

That Ben Jonson also remained a vital force in comedy to the end of the seventeenth century was shown in a study by Paul Mueschke, who pointed out that the traditional emphasis upon Jonson's use of "humors" has hindered the observation of his keen social satire. Using Miss Lynch's discovery of the significance of social consciousness as the basis of his study, Dr. Mueschke demonstrated the presence in Jonson of a hitherto unsuspected social criticism:

> Jonson deliberately relates his characters to social standards. Jonson's utilization of the comic possibilities of social affectation begins in *Every Man in His Humour,* continues through *Every Man out of His Humour,* reaches its culmination in *Epicoene,* and declines in *The Devil is an Ass.* In these four plays are anticipated the social philosophy, the character types, and the dramatic principles out of which the Comedy of Manners was molded. Jonson's contribution to the origin of Restoration comedy is three-fold: in portraits drawn with sufficient skill to serve as models for his contemporaries, he continued the socialization of the Elizabethan gull; with a philosophy cynical enough to attract the sophisticated, he presented a group of wits who consciously formulate and employ an insidious code of seduction; and through a keen sense of dramatic values, he exploited the comic possibilities arising from the juxtaposition of true-wits and would-bes.[57]

William H. Hickerson followed with an analysis of the relation of James Shirley to his predecessors. Fletcherian cynicism and wit centered about a witty woman who affected scorn toward the rakes who pursued her. By her wit she managed to win the one she wanted as a husband. Fletcher repeated this pattern regularly. Shirley's contribution to the Caroline comedy resulted from

---

these situations in nearly identical fashions. Both made use of stock characters, and evidence is clear that the chief characters of the later comedy, the wild gallant and his witty mistress, can have come only from the Beaumont and Fletcher comedy. Artificial characters, in artificial settings, going through amorous intrigues, giving utterance to cynical, gay, often suggestive dialogues—this is Restoration comedy and it is also the comedy of Beaumont and Fletcher."

[57] "Prototypes of Restoration Wits and Would-Bes in Ben Jonson's Realistic Comedy" (1929), p. 192.

his success in combining Jonson and Fletcher. Wits and would-bes created after the model of Jonson were blended with the Fletcherian rakes and witty women.

The plays with which we have been dealing in the second period of Shirley's development show a growth ... toward an artificial socialized comedy ... [which] arises from an attempt ... to depict the manners and the fashionable life of his age....

Out of the pattern of the witty woman and her suitors emerges a pattern containing the principal types of characters made use of in Restoration comedy of manners....

Shirley never created a wit the equal of his witty woman. It remains for the Restoration first to produce its own type of a wit and then to imitate the social product in its own comedy of manners ... [the Restoration] did not produce the would-be ... originally the contribution of Jonson. Jonson, however, portrays the would-be as a humorous gull, and, therefore, it is Shirley's merit that he substituted gentlemen from contemporary life ... and yet retained the fundamental conception of Jonson in depicting them as pretenders.... Consistently Shirley betrays his would-be as a pretender to wit. Out of the would-be Shirley evolved the fop.[58]

Thus the Restoration dramatists found ready-made combinations of the most attractive elements of Jonson and Fletcher in the works of Shirley, whose

... whole plan for the comedy of manners, the union of modernized Jonsonian would-bes and Fletcherian witty women and rakes in an atmosphere full of wit, vigor, and social diversions of contemporary life, set the direction which the Restoration writers of comedy of manners consciously followed.... [Shirley] is the link between the Elizabethans and the Restoration dramatists.[59]

Cogent support of the view has been contributed by Joe Lee Davis in a recent study of minor Caroline imitators of Jonson:

Jonson's influence on English comedy before 1642 is not a mere matter of extensive and chaotic borrowing from his various plays. It is,

---

[58] "Significance of James Shirley's Realistic Plays" (1932), pp. 262-64.
[59] *Ibid.*, pp. 370-72.

rather, an attempt to carry on the traditions of the three distinct genre-types of realistic comedy which his "comedy of humours" represents—comedy of ethical satire, comedy of social satire, and comedy of farcical intrigue.... His Caroline "Sons of Ben" developed an eclectic social comedy whose distinguishing characteristics are that it imitates every chief feature of his comedy of social satire, separates imitation of his comedy of social satire from imitation of his comedy of ethical satire, gives the former more centrality in individual plays than imitation of his comedy of farcical intrigue, combines it in almost every conceivable fashion with other genre-types emphasizing social standards and materials, and thus establishes it as the most dominant force in realistic comic tradition up to the close of the London theaters in 1642. In view of these facts, it is possible to assert that Jonson's influence on English comedy before 1642 makes clear his claim to the title of "father of English social comedy" and warrants the belief that he is one of the most important progenitors of the Restoration comedy of manners.[60]

Recent studies of Wycherley,[61] Shadwell,[62] and Dryden[63] have also indicated a belief that the influence of Molière can be reduced to the status of a single element among many in accounting for the products of these important writers of comedy. But no general treatment of the subject to withstand critical scrutiny has yet been produced.

An investigation is needed that will give accurate information regarding the exact nature and extent of each borrowing from Molière in Restoration comedy, appraise these borrowings judiciously as contributions to the development of each author using him, and show clearly the extent and the limits of his influence on the English comedy of manners. Such is the intention of this study of Restoration plays that reflect, or have been alleged to reflect, in any degree the influence of Molière.

[60] "The 'Sons of Ben' in English Realistic Comedy" (1934), pp. 937-38.
[61] Perromat, *William Wycherley* (1921). Discussed below in Chap. V.
[62] Borgman, *Thomas Shadwell* (1928). My comments will be found, *passim*, Chap. VI.
[63] Allen, *Sources of Dryden's Comedies* (1935).

II: THE METHOD

SOMEONE used to tell the story of the student who asserted that Gray's reference to the curfew in the "Elegy" proved a direct dependence upon Milton, who had mentioned a curfew in "Il Penseroso." After smiling for a moment, one makes a sobering reflection that no one has ever met that student's needs by systematically describing the forms that the common fallacies assume in literary study.[1] Where can any one find a handbook of logic as it applies to the study of literary sources and influences? I stress logic, for honesty and information alone do not lead invariably to truth: sound reasoning must include conscious direction and critical control. Reliance on the instinct that guides the great scholar safely through the hazards of research may wreck the lesser man. And even great scholars have been known to err, where a more explicit technique might have saved them.

Since, for the investigation of literary sources and influences, there is no formulated body of principles to which I can pledge allegiance, it is desirable to state at the outset exactly what methods of weighing, considering, and checking I shall use. As the previous chapter made clear, the problem of Molière's influence on Restoration comedy has been abundantly studied before now. The opinions might have been in harmony if the investigators had used the same methods. At any rate, I hope that by stating the principles that have guided my study I shall make it possible for any one to verify my results.[2] Certainly no one will think the

---

[1] Van Tieghem (*La Littérature comparée,* p. 5) mentions a similar deficiency in discussions of the theory of comparative literature.

[2] For obvious reasons of space and interest, I cannot give much of the evidence upon which my conclusions are based. Nothing can be duller than prolix evidence

less of my conclusions for having been told how they were reached.

The variant and contradictory opinions of my predecessors in the field impress one fact clearly upon me: any tendency to generalize before all the evidence is assembled needs to be strangled at birth. In many instances, I find, foregone conclusions, stowing themselves away in the minds of scholars, rob their unwitting hosts of just that quality that makes research superior to guessing. Some students, for example, appear to think that the tracing of a literary influence is an act of homage to the source;[3] such an assumption is revealed in a tendency to believe things complimentary to Molière's influence and to reject equally good evidence of borrowing where an influence would be no credit to him.[4] Others merely reverse the bias.[5] In short it is probable that conclusions have sometimes controlled the marshaling of facts. Accordingly I have tried to remain objective by regarding literary influence as a simple issue of cause and effect.

Another fact that cannot be overemphasized is the need for clarification of the difference between mere resemblance and demonstrable borrowing. Now a resemblance between the work of a later author and an earlier may justifiably be called a borrowing only when there is no other way to explain it. All likenesses, whether they are verbal parallels, similarities of spirit, of

---

in parallel passages, especially when the parallels are far apart. I have given earlier opinions in conveniently placed footnotes.

[3] Among the later studies, Gillet's *Molière en Angleterre* is the most conspicuous example.

[4] Miles (*Influence of Molière on Restoration Comedy*) believes that Molière was as influential on Etherege and Congreve as on Wycherley and Dryden, although on his own evidence the first two borrowed /relatively little and the other two borrowed extensively (see pp. 60-61, 199-204). He appears to have assumed that the best qualities of Restoration comedy came from Molière; the better the play in which they are found, the more certain he seems to be that an influence exists, and, vice versa, he asserts that minor writers, who he admits borrowed the most, were influenced the least (see pp. 98-99), without indicating any principle by which such a conclusion is reached.

[5] Palmer (*Comedy of Manners*) shows a high admiration for the originality of the Restoration writers and denies any borrowing.

technique, or of thought, or resemblances in style, in an action, or in a character, must be assumed to be casual and fortuitous until a consideration of all the possibilities leaves borrowing as the only intelligent explanation of their existence.[6]

Only one type of likeness, long verbal parallels, can be immediately recognized as indubitable borrowing. In this particular problem there is no disagreement concerning such passages, for whether translated, half-translated, or merely paraphrased speech by speech, they are always found in association with further likenesses. With long verbal resemblances, the existence even of a common source would not contradict the fact of borrowing, for Molière did not follow his sources verbally.[7]

But difficulty arises when no verbal parallelism exists, when the resemblances are merely of method, action, character, dramatic situation, and the like. Caution is needed when dealing with such likenesses, because of the great possibility that both authors are independently availing themselves of an ancient and ever-growing body of commonplaces.

EXAMPLE I: LITERARY COMMONPLACE

The comedy of Plautus and Terence, which entered the stream of Italian literary drama with the Renaissance, was fairly central to the development of Molière's art. Molière also went directly to the Latin classics. But these same classics had been affecting

---

[6] An undue will to believe seems to be clearly proved when a scholar ignores chronology to call a likeness a borrowing. For example, Miles (*op. cit.*, p. 229) has the misfortune to call resemblances of Lacy's *The Dumb Lady* to *Les Fourberies de Scapin* borrowings. Their dates are 1669 and 1671 respectively. Likewise Gillet (*op. cit.*, p. 30) sees the influence of *L'Impromptu de Versailles* (October, 1663), on D'Avenant's *The Playhouse to be Let* (c. August, 1663), but dated 1662 in Gillet. "Hypnotism of the unique source" is the descriptive phrase for this process, introduced by André Morize (*Problems and Methods of Literary History*, p. 88). Paul Van Tieghem (*op. cit.*, p. 190), likewise warns against *similitudes sans influences,* which he ascribes to *causes communes.* He also warns that likenesses of accidental origin must not be considered.

[7] Not even the bitter contemporary accusations of plagiarism in de Visé's *Nouvelles Nouvelles* and *Zélinde* (1663) charge him with verbal theft.

English comedy also for more than a hundred years, and many of their characteristics had become commonplaces of English drama through their use by Ben Jonson and others.[8] Such a problem, involving a likeness to material of classic origin, may be found in a comparison of *The Squire of Alsatia* (May, 1688) by Thomas Shadwell with *L'École des maris*. In his play Molière centers his attention on the subject of a suitable education for young people. He develops his idea of freedom by having each of two brothers, who entertain opposite views, rear a child in his own way; he thus shows the beneficent results of freedom in contrast with the unpleasant consequences of repression. *The Squire of Alsatia* can also be described by exactly the same words. Does this prove that its spirit and matter were borrowed? Not necessarily. The similarity noted above is the result of describing the plots in the most general terms. If we were to retell the action of each play in detail, describing the characters as they appear, no one would ever dream of likening Shadwell's play to that of Molière.

Recalling the *Adelphoe* of Terence, Molière wrote a typically clear thesis play, in which he was discussing such a problem as his own approaching marriage to the beautiful young Armande Béjart, who was only half his own age. Sganarelle may have been a symbol of the jealous, possessive side of Molière's own nature, while Ariste may have stood for his genial, intelligent side. The play revolves solely about the efforts of these two middle-aged men to win the love of their wards so that they can marry them.

---

[8] The same is true, *mutatis mutandis*, of Spanish materials and of the bag of theatrical tricks associated with *commedia dell' arte*, but they do not happen to enter into any of the plays about which this problem centers.

For interesting evidence of the use of *commedia dell' arte* in Elizabethan drama, see Campbell's "*Love's Labour's Lost* Restudied," pp. 21-25. Chambers (*Elizabethan Stage*, II, 261-65) gives an account of Italian companies in England as early as 1573. Smith ("Italian and Elizabethan Comedy," *Modern Philology*, V (1908), 555-67) points out many contacts between the comedy of the two countries. Bader ("Italian Commedia dell' Arte in England, 1660-1700," p. 220) minimizes the extent of its influence, and stresses the diffused and indirect character of what he did find.

In contrast, *The Squire of Alsatia* is one of the most carefully realistic plays of the most carefully realistic playwright of the Restoration. It is a comedy of low life in Whitefriars, the lowest section of London. It is full of the bragging and brawling of scowrers, cheats, and bullies; it contains a group of eager women and rejected mistresses. The author paraded an underworld jargon so obscure that he provided a short "Explanation of the Cant" when he printed the play. Like the authors of dozens of Restoration plays, Shadwell contrasts true gentlemen, Restoration style, with shabby imitations. He provides ladies with whom to reward the gallants. To the Restoration mind, the surest way to breed a fool is to keep him in the country, away from the refining influences of city society; a real gentleman is bred in London by a father wise enough to let him learn by experience in fashionable circles. With experience, some of which may come through reckless excess, a man will live a more sensible life in the city than will a money-minded boor from the country. Realistic writers of comedy are likely to start either with setting or with characters and later develop the action. So when Shadwell needed a plot for his play in which to imbed these ideas, he took over the *Adelphoe* of Terence as a general outline of the action and of the chief relationships.[9]

The extent of Shadwell's indebtedness to Terence may be suggested by again giving an outline that is true of both plays, although not a complete description of either: A surly, ill-mannered, miserly man from the country has allowed his bachelor city brother to adopt one of his sons. The original father believes in strict discipline; and in contrast the adoptive parent prefers kindliness as the best way to educate young men. The

---

[9] Since *The Squire of Alsatia* does not come into the discussion at a later point, it is no more than fair to Shadwell to note that this tracing of the play to Terence does not imply any other than a masterly use of well-known raw materials of drama. Shadwell's play is full of merits and originality due to the talent of the author, who is neither a slavish imitator nor an artless plagiarist.

rustic son secretly escapes from the country to enjoy the entice-
ments of city life. The city son is entangled with a girl whom
he has debauched, but he is able to devise a way to extricate his
simple brother and himself from their troubles, and both are
happily married to the girls of their choice after the apparent
conversion of the country father to the standards of his city
brother. The similarities of *The Squire of Alsatia* to *L'École des
maris* are all in the common source, and the likeness of plot is
not a borrowing from Molière.[10]

EXAMPLE II: COMMONPLACE OF THE THEATRE

Any drama is bound to have many points of similarity to any
other. Methods, materials, devices, limitations, and needs produce resemblances that often have no common origin, or at least
no traceable one. A myopic parallel hunter often lists these conventions of the playhouse as borrowings. *Les Précieuses ridicules*
has been mentioned as the source of Betterton's *The Amorous
Widow, or the Wanton Wife* (c. 1670). The salient features of
Molière's plot are briefly as follows: Madelon and Cathos are
two silly, romance-ridden young *bourgeoises,* who have disas-
trously caught the affectations that emanated from the Hôtel
de Rambouillet under the name of *préciosité,* and who dream of

---

[10] Borgman (*Thomas Shadwell,* pp. 208-9) says, "From the *Adelphoe,* then,
Shadwell takes two contrasting points of view in the training of youth—that based
upon unmitigated severity, and that founded upon kindness tempered with indulgence.
In the original, the follies resulting from the soft method are stressed; in the adaptation, the benefits growing out of the soft method are accentuated. Shadwell's shift
in emphasis may have been due to the influence of *L'École des maris,* Molière's comedy
based upon the *Adelphoe.*" My dissent is with the premise as well as with the conclusion. I grant that Demea (Terence's country father) makes a closing ironic explanation of his sudden generosity that largely, but not wholly, nullifies his personal reform;
this speech, however, can be explained as a bit of final irascibility, comical and human.
It does not completely throw the moral of the comedy against "the soft method," for
after all it was the soft method and Demea's fifth-act acceptance of it that brought
happiness to the young people. But even if the *Adelphoe* did oppose "the soft method,"
there are not enough points of resemblance between Shadwell's play and Molière's, nor
such elements of originality as to bar the likelihood of coincidence, a likelihood that
is heightened greatly by the fact that such a similarity would accord with Restoration
social attitudes.

glamorous young men, worthy of highly refined natures. Coldly rejected, their two substantial *bourgeois* suitors revenge themselves by sending their valets, Mascarille and Jodelet, to impersonate noble suitors under the names of the Marquis de Mascarille and the Vicomte de Jodelet. Mascarille enters first, dressed in the most exaggerated burlesque of the current fashions for French fops. With manners that match his clothes, he talks about literature and poetry, to which he offers his immortally inane addition. Then he shows his skill in literary criticism by discussing the merits of his own composition in great detail. He talks about his clothes, item by item. With Jodelet's entrance the two men shift to talk of military prowess, making magnificent boasts and introducing an element of farce by proposing to show wounds on all parts of their bodies. They finally order fiddlers, that they may dance a few steps. Their false delicacy, silly affectations, and inane gallantries, in which Mascarille is the leader, are extravagant enough to meet the highest expectations of the delighted young ladies. After the proud girls have accepted the social brass of the valets for gold, the masters return, beat the servants, and disclose their identity. The center of the play is the satire of the current affectation of *préciosité;* the plot device of the masquerading servants is a means of making the folly of Madelon and Cathos apparent; their folly lies in their acceptance of *préciosité* as a serious social standard.

In Betterton's play, two young men are unable to woo the ladies of their choice because an amorous old widow, Lady Laycock, insists on a relentless pursuit of every male who approaches her niece. To escape the widow, the men introduce a falconer, Merryman, as the Viscount Sans-Terre. He gives a gay impersonation, monopolizing the attentions of the widow, and finally marries her for her fortune. With no general likenesses of action except the fact that a man of low rank is induced to masquerade as a viscount, there is no more reason to suspect a copy from Molière than there is to recall parallels in earlier English plays. Merryman has none of the essential qualities of Mascarille. However, Betterton may have developed him from Mascarille; the evidence does not enable us to deny that he did. Unable to affirm or to deny that the likeness is a borrowing, we must class it as a possible borrowing, being careful at all times thereafter not to base on it a more definite conclusion than an unproved possibility.

EXAMPLE III: SOCIAL COMMONPLACE

England, Italy, Spain, and France had a considerable amount of social interchange, so that manners, dress, fads, foibles, and even turns of speech took on resemblances that could be copied direct from life in each country and yet look superficially like borrowings from plays. This could be illustrated by reference to another aspect of *Les Précieuses ridicules.* Mascarille is an extreme burlesque of a French fop. He is not a portrait, but a satire of a type. On the Restoration stage we find a type of character often regarded as an imitation of Mascarille—the fop who is full of affectation, but is not a masquerader. Miles, for example, thinks that Sir Fopling Flutter of Etherege's *The Man of Mode* is adapted from Mascarille because Sir Fopling sings, dances, and talks clothes.[11] If fops had not been prevalent in London society and in Parisian society, neither Etherege nor Molière would have staged them. Surely French fops and English fops would both take an interest in dress, and in the current social graces of dancing and singing. Moreover Etherege presents Sir Fopling as a Frenchified Englishman, and as such he would have some of the characteristics currently ascribed to French fops. If there is nothing to prevent Molière's looking about him and sketching Mascarille, what is there to prevent Etherege's looking about and sketching Sir Fopling? It must be remembered that Restoration

---

[11] Miles, *Influence of Molière on Restoration Comedy,* pp. 135-38.

audiences considered Sir Fopling a portrait and tried to identify him with current dandies.[12] Despite the number of likenesses we must deny the borrowing, because the resemblances are social commonplaces and not distinctive in nature or in arrangement.

EXAMPLE IV: COMMONPLACE OF LIFE

Finally, human nature in all lands and in all ages has more points of resemblance than of variance. Observations by different men of a persistent or a recurring element of life may look to the book-minded observer like a borrowing.[13]

In *The Careless Lovers* (March, 1673) by Edward Ravenscroft, there is a borrowing of the bigamy trick of Molière's *M. de Pourceaugnac,* whereby an undesired suitor is put to flight. (Two women enter in succession, each declaring De Boastado has married her. Each supports her claim by producing the alleged offspring of the union.) The fact of this debt, coupled with Ravenscroft's generally known readiness to take anything from any one, especially Molière, would increase the probability that a second likeness is a borrowing. But this second resemblance lies in the fact that Ravenscroft's plot revolves about a stern father who is determined to settle his daughter's marriage for her; this someone has actually ascribed to Molière. It is found in classic, Italian, French, Spanish, Elizabethan, Jacobean, and Restoration drama, because it was in the life of all those times and places. (One might as well try to trace the literary source of the slightly

---

[12] In Cibber's *Lives of the Poets* (1753, III, 34-35) one reads: "... he [Etherege] is said to have drawn ... some of the contemporary coxcombs; and Mr. Dryden ... says, that the character of Flutter is meant to ridicule none in particular, but the whole fraternity of finished fops, the idolators of new fashions. ... Sir Fopling was said to be drawn for one Hewit, a beau of those times ... the town's asscribing them [Sir Fopling, Dorimant, and Medley] to some particular persons ... at least demonstrated a close imitation of nature." See also Verity's *Works of Sir George Etheredge,* p. xiv n.

[13] See Dodge, "A Sermon on Source-hunting," *Modern Philology,* IX (1911-12), 211-23; Stoll, "Certain Fallacies and Irrelevancies in Literary Scholarship," *Studies in Philology,* XXIV (1927), 485-508; Oliphant, "How Not to Play the Game of Parallels," *Journal of English and Germanic Philology,* XXVIII (1929), 1-15.

more commonplace fact that girls have fathers.) The likeness must not be considered as even a possible borrowing.

EXAMPLES V AND VI: IDENTIFYING PECULIARITIES

Even when a likeness has not been eliminated by one of the foregoing considerations, it is still unacceptable as a borrowing unless it has identifying peculiarities. In Sir Charles Sedley's *The Mulberry Garden* (May, 1668) there is a resemblance to *L'École des maris*. Molière's play opens with a rather spirited argument between the brothers, Sganarelle and Ariste, each the guardian of a girl he hopes to marry. Old-fashioned Sganarelle ridicules Ariste for his stylish dress. As the young ladies appear on their way outdoors for a pleasant stroll, Sganarelle orders his ward to stay inside. He advocates forceful repression and strict adherence to household duties as the best way to teach a girl to be a faithful wife, while Ariste argues for freedom and kindness. The young ladies are present during the discussion in which Sganarelle predicts disaster to Ariste for the freedom he allows his ward.

The rising curtain of Sedley's *The Mulberry Garden* reveals Sir John Everyoung, a cavalier of the last days of the Commonwealth, who has taken to foppish dress, and his brother-in-law, Sir Samuel Forecast, who still affects the Puritan ways. They argue about the proper way to rear and to dress Everyoung's daughters, Forecast's nieces. These daughters soon enter to ask for the coach in which they wish to take a drive in the park. Forecast remarks that his own daughters are locked up at home, and the men resume the controversy about proper freedom for young ladies. Here the number of likenesses is too great for coincidence. Characters, subject of discussion, and order of events through four pages are almost identical, although there are no verbal parallels. These four pages are undoubtedly a borrowing from Molière.

Another example can be found in a comparison between Shad-

well's *Bury Fair* (*c.* April, 1689) and *Les Précieuses*. Lady
Fantast and her daughter have a silly desire to ape the refinements of the French. As Lady Fantast's stepdaughter, Gertrude,
and Wildish, suitor to the latter, cannot endure the postures and
pretenses, they determine to use ridicule. Wildish induces La
Roche, a French barber, to masquerade as a count and woo Lady
Fantast's daughter. Much original fun develops from the barber's inability to keep exactly in character. But La Roche wins
the attention of the ladies, although it is at the price of a beating
from their admirers. When the rumor of his being a barber
spreads and Wildish admits the hoax, the duped ladies leave
Bury in confusion and dismay. The differences between La Roche
and Mascarille are many; yet the similarities are distinctive of
Molière's invention, and their repetition in Shadwell is inexplicable as coincidence. We note that, by the same device, both
authors ridicule two silly women for their affectations, having
them trapped into receiving the courtship of false counts whose
affectations are evident to everyone else. The pretenders are further induced to undertake the action by suitors whom the affected
women have despised; the opportunity appeals to the natural vanity of the counts, and their enthusiastic responses makes them
secondary butts; their unmasking brings about the social debacle
of the pretenders and the chagrin of the affected women. Any
one of these elements separately could be fortuitously hit upon
by two men, but their entire combination could not. Shadwell
has undoubtedly borrowed the material.

Thus even a fairly close likeness between Restoration authors
and Molière must be treated with calm skepticism and denied
the name of borrowing, unless the similarity is peculiarly marked
with identifying traits that cannot be reasonably explained as the
independent use of commonplace materials of literature, of the
theatre, or of life. Or, to state it positively, *a likeness to Molière
is accepted as a borrowing when the thought, the wording, the*

action, the situation, or the dramatic device has, in isolation or in combination, enough points of resemblance or such identifying peculiarities as to bar the likelihood of coincidence in observation or in the use of commonplaces. Somewhat less convincing resemblances are noted as possible borrowings, not proved; but commonplaces of literature, of the stage, or of the times are excluded from this classification.[14]

LITERARY INFLUENCE

After the extent of borrowing from a work has been established, the tracing of literary influence can be controlled by the simple principle that *a literary influence exists when borrowings have helped to form results.* The influence is identified when the tracing of borrowing enables us to perceive what elements in the product of the borrowing author are definitely due to his encounter with the source.

As influences are of all kinds and degrees, they must be classified and studied before their natures can be intelligently determined. Borrowings are here placed under the three heads traditional in literary criticism, the *spirit,* the *matter,* and the *form.* By these terms are intended what Goethe and Herder meant by *Gehalt, Stoff,* and *Form.*[15] Although the product of the creative imagination cannot be separated dichotomously into thought and embodiment, it can be examined from different points of view.

Under spirit (*Gehalt*), I include any aspect of the author's thought as a whole, so far as it can be distinguished from the particular kind of objectivity which he gave it. This is the most

[14] The foregoing definitions and principles doubtless reflect the opinions of more scholars than I am aware of. In addition to those cited from time to time above, I feel specific debt, for some suggestion or support, to the following: Baldensperger, "Littérature comparée—le mot et la chose," *Revue de littérature comparée,* 1ʳᵉ année, pp. 1-29; Lanson, "Etudes sur les rapports de la littérature française," etc.; *Revue d' histoire littéraire,* III (1896), 45-70; Price, *English-German Literary Influences,* pp. 119-23.

[15] The example of Gundelfinger [*pseud.* Gundolf], *Shakespeare und der Deutsche Geist,* is followed in this division.

valuable and most imperishable aspect of literature. Influences of spirit have a higher value, therefore, than those of matter or form. The greatest are formative of the mind and spirit of a great man. Of this kind is the effect of the social philosophy of William Godwin on Shelley, or the influence of Ibsen's *Ghosts* on *Das Friedensfest* of Gerhardt Hauptmann.

By matter (*Stoff*) I mean the particular objectivity the artist has given his literary spirit. In drama this consists of the action, the characters, the incidents, the situations, the scenery—everything that comprises the audible or visible medium by which the author's intention (*Gehalt*) reaches the audience. Borrowings of matter may or may not be very influential, depending largely upon the amount of spirit that goes with them. Without evidence of influence on a man's thought, no great importance can be attached to borrowing. Shakespeare, for example, borrowed matter from Lodge, from Kyd, from Bandello, from Rabelais, and from Montaigne; but we must insist on finding likenesses of spirit before we believe there are prospects of discovering a great influence. In the field of seventeenth-century drama, the use of incidental material is often a factor of very little importance. The limitations of the dramatic genre make originality in plot elements difficult; the urgent necessity of theatrical success makes a playwright eager to use any tested device. A slightly relaxed standard of literary honesty in drama, in comparison with other types of literature, seems to have been the rule.[16] The result is that even lavish borrowings of plot detail may have little influence. Perhaps this lack of force comes about because a borrower in search of new material does not surrender to the spirit of the text, as he may when his reading lacks a practical motive.

Under *form* I place those aspects of literature that relate primarily to manner and method, so far as they are separable from

---

[16] See preface to *An Evening's Love* in *Dramatic Works of Dryden*, ed. by Scott-Saintsbury, III, 249.

matter. An author considers form when deciding to express an idea in a sonnet rather than in an essay or a story, as when the Elizabethans turned to sonnet sequences after the example of Petrarch. Form, of course, is always intimately related to matter and spirit. In drama it is largely barren as a separate concept because all plays are similar externally. But the sort of dialogue, the style of language, the manipulation of scenes, the plan of exposition, and the selection of elements for direct or narrated action are primarily in the category of form. In the discussion of the value of an influence, with which we are chiefly concerned, no a priori precedence can be given to either matter or form, although both must be placed far below spirit.

After classifying the borrowings under spirit, matter, or form, I study them for their influence in determining the character of the literature in which they were used. The weighing of the influence of these elements is guided by three criteria, to which I give a priori acceptance. In using these criteria, one must keep in mind that separately they do not reach the truth. After applying all three separately, I undertake to synthesize the partial answers into a final judgment that takes all the evidence into due consideration.

Criterion I.—The degree of influence depends upon the extent and centrality of the borrowed elements in the works of the source. In this particular study the estimation of the degree of influence is simpler because the source is the work of just one man. But even with our single author, the value of different works is far from the same. At the top stand his great comedies of character and of manners. The most direct influence must be central to the art of the author borrowed from, if his special personality is to be a force. Marginal matters often bear no stamp of an author's own genius. For Molière this means that the most significant influence must come from a great comedy, not from a minor one. A borrowing from *Le Dépit amoureux* could

scarcely match one from *L'Avare*. To be most potent, a borrowing, however, must also be central to the art of the particular
work from which it is taken, for the significance of a play as a
whole does not necessarily appear in every detail; thus a borrowing may be made from a very fine play and yet be of no importance at all. For example, in *Le Tartuffe* the husband is
concealed under the table so that he can be shown Tartuffe's
villainy. For a Restoration playwright to reproduce the stage
devices of this scene does not argue for any very considerable
influence, as a common French farce might have suggested the
same action. Molière's greatest plays incidentally contain examples of his unerring skill in pleasing his customers with clever
theatrical devices, and material could be borrowed from the best
plays without touching upon the man's greatness. The farces, the
comedies of intrigue, parts of the *comédie-ballets,* and much of
the cleverness and skill of the great comedies are much less
central to Molière's art than the main elements of the comedies
of character and manners.

    *Criterion II.—The degree of influence depends upon the extent
and centrality of the borrowed elements in the works of the borrower.* For example, in attempting to determine the degree of
influence of Molière upon Dryden, one first assembles the list
of established borrowings in Dryden's plays and applies Criterion
I to see whether it was the great Molière or merely the clever
Molière who was at work in Dryden. One next weighs Dryden's
works separately to see what their essential qualities consist of,
and then one refers to the borrowings to see which of these
qualities, if any, came from Molière. One tries to imagine Dryden's plays with the borrowings from Molière left out. One
asks if Dryden could have replaced the deficiencies from his own
resources or if he would have been as impotent as Medbourne
would have been without a *Tartuffe* to translate. If Dryden with
the borrowings is more than Dryden without them, the differ-

ence measures the influence, the result of the later author's acquaintance with the works of the earlier. The more central this
difference is to Dryden's peculiar and essential culture, the
greater Molière's influence upon him. The need here is to keep
the whole of the borrowing author's work in mind and to avoid
a distortion that will certainly come if one concentrates upon
the borrowings to the neglect of the proportion they bear to the
whole. In *The Tempest* Shakespeare copied a passage of Montaigne almost literally. What is the importance of this passage
in the whole? The play would not be very different, nor would
the rôle of Gonzalo be much weaker if Montaigne had been
left out. Surely, we must always consider the extent to which
borrowed elements loom up in an examination of the whole in
proper perspective. While it would not be hard to demonstrate
that there is much difference in spirit, the amount of matter
from Plautus in *The Comedy of Errors* is very high. But before
we commit ourselves too far in thinking Plautus highly formative of Shakespeare's comic art, we must read all the comedies
of the latter and allow for the fact that the ratio to the total
drops with every additional play, for Plautus ceased to influence
Shakespeare.

*Criterion III.—The influence of borrowings upon a larger mass
of literature,* such as the comic drama of a period, *must be studied
in the light of the whole of that literature,* not merely of that
in which borrowings occur.[17] After a clear idea is gained of the
whole influence upon each separate author, an attempt must
be made to relate these influences to the entire work of the age.
For this aspect, the natural approach seems to be chronological.
All the comedies of the Restoration have therefore been arranged
by years.[18] Summaries of the spirit, matter, and form of the comic

[17] Van Tieghem seems to be assuming the same principle when he insists upon the
student's need for a broad knowledge of contemporary literature in the *pays récepteur*
(*op. cit.,* p. 64).
[18] See Appendix B for this list.

writing of the English authors are considered, first by single years, then by larger units of time, and finally for the whole period. The relation of Molière to each of these groups of plays can be decided with some precision. The degree of influence on an age will be affected by the significance of the borrowers. The value of a servile imitation by a hack cannot be great unless it becomes an intermediate source of influence on an important author. Even this is unlikely to occur, as we shall see from the sterility of Medbourne's *Tartuffe, or the French Puritan* (*c.* April, 1670), because the hack generally fails to transmit any of the essential greatness of the original. A translation or a complete adaptation drawn from an unimportant work of Molière's is not a valuable influence. Such is Otway's *Cheats of Scapin.* Neither would an influence on a minor writer of comedy like Otway have the value of an equal influence upon a Wycherley or a Congreve. We must remember also that the influence on an age has a relation to the centrality of the borrowings in what is transmitted to the borrowers' fellows and successors. We must concern ourselves with the extent to which those elements borrowed from Molière affected the nature of the total comic writing of the Restoration. A comparison must be made between what is central to the age and what is borrowed, to see what effects the borrowings produced. If the essential qualities of Wycherley, Dryden, Shadwell, and Congreve, for example, were the things directly or indirectly borrowed from Molière, they would have transmitted much of him to their age, and his influence would be very high. But the farther the borrowings are from the center of their productions, the slighter his influence would be, for to have been influential in a high degree he must have greatly changed the total product from what it would have been without him. The visibility of Molière's influence when the perspective is true to the facts, when all the comedies are seen in their true relation, is the final test.

III: ILLUSTRATIVE ADAPTATIONS
OF MOLIÈRE

RECENT studies of British drama seem to make it clear that when the two Restoration companies began playing in 1660, they met the shortage of new plays by depending upon pre-Restoration staples. Fletcher, Jonson, Shirley, Shakespeare, Brome, and Middleton provided the bulk of the comic offerings. New writers, as they arose, naturally made their inventions conform to those elements in the old drama which satisfied current taste. But it is an incontrovertible fact that Molière's comedies were repeatedly levied upon also. What did each Englishman take? What did he do with it? What did he like about it? With such questions as these in mind, let us examine some early Restoration plays that indubitably borrow from him:[1] Dryden's *Sir Martin Mar-All, or the Feigned Innocence* (August, 1667), Flecknoe's *The Damoiselles à la Mode* (September, 1668), Lacy's *The Dumb Lady, or the Farrier Made Physician* (1669), Caryl's *Sir Salomon, or the Cautious Coxcomb* (c. 1669), Betterton's *The Amorous Widow, or the Wanton Wife* (c. 1670), Medbourne's *Tartuffe, or the French Puritan* (c. April, 1670), and Shadwell's *The Miser* (January, 1672). They provide examples of Molière's fate in the hands of typical English adapters.

SIR MARTIN MAR-ALL

After the rather indifferent reception of *The Wild Gallant* (February, 1663), John Dryden scored the greatest theatrical success of his long dramatic career with the farcical *Sir Martin Mar-*

---

[1] I have chosen these plays from the complete list of early borrowings from Molière because they offer a suitable variety of methods of adaptation and of results.

All, an adaptation from Quinault and Molière. The process of adaptation is interesting. A play of Italian provenience, *L'Inavvertito* of Nicolò Barbieri, had been rendered into French by Quinault under the title of *L'Amant indiscret* and by Molière as *L'Étourdi.* Dryden based the first two acts on Quinault, and then shifted to Molière for the rest.[2] To this he added a minor action of his own that brings enough spice of indecency to provide the second title and to balance the innocence of the borrowed fun. Barbieri's play had provided Molière with a combination of Italian comedy and classical material. The fundamental situation is that of a rather stupid young man in love with a pretty slave girl, but without money to buy her. His clever servant tries to bring about the desired result, although the young man's father wishes him to marry another girl. This is all conventional stuff of ancient drama. The interest in the play arises from the resourcefulness of the servant in rapidly bringing forward a dozen or fifteen successive plans for extricating his master, who stupidly spoils each design, except the last, by a farcical capacity for ineptitude and misunderstanding. According to Toldo, Molière gave his young man much more intelligence than Barbieri,[3] and then adapted his plot so that some of the trouble was sheer bad luck and some due to inadequate coöperation between servant and master. Thus Molière made a happy ending acceptable. Molière also enlivened this example of Italian literary drama with devices drawn from *commedia dell' arte.* Barbieri's speeches were shortened, shorn of their pseudophilosophical elements, and replaced by brisk action. Despite these changes and despite its appeal everywhere, neither the tone of *L'Étourdi* nor the matter suggest localized manners.

[2] I am indebted to N. B. Allen for first calling my attention to this point. Scott wrote exactly about the relation of Quinault and Molière to Dryden's play, but he has apparently been misread; hence Quinault is often erroneously credited with the racy underplot. In *Sources of Dryden's Comedies* (p. 220 n), Allen explains the relationship of the plays in detail.

[3] Toldo, *L'Oeuvre de Molière et sa fortune en Italie,* pp. 20-27.

In this respect Dryden has happily improved Molière, who had not imported his characters into France, but had given them a vague and unreal background called Messina. *Sir Martin Mar-All* is as essentially English as most farces of native origin. The characters are British people, their actions, though farcical, are based on life in England, and the merry tone is a common one in the Stuart theatre. Less than half the tricks employed by Mascarille are retained in any form, and these are adapted to the British background. The tricks added to piece out the plot are as good as Molière's, and one deserves Genest's praise for superiority.[4] To prove that he is a wit, Sir Martin must serenade Millisent. As he can neither sing nor play, he goes through the gestures and grimaces while his clever Warner plays and sings from concealment. But Sir Martin misses the signal and ecstatically continues his gestures long after the music ceases. Dryden realized the impossibility of making Mar-all a sympathetic character. Instead he made him the typical silly country knight of Restoration plays, following the tradition of the Jonsonian characters of little social insight. He completely mars all when he marries the maid, thinking he has won the mistress. The mistress has used this plan to wed Warner, the servant, whose true wit attracts her in accordance with Restoration notions, and who proves to be of good family and laughingly insists that he has been the master all the time. Thus true-wits are rewarded.

If one were to adapt Dryden's play to modern America, with all the changes needed to make the farce appear contemporary in actions and dialogue, the revision would be comparable to the revision he imposed on Quinault and Molière. Dryden wrote more than half of the first two acts with Quinault open. He adapted speech by speech, idea by idea, and when he wished, word for word. The first meeting of Sir Martin and his rival, Sir John, for example, is directly after the similar meeting of cognate characters

---

[4] Genest, *Some Account of the English Stage,* I, 75-76.

in *L'Amant indiscret*. The parallel passages from the two plays follow:

Cléandre. Est-ce vous, cher Lisipe, est-ce vous que je voy?
Ne m'abusay-je point?
Lisipe.   Non, Cléandre, c'est moy.
Cléandre. Quelle heureuse rencontre! Eh quoy! dans cette ville!
Lisipe. J'ay fait assez longtemps un mestier inutile,
Où je n'ay rien gagné, si ce n'est quelques coups;
Il est temps que chez moy je cherche un sort plus doux.
Je me sens tout usé d'avoir porté les armes,
Et pour moy, désormais, le repos a des charmes.
Je suis prest d'épouser une rare beauté
Où je borne mes voeux et ma félicité,
Et j'ay fait de Paris le voyage avec elle,
Pour vuider un procez qui dans ce lieu l'appelle.
Cléandre. Depuis trois ans passés vous estes hors d'icy,
Sans nous avoir écrit!
Lisipe.   Cléandre, il est ainsi;
Mais les mains qu'on employe à servir aux armées
D'écrire bien souvent sont désaccoutumées;
Puis on a de la peine à les faire tenir.
Cléandre. Et puis de ses amis on perd le souvenir.
Lisipe. Point du tout, j'eus toujours Cléandre en ma mémoire.
Cléandre. C'est m'obliger beaucoup que me le faire croire.
Lisipe. Hé bien! l'on m'a conté que vous jouez toujours.
Comment va la fortune?
Cléandre.   Elle est dans le décours:
Ma maison de Paris, depuis un mois vendue,
En beaux deniers comptans dans mes mains s'est fondue.
Lisipe. Lorsque le malheur dure, il est bien affligeant.
Cléandre. Quand je jette les dez, je jette mon argent,
Et si je m'émancipe à dire tope ou masse,
Le malheur qui me suit ne me fait point de grâce.
Si je joue au piquet avec quelque ostrogot,
Il me fera vingt fois pic, repic, et capot;
En dernier il aura deux quintes assorties,
Et vingt fois pour un point je perdray des parties.

Lisipe. Le jeu n'est pas plaisant lorsque l'on perd ainsi.
Cléandre. J'ay perdu le désir de plus jouer aussi,
Et j'en ay fait serment au moins pour six semaines.
Lisipe. Les sermens d'un joueur sont des promesses vaines:
Je suis fort asseuré que vous n'en ferez rien.
Cléandre. Je prétends ménager le reste de mon bien,
Et n'iray plus tenter un hasard si nuisible.
Lisipe. Ha! cette retenue est du tout impossible:
Vostre âme pour le jeu sent trop d'émotion.
Cléandre. Elle est pleine aujourd'huy d'une autre passion.
Lisipe. D'ambition? d'amour?
Cléandre.   C'est d'amour, cher Lisipe.
Lisipe. Dans ce jeu bien souvent, comme aux autres, on pipe,
Et parfois tel amant s'embarque avec chaleur,
Qui perd souvent son fait, et joue avec malheur.
Est-ce pour une veuve, ou bien pour une fille?
Cléandre. C'est pour l'unique enfant d'une bonne famille,
Pour une fille riche et belle au dernier point.
Lisipe. Et qui souffre vos soins?
Cléandre.   Et qui ne me hait point.

L'Amant indiscret, Act I, scene 4.

Sir John. Sir Martin Mar-all! most happily encountered! how long have you been come to town?

Sir Mart. Some three days since, or thereabouts: But, I thank God, I am very weary on 't, already.

Sir John. Why, what's the matter, man?

Sir Mart. My villainous old luck still follows me in gaming; I never throw the dice out of my hand, but my gold goes after them: If I go to piquet, though it be but with a novice in't, he will pique and repique, and capot me twenty times together: and, which most mads me, I lose all my sets when I want but one of up.

Sir John. The pleasure of play is lost, when one loses at that unreasonable rate.

Sir Mart. But I have sworn not to touch either cards or dice this half year.

Sir John. The oaths of losing gamesters are most minded; they forswear play as an angry servant does his mistress, because he loves her but too well.

Sir Mart. But I am now taken up with thoughts of another nature; I am in love, sir.

Sir John. That's the worst game you could have played at; scarce one woman in an hundred will play with you upon the square. You venture at more uncertainty than at a lottery: For you set your heart to a whole sex of blanks. But is your mistress widow, wife, or maid?

Sir Mart. I can assure you, sir, mine is a maid; the heiress of a wealthy family, fair to a miracle.

Sir John. Does she accept your service?

Sir Mart. I am the only person in her favour.

Dryden's *Dramatic Works,* III, 10-11.

Such rewriting is evidently masterly in its attempt to produce an English effect from a French original. It condenses much more than the following parallel, which is probably as close as any:

Lisipe. Vous ne m'avez pas dit l'heure du rendez-vous.
Maie que veut ce maraud?
Philipin.   C'est vous que je demande,
Pour vous dire deux mots d'importance fort grande.
Lisipe. Parle.
Philipin.   C'est en secret que je vous dois parler.
Rosette. Je le tiens fort subtil, s'il peut s'en démesler.
Philipin, a Lisipe. Par l'ordre de Cléandre, avec beaucoup
    d'adresse,
Je suis venu sonder la vertu de Lucresse,
Et j'ay par mes discours si bien sceu l'émouvoir,
Que mon maistre a receu rendez-vous pour la voir.
Mais sçachant vostre amour, loin de vous faire outrage,
Il renonce pour vous à ce grand advantage,
Et veut vous faire voir, par ce prompt changement,
Qu'il est meilleur amy qu'il n'est discret amant.
Il ne prétend plus rien au coeur de cette belle,
Et vous fait advertir d'avoir l'oeil dessus elle.
Lisipe. Pour un si bon advis reçois ce diamant.
Que ton maistre m'oblige!
Philipin.   O Dieu! quel changement!

Lisipe. Madame, Philipin, de la part de Cléandre,
Touchant le rendez-vous vient de me tout apprendre.
Le croyant mon amy, je n'étois pas trompé.
Lucresse, à part. La défaite est fort bonne, et Lisipe est dupé.

L'Amant indiscret, Act II, scene 6.

Sir John. Half my business was forgot; you did not tell me when you were to meet him. Ho! what makes this rascal here?

Warn. 'Tis well you're come, sir, else I must have left untold a message I have for you.

Sir John. Well, what's your business, sirrah?

Warn. We must be private first; 'tis only for your ear.

Rose. I shall admire his wit, if in this plunge he can get off.

Warn. I came hither, sir, by my master's order,——

Sir John. I'll reward you for it, sirrah, immediately.

Warn. When you know all, I shall deserve it, sir: I came to sound the virtue of your mistress: which I have done so cunningly, I have at last obtained the promise of a meeting. But my good master, whom I must confess more generous than wise, knowing you had a passion for her, is resolved to quit: And, sir, that you may see how much he loves you, sent me in private to advise you still to have an eye upon her actions.

Sir John. Take this diamond for thy good news; and give thy master my acknowledgments.

Warn. Thus the world goes, my masters! he, that will cozen you, commonly gets your good-will into the bargain.   [*Aside.*

Sir John. Madam, I am now satisfied of all sides; first of your truth, then of Sir Martin's friendship. In short, I find you two cheated each other, both to be true to me.

Mill. Warner is got off as I would wish, and the knight overreached.

[*Aside.*

Works, III, 26-27.

In the second half, the need of integrating borrowed plot with original subplot apparently made it impossible for Dryden to follow Molière as closely as he had Quinault. But he used the greater man in the same general manner, as the following parallels show:

Léandre.　　　　Je ne sais; mais enfin,
Si quelque obscurité se treuve en son destin,
Sa grâce et sa vertu sont de douces amorces,
Qui pour tirer les coeurs ont d'incroyables forces.
Mascarille. Sa vertu, dites-vous?
Léandre.　　　　　Quoi? que murmures-tu?
Achève, explique-toi sur ce mot de vertu.
Mascarille. Monsieur, votre visage en un moment s'altère,
Et je ferai bien mieux peut-être de me taire.
Léandre. Non, non, parle.
Mascarille.　　　　Hé bien donc! très-charitablement
Je vous veux retirer de votre aveuglement.
Cette fille....
Léandre.　　Poursuis.
Mascarille.　　　　N'est rien moins qu'inhumaine;
Dans le particulier elle oblige sans peine;
Et son coeur, croyez-moi, n'est point roche, après tout,
A quinconque la sait prendre par le bon bout.
Elle fait la sucrée, et veut passer pour prude;
Mais je puis en parler avecque certitude:
Vous savez que je suis quelque peu d'un métier
A me devoir connoître en un pareil gibier.
Léandre. Célie....
Mascarille.　　　　Oui, sa pudeur n'est que franche grimace,
Qu'une ombre de vertu qui garde mal la place,
Et qui s'évanouit, comme l'on peut savoir,
Aux rayons du soleil qu'une bourse fait voir.
Léandre. Las! que dis-tu! croirai-je un discours de la sorte?
Mascarille. Monsieur, les volontés sont libres: que m'importe?
Non, ne me croyez pas, suivez votre dessein,
Prenez cette matoise, et lui donnez la main:
Toute la ville en corps reconnoîtra ce zèle,
Et vous épouserez le bien public en elle.
Léandre. Quelle surprise étrange!

　　　　　　　　　　L'Étourdi, Act III, scene 2.

Sir John. When she is once mine, her virtue will secure me.
Warn. Her virtue!

Sir John. What, do you make a mock on 't?

Warn. Not I; I assure you, sir, I think it no such jesting matter.

Sir John. Why, is she not honest?

Warn. Yes, in my conscience is she; for Sir Martin's tongue's no slander.

Sir John. But does he say to the contrary?

Warn. If one would believe him,—which, for my part, I do not,—he has in a manner confessed it to me.

Sir John. Hell and damnation!

Warn. Courage, sir, never vex yourself; I'll warrant you 'tis all a lie.

Sir John. But, how shall I be sure 'tis so?

Warn. When you are married, you'll soon make trial, whether she be a maid or no.

Sir John. I do not love to make that experiment at my own cost.

Warn. Then you must never marry.

Sir John. Ay, but they have so many tricks to cheat a man, which are entailed from mother to daughter through all generations: there 's no keeping a lock for that door, for which every one has a key.

Warn. As, for example, their drawing up their breaths, with—oh! you hurt me, can you be so cruel? then, the next day, she steals a visit to her lover, that did you the courtesy beforehand, and in private tell him how she cozened you; twenty to one but she takes out another lesson with him, to practise the next night.

Sir John. All this while, miserable I must be their May-game!

Warn. 'Tis well, if you escape so; for commonly he strikes in with you, and becomes your friend.

Sir John. Deliver me from such a friend, that stays behind with my wife, when I gird on my sword to go abroad.

Works, III, 59-60.

Lélie. Du chagrin qui vous tient quel peut être l'objet?

Léandre. Moi?

Lélie.   Vous-même.

Léandre.   Pourtant je n'en ai point sujet.

Lélie. Je vois bien ce que c'est, Célie en est la cause.

Léandre. Mon esprit ne court pas après si peu de chose.

Lélie. Pour elle vous aviez pourtant de grands desseins;

Mais il faut dire ainsi lorsqu'ils se trouvent vains.

Léandre. Si j'étois assez sot pour chérir ses caresses,
Je me moquerois bien de toutes vos finesses.
Lélie. Quelles finesses donc?
Léandre.   Mon Dieu! nous savons tout.
Lélie. Quoi?
Léandre.   Votre procédé de l'un à l'autre bout.
Lélie. C'est de l'hébreu pour moi, je n'y puis rien comprendre.
Léandre. Feignez, si vous voulez, de ne me pas entendre;
Mais, croyez-moi, cessez de craindre pour un bien
Où je serois fâché de vous disputer rien;
J'aime fort la beauté qui n'est point profanée,
Et ne veux point brûler pour une abandonnée.
Lélie. Tout beau, tout beau, Léandre.
Léandre.   Ah! que vous êtes bon!
Allez, vous dis-je encor, servez-la sans soupçon:
Vous pourrez vous nommer homme à bonnes fortunes.
Il est vrai, sa beauté n'est pas des plus communes;
Mais en revanche aussi le reste est fort commun.
Lélie. Léandre, arrêtons là ce discours importun.
Contre moi tant d'efforts qu'il vous plaira pour elle;
Mais sur tout retenez cette atteinte mortelle:
Sachez que je m'impute à trop de lâcheté
D'entendre mal parler de ma divinité,
Et que j'aurai toujours bien moins de répugnance
A souffrir votre amour qu'un discours qui l'offense.
Léandre. Ce que j'avance ici me vient de bonne part.
Lélie. Quiconque vous l'a dit, est un lâche, un pendard:
On ne peut imposer de tache à cette fille;
Je connois bien son coeur.
Léandre.   Mais enfin Mascarille
D'un semblable procès est juge compétent:
C'est lui qui la condamne.
Lélie.   Oui?
Léandre.   Lui-même.
Lélie.   Il prétend
D'une fille d'honneur insolemment médire,
Et que peut-être encor je n'en ferai que rire?
Gage, qu'il se dédit.

Léandre.   Et moi gage que non.
Lélie. Parbleu je le ferois mourir sous le bâton,
S'il m'avoit soutenu des faussetés pareilles.
Léandre. Moi, je lui couperois sur-le-champ les oreilles,
S'il n'étoit pas garant de tout ce qu'il m'a dit.

L'Étourdi, Act III, scene 3.

Sir Mart. You are very melancholy, methinks, sir.

Sir John. You are mistaken, sir.

Sir Mart. You may dissemble as you please, but Mrs. Millisent lies at the bottom of your heart.

Sir John. My heart, I assure you, has no room for so poor a trifle.

Sir Mart. Sure you think to wheedle me; would you have me imagine you do not love her?

Sir John. Love her! why should you think me such a sot? love a prostitute, an infamous person!

Sir Mart. Fair and soft, good Sir John.

Sir John. You see, I am no very obstinate rival, I leave the field free to you: Go on, sir, and pursue your good fortune, and be as happy as such a common creature can make thee.

Sir Mart. This is Hebrew-Greek to me; but I must tell you, sir, I will not suffer my divinity to be profaned by such a tongue as yours.

Sir John. Believe it; whate'er I say, I can quote my author for.

Sir Mart. Then, sir, whoever told it you, lied in his throat, d'ye see, and deeper than that, d'ye see, in his stomach, and his guts, d'ye see: Tell me she's a common person! he 's a son of a whore that said it, and I'll make him eat his words, though he spoke 'em in a privy-house.

Sir John. What if Warner told me so? I hope you'll grant him to be a competent judge in such a business.

Sir Mart. Did that precious rascal say it?—Now I think on 't, I'll not believe you: In fine, sir, I'll hold you an even wager he denies it.

Sir John. I'll lay you ten to one, he justified it to your face.

Sir Mart. I'll make him give up the ghost under my fist, if he does not deny it.

Sir John. I'll cut off his ears upon the spot, if he does not stand to 't.

Works, III, 64-65.

The result of this borrowing is not a transfer of Quinault's or of Molière's method, style, or excellence. The farce is just as truly British, just as truly in Dryden's vein, as it would have been if Dryden had invented all of it. Not much of the immortal Molière could have reached England by means of a vehicle as far from the center of his art as *L'Étourdi,* even if the play had come over entire. The degree of influence is reduced by Dryden's success in making the play seem British. Material not central to Molière's art was borrowed to form part of the matter, but none of the form or spirit of Dryden's play.[5]

THE DAMOISELLES À LA MODE

The Damoiselles à la Mode (September, 1668), printed in 1667, Richard Flecknoe's only comedy, is an avowed attempt to bring Molière to England.[6] The play is a close adaptation of *L'École des maris* and *Les Précieuses ridicules,* with a few suggestions from *L'École des femmes.*[7] All this is frankly set forth in the preface.[8] Since Langbaine did not know that it had ever been acted, there is reason to believe that it had little success with the public. Copies of the play are rare. Writing with Molière's works open before him, Flecknoe avoided making a literal translation

---

[5] Allen (*op. cit.,* pp. 210-25), offers a more detailed analysis of the relation of Dryden's play to Molière's.

[6] This rare book has never been sponsored by a publisher. I have used a photostat of the British Museum copy of the sole edition, which was printed for the author, London, 1667.

[7] I cannot believe the vague similarities cited by Gillet show the use of *Sganarelle, Le Médecin malgré lui,* and *Le Misanthrope.* See *Molière en Angleterre,* pp. 43-44; Appendices I and II, pp. 144-99.

[8] "This *Comedy* is taken out of several Excellent Pieces of *Molière.* The main plot of the *Damoiselles* out of his *Pretieusee's Ridiculee's;* the Counterplot of *Sganarelle,* out of his *Escole des Femmes,* and out of the *Escole des Marys,* the two *Naturals;* all which like so many *Pretieuse* stones, I have brought out of *France;* and as a Lapidary set one Jewel to adorn our *English Stage:* And I hope my setting them, and giving them an *English* foyle, has nothing diminisht of their native luster. And I have not only done like one who makes a posie out of divers flowers in which he has nothing of his own (besides the collection, and ordering them) but like the *Bee,* have extracted the spirit of them into a certain Quintessence of mine own ... and I hope with that success, as I have not only made the Language of the Author, *English,* but even the spirit, life, and quickness of it too."

at any time. He wrote clear, idiomatic English, in which the longer speeches of Molière are regularly shortened and simplified. He added a few jests and occasionally he added a new figure of speech, but, in general, the matter belongs to Molière.

The play opens with the plot of *L'École des maris,* Bonhomme and Sganarelle arguing about the way to educate young girls. Bonhomme is the genial father, and his two daughters, Mary and Anne, ungraciously reward him by being veritable *précieuses.* They are wooed by Du Buisson and La Fleur; *Les Précieuses ridicules* is repeated in substantial entirety, with Mascarille and Jodelet as the masquerading valets. Meanwhile Sganarelle and his daughter Isabella, who is described in the *dramatis personae* as "a witty Damoiselle," are going through the essentials of the action of *L'École des maris.* Isabella's successful lover is called Valerio. A friend to Valerio, named Egasto, replaces the valet in Molière. The comic business of Alan and Georgette in relation to Arnolphe, in *L'École des femmes,* has been largely transferred to "Two Natural Fools" and Sganarelle. The place of the action is Paris.

Flecknoe lost the spirit of Molière, although he says he tried to keep it. The assignment of the action of two characters from Molière to a single person in the combined play works havoc with all characterization. The combination of the two plays diminishes the significance of the mixture far below the level of either of the original components. Bonhomme, for example, cannot be a plain bourgeois like Georgibus and yet a broad-minded man like Ariste. He has been lenient with his daughters and does not deserve to have them turn into silly *précieuses.* The decision to have Mary and Anne finally marry Du Buisson and La Fleur removes the sting from Molière's Madelon and Cathos; it also makes the piqued young men absurd for trying to punish the girls and then for taking them with their affectations undimin-

ished. The pain is gone from Sganarelle's loss of Isabella, for
Bonhomme has been through his troubles too. In Molière some
farcical elements exist, but they do not blur the satiric lesson of
either play. Molière's audience knows a man is a fool to try to
win a girl's love by force and that women are silly to confuse
romance and *préciosité* with actual marriage and sensible human
speech. Flecknoe's audience could wonder whether any man
knows how to rear young women and might infer that love
is so strong that suitors will swallow any amount of nonsense to
marry the young women of their fancy. One may charge the
failure of Flecknoe to his incompetence, but in his defense it
can be demonstrated that his avoidance of didactic implications
and his development of a bustling intrigue is like the work of
almost any of the "Sons of Ben." Flecknoe's preface may be
interpreted as indicating his inability to judge his own work,
although it may also suggest, what Dryden's treatment suggests,
that the early adapters had no discernible respect for Molière.
Flecknoe used matter high in Molière's art and might have been
greatly influenced, if matter, spirit, and form had not sunk under
the weight of the adapter's bad judgment.

THE DUMB LADY

During the year following the staging of Flecknoe's extraordinary play, John Lacy adapted *Le Médecin malgré lui* to the
English scene and taste. To this he gave the title *The Dumb
Lady, or the Farrier Made Physician* (1669). Ward thinks it
shows

what kind of entertainment so experienced a comedian thought most
likely to suit the tastes of the public for whom he catered.... In other
words, he is uniformly and unblushingly coarse, and whatever he has
of wit is lost in his grossness.[9]

The public taste which Ward deplores is apparently like that of

[9] Ward, *English Dramatic Literature*, III, 449.

Gerard Langbaine, who wrote that the reader "will easily see that our Author has much improv'd the French play." [10]

Le Médecin malgré lui is a rollicking three-act farce revolving about the unusual revenge that comes to Sganarelle, a drunken fagot-cutter, because his wife resents his beating her. Sganarelle, she tells Valère when he is urgently seeking a doctor to cure Lucinde of a sudden fit of dumbness, is a great doctor, but he has a foible for disguise and will not acknowledge his profession until he is beaten into it. Once beaten into it, Sganarelle plays the physician in the grand style, makes money, flirts outrageously with the servant women, beats rich Géronte to make him a doctor too, and finally cures his patient, who was merely feigning until she could marry Léandre instead of Valère. The satire appears when Sganarelle and Léandre burlesque the hocus pocus of doctors. At the close of this strange interlude, his wife leads Sganarelle back to his fagots.

Lacy's method of dramatic composition here consisted essentially of taking Molière's farce, stretching it to five-act length and then filling up the gaps with additional material copied from the life of the time. Occasionally the reader will catch echoes of Molière's phrasing, but the bulk of the dialogue is thoroughly made over. Nearly all of Molière's situations and episodes are retained. The satire against the medical profession is blunted and shortened. Sganarelle's unimportant equivocal advances to the nurse Jacqueline are elaborated, amplified, and reciprocated with a bald relish for indecency. The unwelcome suitor of Lucinde is brought forward in the character of Squire Softhead, as ignorant, as boastful, as poltroonish a specimen of the country gull as one can find. His usual oath, "by the heart of a horse," had comic reiteration in inept places. Many changes, of which these are typical, when combined with little alterations and additions of slighter character on every page, give a thoroughly English

[10] *Account of the English Dramatick Poets,* p. 318.

picture on a well-covered French canvas. None of Molière's spirit or peculiar method reappears, but much of the farcical basis in his plot is clearly seen. *L'Amour médecin* also provided an episode which shows how a closely imitated passage follows and yet misses the excellence of the original crisp dialogue:

Lisette. [suivante de Lucinde qui est la fille de Sganarelle] Ah, malheur! Ah, disgrâce! Ah pauvre Seigneur Sganarelle! où pourrai-je te rencontrer?

Sganarelle. Que dit-elle là?

Lisette. Ah! misérable père! que feras-tu, quand tu sauras cette nouvelle?

Sganarelle. Que sera-ce?

Lisette. Ma pauvre maîtresse!

Sganarelle. Je suis perdu.

Lisette. Ah!

Sganarelle. Lisette!

Lisette. Quelle infortune!

Sganarelle. Lisette!

Lisette. Quel accident!

Sganarelle. Lisette!

Lisette. Quelle fatalité!

Sganarelle. Lisette!

Lisette. Ah, Monsieur!

Sganarelle. Qu'est-ce?

Lisette. Monsieur.

Sganarelle. Qu'y a t-il?

Lisette. Votre fille.

Sganarelle. Ah, ah!

Lisette. Monsieur, ne pleurez donc point comme cela; car vous me feriez rire.

Sganarelle. Dis donc vite.

Lisette. Votre fille, toute saisie des paroles que vous lui avez dites, et de la colère effroyable où elle vous a vu contre elle, est montée vite dans sa chambre, et pleine de désespoir, a ouvert la fenêtre qui regarde sur la rivière.

Sganarelle. Hé bien?

Lisette. Alors, levant les yeux au ciel: "Non, a-t-elle dit, il m'est impossible de vivre avec le courroux de mon père, et puisqu'il me renonce pour sa fille, je veux mourir."

Sganarelle, Elle s'est jetée.

Lisette. Non, monsieur: elle a fermé tout doucement la fenêtre, et s'est allée mettre sur son lit. Là elle s'est prise à pleurer amèrement; et tout d'un coup son visage a pâli, ses yeux se sont tournés, le coeur lui a manqué, et elle m'est demeurée entre les bras.

Sganarelle. Ah, ma fille!

Lisette. A force de la tourmenter, je l'ai fait revenir; mais cela lui reprend de moment en moment, et je crois qu'elle ne passera pas la journée.

Sganarelle. Champagne, Champagne, Champagne, vite, qu'on m'aille querir des médecins, et en quantité: on n'en peut trop avoir dans une pareille aventure. Ah, ma fille! ma pauvre fille!

L'Amour médecin, Act I, scene 6.

Nib[*by,* a niece to Gernette, the father of Olinda]. O wo is me, and wo unto us all, O this Uncle, this wicked Uncle.

Ger[*nette*]. Alack, what's the matter?

Nib. O cruel destiny! O fatal fortune!

Ger. Why, Niece *Nibby,* what's the matter?

Nib. That ever I should live to see this day.

Nur[*se*]. O my dear Mrs. *Nibby,* what's the misfortune?

Nib. O where should I find this cursed Uncle of mine?

Ger. Here I am Nibby, what's the danger?

Nib. You are undone and ruin'd.

Ger. How, undone and ruin'd? do not delay me.

Nib. O your daughter, your daughter you wicked wretch, I am not able to say more for grief.

All. Ah, Oh, ah, ah. (All weep.)

Ger. Tell me quickly what's the matter.

Nib. Why, your daughter's grown desperate mad at your unkindness; ran to the window that stands over the River, and there opening the great casement.

Ger. O what did she then?

Nib. Why, lifting up her hands and eyes to that good place, where you will never come Uncle; she loudly cryed; Since my father has abandon'd me, 'tis time for me to quit this life of mine.

Ger. And so threw her self into the River?

Nib. No, it seems she did not like that kind of death.

Ger. Why, what then?

Nib. Why then she ran like lightning to the Table, where your Pocket-Pistol lay.

Ger. And so shot her self with that?

Nib. No, it seems there was no powder i' th' pan, but bitterly sighing and weeping, at last she ran and desperately threw her self upon her bed, and then growing paler and paler, by degrees fell into a deadly sound.

Ger. And so dyed?

Nib. Stay, stay, you'r too quick for your daughter; but with much rubbing, tumbling, and tossing her, I brought her to life again; so leaving her at deaths door, I came to tell you the news.

Ger. Where are my servants? run, bid 'em run, [etc., etc.]

> *The Dumb Lady,* Act IV (1672 quarto, pp. 63-64).

The Lacy capable of taking the edge from sharp lines, as he obviously does in the above translation, would have had no applause. But there was another Lacy, a man with a talent, different from Molière's, it is true, but pleasing to his time. He was able to present gross sexual flippancies with sufficient wit to make them palatable to his age. Without attempting any defense of the vogue for such material, the historian may properly note that Lacy is facile in his smut and occasionally witty. Many may still be amused at the injured pride of Isabel who weeping exclaimed, "To think that ever I should live to be call'd baud; if he had call'd me whore, 'twould ne'er have vext me; but to be call'd baud, is to be thought an old woman unworthy of copulation." [11]

There is ribald laughter in Drench's prenuptial vows to the Nurse, who was already married to Jarvis and cuckolding him with the latter's master:

Doct. . . . and now I am resolved to marry thee Nurse, for I see thou lovest me truly.

[11] Lacy, *The Dumb Lady,* Act II (1672 quarto, p. 38).

Nurse. I, but Doctor, you know I've a Husband.

Doct. Hang him, I were a pitiful Doctor to suffer any body to live that I have occasion to have dead.

Nurse. If it could be done with a safe conscience.

Doct. Why, if it be safely done, it's done with a safe conscience; I see thou'rt a fool and knows nothing.

Nurse. You Learned men know best, I leave all to you.

Doct. Thou shalt lead the sweetest life Nurse; first I will get my son and heir my self Nurse, and then thou shalt have a brave gallant with a fine white Periwig that cost twenty pound Nurse.

Nurse. O dear Doctor, how sweetly you express your love to me.

Doct. And then your gallant shall carry you abroad, and bring you home o'nights; so well pleas'd, Nurse!

Nurse. O my most obliging Doctor!

Doct. And then thou shalt throw that gallant off, Nurse, and have one with a brave brown Periwig, Nurse.

Nurse. Did ever man shew such true love to a woman? let all husbands take example by this dear Doctor.

Doct. And then thou shalt have one with a brave black Periwig, Nurse, so that thou shalt have children of all colours i' th' Rain-bow: but why does thou weep, Nurse?

Nurse. I weep for joy to think what a comfortable life I shall lead with you.

Act IV (p. 54).

Such passages as these, which are central to Lacy's coarse spirit, are derived from English influences; and so Molière's material, extensive as it is, does not stand at the center of Lacy's play. Instead, the English fondness for low intrigue and bawdy talk in the theatre is fully satisfied by a play that depends upon Molière for its framework. Lacy has covered Molière's dramatic skeleton with a body that is no credit to Lacy and too remote to be a discredit to Molière.

THE CAUTIOUS COXCOMB

Sir Salomon, or the Cautious Coxcomb (*c.* 1669), by John Caryl, is the second adaptation by a Restoration playwright in which the author promptly acknowledged the use of Molière.[12] *L'École des femmes* undoubtedly inspired Caryl's play and provided most of the details of the major plot. Many passages are little more than free translations. The prominent subplot utilizes other material from Molière's play, but is substantially original in the limited sense that it is conventional material of the English theatre, adapted to the situation. The characters are adequately Anglicized in manners, and British place names are carefully substituted; no foreign trace is discernible to a spectator. It is an amusing fact that the only play of Molière's to arouse complaint in France for alleged verbal indecency was here rendered inoffensively. Not a remnant of the *potage,* the *enfants par l'oreille,* and the *chaudières bouillantes* is found; and the inept translation of the *il m'a pris* passage would destroy the chance for Célimène's obscene imagination. Genest reports that the play was successfully staged and well received when it was produced.[13]

An examination of Caryl's changes, rather than of his borrowings, may give us some clue to the temper of the age. In *L'École des femmes* we have an intensely serious moral purpose standing out clearly above a characteristically simple but well-motivated intrigue. Arnolphe's character is fully developed and always the chief interest. But there is also a bustling intrigue that satisfies interest on a lower level. A master of theatrical necessities, Molière floats his high seriousness on a sea of French farce and *commedia dell' arte,* both of which came readily from his ample memory. The action is brisk, full of comings and goings, mistakes in identity, unconscious betrayals, and even lively cudgels on Arnolphe's back. But this is not really Molière's *L'École des femmes;* it is theatrical sugar-coating; Molière's real medicine is the satiric development found largely in Arnolphe's

---

[12] See quotation from the epilogue, above, p. 2.
[13] *Some Account of the English Stage,* I, 98.

talks with Chrysalde, in his long soliloquies, in his asides, and in the total effect of the play.

Caryl omits the character of Chrysalde.[14] As Sir Salomon Single (Arnolphe) has an estranged son, his desire to disinherit him by begetting a new heir beclouds the issue of educating a young woman. Mrs. Betty (Agnès) is ignorant, but the point is incidental and unimportant. The cast-off son, Mr. Single (Horace), loves Julia, the daughter of Wary, and their difficulties make Sir Salomon's education of Mrs. Betty seem still less important. Sir Salomon's quarrel with his son and his rôle of unreasonable father remove the emphasis from the comic fear of being cuckolded that motivated Arnolphe. The addition of Sir Arthur Addel, a typical Restoration would-be without wit or courage, obscures Molière's contribution still more. Molière's extended satiric treatment of *Les Maximes du mariage* is debased and shortened. Similarly the naïve love of Agnès for Horace loses its charm in Mrs. Betty, who is an innocent but commonplace country girl. Ralph (Alain) and Allice (Georgette) follow their low comedy way with little change, but no motive at all is given for Sir Salomon's keeping them with Mrs. Betty in a separate house, where he was known as Evans. The beating of Horace and his feigned injury is transferred by Caryl to Sir Arthur Addel, the gull and the butt of what feeble wit the play possesses.

L'École des femmes, the source of the plot of *Sir Salomon,* inspired the play, if a totally uninspired product may be so described. But those qualities in *L'École des femmes* which caused Molière to be called the Shakespeare of France did not reappear. Caryl drew from Molière what he might have drawn from

---

[14] In identifying Wary with Chrysalde, Miles (*Influence of Molière on Restoration Comedy,* p. 237), makes a common mistake in tracing borrowings. A character is not borrowed or imitated if he is merely assigned the same action in the same plot device. Plot elements are very often transferred without any transfer of the character to whom the actions or speeches originally belonged. Chrysalde exists solely as a confidant of Arnolphe. Wary is not a friend of Sir Salomon, although the latter does once talk to him much as Arnolphe did to Chrysalde.

Scarron, a facile plot with effective situations beyond Caryl's feeble powers of invention. As Caryl seems to be the first ever to compare Molière to Shakespeare, one wonders whether he saw Molière's excellences, or rejected them as not to the Restoration purpose. Caryl's borrowings from *L'École des femmes*, extensive as they undoubtedly are, do not come from central or essential elements. He borrowed Molière's skill in farce from a play in which farce is an incidental means to a comic end of greater import. But he did not borrow Molière's real matter, nor Molière's form and spirit. The end, the form, the spirit, and even the matter of Caryl's play are essentially British. It is impossible to trace to Molière's influence even the slightly unusual fact that this Restoration play is clean verbally and free from mockery of conventional moral standards.

THE AMOROUS WIDOW

The next play under consideration, *The Amorous Widow, or the Wanton Wife* (*c.* 1670), by Thomas Betterton, is a typical seventeenth-century story of an eager widow, Lady Laycock, with plenty of money and no sense of the ridiculous in her pretensions to youth and beauty. She relentlessly pursues the young men who court her niece, wavering between Lovemore, an admirer of Brittle's faithless wife, and Cunningham, a suitor for the hand of Philadelphia, her niece. They finally dupe her with Merryman, actually a falconer, who poses as the Viscount Sans-Terre and helps the lovers with his gay impersonation.[15] *George*

15 The rôle has been ascribed to Mascarille of *Les Précieuses ridicules*. This is possibly the source, but there are so many parallels to other plays and so many differences from this one that internal evidence is inadequate proof of any particular origin. As a type Lady Laycock is found in Jonson and many of his successors. Beaumont and Fletcher taught others the device of marrying a gentleman gull to a low creature parading as a high. Would not Lady Laycock's masculine aggression suggest to Betterton that she be meted the same punishment as Sir Gregory Fop in *Wit at Several Weapons* (*c.* 1608)? Would not this suggestion automatically produce a Viscount Sans-Terre in Betterton's mind without any thought of Molière? Betterton's denouement resembles neither. Unlike Madelon and Cathos, Lady Laycock is irrevocably wedded

Dandin, ou le mari confondu provided what Betterton obviously intended to be the second plot. George Dandin, a rich farmer, has married into the decayed nobility to further his own social ambitions. His money has saved his wife's family from ruin, but has not brought him any respect from his new relations. His wife boldly asserts her freedom from bourgeois social standards by cuckolding him with Clitandre. Whenever Dandin complains to her parents, he is embarrassed by their ready belief in her transparent falsehoods and in his low-born incapacity to deserve or to understand her. When his final attempt to lock her out of the house results in her locking him out and charging him with drunkenness, he is forced to beg her pardon on his knees and promise to do better. Then he knows there is no escape; he might as well go drown himself.[16]

The actor-playwright converted the whole of *George Dandin* into a secondary plot without essentially changing it. The French text is followed pretty closely in entrances, exits, stage business, and the order of speeches. While adaptations and additional matter are found, the speeches can generally be described as free translation. The language is slightly coarsened in some details. Two incidents in Molière that recall French farce, Angélique's beating Dandin while pretending to strike Clitandre,[17] and the amusing mistakes of identity because of darkness, are reduced almost to the vanishing point. Molière's material fills only thirty of the seventy-eight pages in the 1737 quarto. The primary intrigue comprises the whole of the first two acts, the last six pages of Act III, the last ten pages of Act IV, and the first four and

to her pretender. Unlike Sir Gregory and his type, she is spared a last-scene unmasking of her low-born mate.

[16] The evident resemblance of this action to Boccaccio, *The Decameron,* seventh day, fourth novel, is of no importance in this study. Betterton used Molière. Molière used his own early farce, *La Jalousie du Barbouillé,* which he had probably based on Italian scenarios. These came more or less directly from Boccaccio, who derived the plot from its apparent origin in India, by means of *The Book of Sinbad,* directly or indirectly. See Despois-Mesnard, ed., *Oeuvres de Molière,* VI, 481-91.

[17] Act II, Scene 8.

the last three of Act V.[18] The secondary plot from *George Dandin* is well linked to the widow intrigue by the appearance of Lovemore (Clitandre) in both actions and by the placing of all events in one scene. The total impression of the play is an interesting study in emphasis. Molière's clear presentation of the folly of marriage out of one's class, with its incidental satire of decayed nobility and of marriage without love between the principals, is clouded by the presence of the widow. By these associations, a satire on marriage degenerates into a mere dramatic *conte à rire*. As a guide to Restoration taste, *The Amorous Widow* shows that elements in Molière could be taken over unchanged, when change was not needed to meet English standards. *George Dandin* happens to be the only play of Molière's to contain an intriguing, adulterous wife. Moreover she is presented as victor in all battles of wits with her jealous husband. Molière revealed his broad moral intention only by a clear, pitiless irony that no one can easily misinterpret, but Betterton distorted him completely and yet copied him whole. This first major translation of Molière is therefore a masterpiece of plagiaristic economy, producing a great distortion with little change. Betterton's failure to catch any of the essential spirit of Molière's high comedy is very significant. He had been sent to Paris some years before on a theatrical commission to study the French stage and to bring back all he could for use in England. Was Betterton, the greatest actor in Restoration England, and the most respectable morally, incapable of perceiving Molière's earnestness behind his satiric laughter, or did he realize that moral earnestness had no appeal to the Restoration theatre goers? In either case the age is clearly characterized, and its peculiar use of Molière is illustrated. For

---

[18] Genest (*op. cit.*, I, 108) makes the misleading statement that Betterton added an underplot to Molière's play, whereas Molière's play became the underplot to Betterton's major plot. Van Laun (*Dramatic Works of Molière Rendered into English*, IV, 336) and Charlanne (*L'Influence française au xviiᵉ siècle*, p. 287) repeat the error. Miles (*op. cit.*, p. 225) corrects it.

Betterton, as well as for the other authors, Molière provided comic matter, farcical plots, and theatrically effective situations. Molière's classic simplicity, his satire of the social follies, and his insistent social sanity, which is central to the spirit of his great comedies, were never adequately appreciated by Restoration England.

TARTUFFE

In contrast with such triviality as Betterton's, we place Medbourne's version of *Le Tartuffe*. In Molierè's play, which is close to the center of his greatness in spirit, matter, and form, the reader will recall, we find the story of Orgon, who has been taken in by the religious pretensions of the impostor Tartuffe to such an extent that his own mother, his brother-in-law, and even his wife have not been able to undeceive him. Orgon insists that he will break the engagement of his daughter to Valère, whom she loves, in order to award her to the hypocritical Tartuffe. He even turns out his own son and deeds his property to the villain. Orgon's wife undertakes a denouement. Concealing her unbelieving husband beneath the table, she permits him to witness Tartuffe's unmistakable amatory advances, his renunciation of religious sincerity, and his boast that he can lead Orgon by the nose. Like the most ordinary seducer, he argues that "le mal n'est que dans l'éclat qu'on fait." Orgon's recovery of his sanity, though tardy, is instant and complete. With unmasked selfishness Tartuffe claims legal title to the property, but through the wise goodness of the king he is exposed as a felon in disguise, the property is recovered, and the family returns to normal life.

Let us see what the Restoration can make of this. Matthew Medbourne, an actor in the company at the Duke's Theatre, translated *Le Tartuffe* under the title of *Tartuffe, or the French Puritan* (*c.* April, 1670). Ready about a year after Molière finally triumphed over temporary suppressions,[19] Medbourne's play is bad enough as translation or as English verse to merit any amount of abuse, but it is the first attempt made during Restoration times to transfer the high seriousness of the French comic master to the English stage. In his dedication he says:

MY LORD, I Here Present Your Honour with the Master-Piece of MOLIERE'S Productions, or rather that of all *French Comedy.*

What considerable Additionals I have made thereto, in order to its more plausible Appearance on the *English Theatre,* I leave to be observed by those who shall give themselves the Trouble of Comparing the several Editions of this Comedy. How Successful it has prov'd in the *Action,* the Advantages made by the *Actors,* and the Satisfaction receiv'd by so many *Audiences,* have sufficiently proclaim'd.

The "Additionals" are not very great in bulk, and yet they follow a consistent plan. Molière's *dramatis personae* are reproduced, even in spelling, except that Elmire, Mariane, Valère, Cléante, Dorine, and Flipote are slightly altered to Elmira, Mariana, Valere, Cleanthes, Dorina, and Flypote respectively. Molière mentioned Laurent, but kept him off stage; Laurence becomes Medbourne's only actual additional character. The wretched, inept, and often stupid translation proceeds speech by speech with entrances, exits, and scene divisions as in Molière. Even the stage directions are generally carried over. So close is the rendering that he gives the direction, "Fillips," where modern editors of Molière indicate a snap of the fingers was implied.[20] There are some distinct changes. Four lines are added at the end of Act I, scene 4,[21] to introduce Laurence. In Act I, scene v, an index finger in the margin points out a two-line speech of Orgon's

[19] The five-year struggle (from May 12, 1664, when three acts of *Le Tartuffe* were given in the festival series at Versailles, to February 5, 1669, when royal authorization was granted for public performance) makes the exact dating of its appearance impossible.

[20] Cf. Despois-Mesnard, ed., *Oeuvres de Molière,* IV, 417, note 2, with Medbourne's *Tartuffe,* p. 8. My references to Medbourne are to the second quarto, 1707. I have not seen the first, 1670.

[21] *Ibid.,* p. 7.

used solely to divide a long speech of Cléante's (fifty-six lines in Molière). He also permits Cleanthes to drop two lines of classic allusion. A second index finger points also to an added meeting between Laurence, Dorina, and Tartuffe, with which Act I, scene v closes.[22] The second act also closes with added matter between Dorina and Laurence, the devout-seeming servant of the professional *dévot*. The Restoration tone will appear in a short quotation:

Laur ... Though I am *Tartuffe's* Man, and receive Wages of him,
His Agreement with my Friends was otherwise; but since he
Has got me fast, he uses me at his Pleasure. I perceiving
This, and to creep into his Favour, pretended by his Sanctity
To be a Convert, and took upon me the Humour you have
Seen: and by this means have won so much upon him,
That I am his Secretary, the Repository of his Privacies, and
What not? and (I must tell you) among his Acquaintance
Have an Interest.
Dor. But *Laurence,* all this concerns me nothing; this Interest
That you boast of, is the main thing I fear: the Austerity
Of your Life, I doubt, will ne're bear with my merry Disposition.
Laur. For that, *Dorina,* trouble not your self;
I see you know me not; for if you did,
You'd say that your Temper and mine were both
Modell'd alike: for I can be as Blithe
And Frolicksome as the most wanton Courtier.
          [*Sings with Antick Postures, and after Dances a Jig.*]

SONG

Spend not thy Time in vain, my Love,
     But answer my Desires:
Be Bucksome, Blithe, my pretty Dove,
     Meet me with equal Fires.

[22] *Ibid.,* pp. 11-13. Tartuffe does not appear in Molière's play until Act III, scene 2. In the preface Molière explains (*op. cit.,* IV, 375) "...j'ai mis tout l'art et tous les soins qu'il m'a été possible pour bien distinguer le personnage de l'Hypocrite d'avec celui du vrai Dévot. J'ai employé pour cela deux actes entiers à préparer la venue de mon scélérat."

> For if thou longer dost delay,
>   Thy Beauties soon will fade thee:
> In Honour thou are bound to pay
>   Those Debts which Nature made thee.
>
> Since my Designs are fair and just,
>   How canst thou well Deny me?
> In faithful *Laurence* thou may'st trust,
>   Then come and lie down by me.

This is a touch to shew you that I can ...
Dor. Yea, marry, this is somewhat like; I perceive there
May be some hopes in the matter;

Thus she draws out damaging knowledge about Tartuffe and then goes hastily to tell Orgon's anxious family as the act closes.

The translation is again interrupted in Act IV, scene 2, with a scene in which Laurence betrays Tartuffe more definitely to Dorina and advises the family to arrange a scene between Elmira and Tartuffe with Orgon as a concealed witness, a needless additional motivation. The matter at the beginning of the last act is rearranged to show Dorina with Cleanthes, but after a few pages it returns to Molière's scene division and speeches. This act undergoes more change than the others. Laurence enters with a box of papers he has stolen from his master to prove his fidelity to Dorina. Finally Medbourne inserts a "Dance of Eight," which Orgon witnesses. Then Orgon arises and delivers the translation of Molière's last speech. The epilogue, credited to Sedley, deserves full quotation:

> Many have been the vain Attempts of Wit,
> Against the still-prevailing Hypocrite.
> Once (and but once) a Poet got the Day,
> And Vanquish'd *Busy* in a Puppet Play.
> But *Busy* Rallying, Arm'd with Zeal and Rage,
> Possest the Pulpit, and Pull'd down the Stage.
> To Laugh at English knaves is dangerous then,
> Whilst English Fools will think 'em Honest Men.

But sure no Zealous Rabby will Deny us
Free Leave to Act our Monsieur *Ananias.*
A Man may say (without being thought an Atheist)
There are damn'd Rogues amongst the French and Papist,
That fix Salvation to short Bands and Hair,
That Belch and Snuffle to prolong a prayer.
That use (enjoy the creature) to express
Plain Whoring, Gluttony, and Drunkenness;
And in a decent way Perform 'em too,
As well, nay better far, alas, than you:
Whose fleshly Failings are but Fornication;
We Godly Phrase it, Gospel Propagation;
Just as Rebellion was call'd Reformation.
Though Zeal stand Centry at the Gate of Sin,
Yet all that have the Word, pass freely in;
Silent and in the Dark for fear of Spies
We march, and take Damnation by Surprize:
There's not a Roaring Blade about the Town
Can go so far towards Hell for Half-a-Crown,
As I for Six-pence, 'cause I know the Way:
For want of Guides Men are too apt to stray.
Therefore give Ear to what I shall Advise.
Let every Married Man that's Rich and Wise,
Take a *Tartuffe* of known Ability,
To Teach, and to Encrease his Family;
Who may, to settle lasting Reformation,
First Get his Son, then Give him Education.[23]

It has often been remarked that *Le Tartuffe,* despite Molière's insistence that he was only attacking hypocrites who affect a false piety, is always in the mind of any Frenchman who turns against the church and its representatives. Many think it was the author's real intention to attack piety by associating it closely with hypocrisy, and that his prefatory protestation against such

[23] Gillet (*op. cit.,* p. 107 n.) says "L'épilogue est attribué à Sedley (Works, 1722, t. I, p. 11; *The Works of the Most Celebrated Minor Poets,* 1749, t. I, p. 118). D'autre part, une note dans une autre édition de Sedley (1716, t. I, p. 14), ainsi que Jacob (*Poetical Register,* p. 180), Whincop (List, p. 260), Davies (t. II, p. 63), et le *Dict. of Nat. Biogr.* l'attribuent à Lord Dorset."

a purpose was a tactful defense. Later imprisoned for his Catholicism, Medbourne probably felt a considerable degree of opposition to Puritanism and made its satire the purpose of his translation. Incidentally this is the only interpretation that would have had any meaning in England. In France *Le Tartuffe* may have been an attack on *la cabale des dévots,* on the Port-Royal Movement, or on the Catholic Church proper. Of all this Medbourne himself, if we may judge by his crude knowledge of the French language, probably knew nothing. A satire on the Puritans would appeal to the old Cavalier spirits, who were thick about the court and the playhouses. Medbourne's sub-title reveals his interpretation, and the epilogue drives home the application.

On the side of technical dramaturgy, one would naturally hope that a close translation would provide an influential model. Medbourne's rather slight alterations were generally in the direction of normalizing the play to English standards. Molière proudly pointed to the delay of Tartuffe's entrance until the third act. Medbourne sent him across the stage at the end of Act I. Tartuffe's servant Laurent was mentioned as an off-stage person by Molière. Medbourne developed him into an accomplice of Tartuffe acting as his servant, who for love of the pert Dorina turned traitor to the evil cause. Molière was content with a sudden denouement, based on royal intervention. Medbourne tried to motivate the end more fully by having Laurence (Laurent) and Dorina secure the cabinet of valuable papers, so that the retained intervention is redundant. Medbourne mentions a sister of Valère as marrying Damis, so that three weddings close the story instead of one. The dance of eight people and Laurence's proof of his true character as a "wanton courtier" behind a mask of Puritanism join these other elements to destroy some of the unity of plot and to cloud the clear singleness of Molière's purpose. It was unlikely that English playwrights would find any novel model of structure here.

THE MISER

In *The Miser* (January, 1672) Shadwell succeeded in transferring to the English scene most of the material and little of the spirit of *L'Avare*. The considerable alterations, aside from the necessary changes in local color, have the general effect of lowering the social and moral tone. Goethe may speak of *L'Avare* as a sublime tragedy, but the level of *The Miser* is that of realistic comedy. Shadwell seems a bit niggard in his gratitude to his source, when he says in his preface:

The Foundation of this Play I took from one of *Moliere's* call'd *L'Avare;* but that having too few Persons, and too little Action for an *English Theatre,* I added to both so much that I may call more than half of this Play my own, and I think I may say without Vanity, that *Moliere's* Part of it has not suffer'd in my Hands; nor did I ever know a *French* Comedy made use of by the worst of our Poets, that was not better'd by 'em. 'Tis not Barrenness of Wit or Invention, that makes us borrow from the *French,* but Laziness.[24]

As the dialogue was essentially reconstructed throughout and an extensive subplot was added, Shadwell was not necessarily dishonest. The most astounding element in his complacence is his blindness to the values of Molière's classic character comedy. To him the play was an intrigue, an interesting set of incidents that involved the dramatic excellence of novelty, suspense, and surprising turns of fortune. Apparently nothing more. In the original prologue he confesses shame at "stealing from the *French*" and conceals his name from the audience, not because of mere theft but because of the shamefulness of using such matter,

> ... in which true Wit's as rarely found,
> As mines of Silver are in *English* Ground.

Twice in this prologue he refers to farce from France and indicates clearly that he thinks *L'Avare* mere "French nonsense"

24 *Works of Shadwell* (1720), III [7].

that should please because it has "small Stock of Brain." [25] Evidently piqued at the failure of *The Humorists* (*c.* December, 1670), he resolved to abandon the memory of Jonson for the profits of Lacy, Caryl, and Betterton, whose use of material from Molière he frankly imitated.

L'Avare, based on the *Aulularia* of Plautus, presents the miser Harpagon willing to sacrifice even his family for money. He would compel his daughter Élise to wed the senile Anselme, for the latter demands no dowry. He competes with his son Cléante for the lovely young Mariane. Élise's lover Valère has entered Harpagon's domestic service in order to be near his beloved. Molière develops much incidental comedy from Harpagon's astounding penuriousness in his household, but he clearly shows the complete disintegration of the family because of the father's character. In the end, the son's valet conceals a casket of the miser's treasure. Wealthy Anselme proves to be the long-lost father of Mariane and Valère. The lovers are happily united, the casket is restored to the distracted father, and the curtain falls as Anselme agrees to pay all wedding costs, including a new suit for Harpagon.

To Molière's mind, the essential social unit was the family, and like many a French author down to the present day, he thought he had proved the iniquity of any action if he showed that it led to domestic disintegration. In *L'Avare* Harpagon's avarice forces his children to resort to every sort of subterfuge to gain those decent resources that a wise father would be solicitous to provide. Respect for parental authority, confidence in the goodness of the children, pleasure in each other's company, and love for the other members of the family have all disappeared in the family debacle. Molière regarded this domestic anarchy as proof that Harpagon was a very foolish man. Such intense interest in the integrity of home life escaped Shadwell completely,

[25] *Ibid.,* III [8].

for he was content to invite our admiration for a son and a daughter who are too heartlessly shrewd for their miserly father. Shadwell shifted the emphasis from Goldingham (Harpagon) to the son and daughter, who are clever, calculating, and heartless, fit for Restoration approval. The addition of cheating gamblers, seen in English theatres ever since Jonson's *Bartholomew Fair,* three cheap wenches, and a silly citizen's son to be gulled draws the attention to the usual English complicated plot. The degradation of tone and the substitution of ribald mockery for satiric earnestness show how far Shadwell had turned from his first two plays. As Dr. Borgman says,

> The final impression is that Shadwell's play concerns itself as much with the cheats and the fools as with the miser and his household. That the English writer neglected the opportunity for humour-portraiture inherent in the character of the miser and that he was willing to give so much space to riotous scenes in taverns and stews shows how he was turning from the type of play which he had praised so highly in the preceding year to a form of comedy based upon a less strict theory.[26]

This final impression to which Borgman refers is very far from Shadwell's source in either spirit or matter. Neither does it recall French dramatic form. His attempt to naturalize the great Molière is a failure.

SUMMARY

The seven Restoration plays discussed in this chapter were written and staged while Molière was still alive and appearing regularly on the Parisian boards. The sources were furthermore in print before they were adapted. Communication between France and England was so easy that one must believe some of the playwrights had been in Paris and availed themselves of the best possible way of finding out what Molière had to say. But note what the adaptations are like:

[26] *Thomas Shadwell,* p. 146.

1. Molière is respected a little less than Quinault in *Sir Martin Mar-All;*

2. *The Damoiselles à la Mode* jumbles two plays into one and ruins both of them;

3. a short farce has been padded to a full-length farce, *The Dumb Lady,* by the injection of conventional English stage realism and English smut;

4. a great comedy of manners is debased into a mere comedy of intrigue called *The Cautious Coxcomb;*

5. another thoughtful comedy of manners is reduced to a farcical underplot of *The Amorous Widow,* which is a commonplace comedy in the conventional style of the Restoration;

6. Medbourne's *Tartuffe* is a serious but blundering effort to bring the great Molière across The Channel; and

7. *The Miser* is a degradation of an immortal comedy of character into a ribald farce of London realism, garnished with the conventional English stage types.

To fix in his memory the unbridged chasm between the art of Molière and these English adaptations, the reader is invited to compare the seven plays named above in form, in spirit, and in total matter with the following from which they have undoubtedly borrowed: *L'Étourdi, Les Précieuses ridicules, L'École des maris, L'École des femmes, Le Médecin malgré lui, George Dandin, Le Tartuffe,* and *L'Avare.*

While the last two English plays fail most egregiously to import spirit, manner, tone, or morality, they differ from the other five chiefly in the fact that the authors tried to understand Molière and failed; the first five made no effort to respect the source. Several conclusions are clear. The form of Molière left no least trace upon any of the seven plays. His spirit cannot be discovered to an appreciable degree in any one of them. His matter was used freely, but with a distortion into something of different import and with different values. It is recognizable, but it lacks significance. It makes the reader think of similes about breaking up great statuary into material to build stone fences with. Since these are precisely the most extensive efforts to Anglicize Molière during his lifetime, the fact that none of them is ever ranked high in the history of Restoration comedy suggests that he was hardly the great model and example for the peculiar excellence of Restoration comedy. Was Molière inherently unfriendly to the Restoration comic *Zeitgeist?*

IV: SIR GEORGE ETHEREGE

THE VOGUE of plays that mirrored the latest manners of the London court was due in large measure to Sir George Etherege's comedies. A clear-eyed, witty observer of the social scene, Etherege had the gift of putting social trifles into epigrams of telling cadence. He raised the English comedy of manners to a high artistic level by his style and by his realistic reflection of the most amazing social life England has ever known. Some have asserted that this comic realism and this prose style came from Molière. Obviously, to show that a literary influence produced such vague and pervasive qualities as style, or realism, one must demonstrate that the second author was acquainted with the first and that no other influences existed that could produce these results. Lightness, brilliance, delicacy of touch, and keenness of observation are too intangible for easy tracing. It is needless to add that only the deepest "hypnotism of the unique source" [1] would induce a scholar to insist that Etherege's style must have leaned heavily upon Molière's merely because it is also decidedly good.

But even the fact that Etherege's style is good had dropped from the minds of men, with the exception of Hazlitt's, for more than a century. More than any one else, the late Sir Edmund Gosse, in his influential article in *The Cornhill Magazine,* [2] deserves credit for restoring him to his rightful place in the history of Restoration drama. About 1880 Gosse discovered Etherege's

---

[1] The phrase is from Morize, *Problems and Methods of Literary History,* p. 88.

[2] "Sir George Etheredge. A Neglected Chapter of English Literature," *The Cornhill Magazine,* XLIII (March, 1881), 284-304. Reprinted in Gosse's *Seventeenth Century Studies,* pp. 259-98. Later citations refer to the second printing.

manuscript *Letterbook*[3] in the British Museum Library and gained from it a keen admiration for the wit of the author. He also unearthed a 1664 quarto of Etherege's *The Comical Revenge; or, Love in a Tub* (March, 1664), which he said had been previously assigned to 1669,[4] and thought he had thereby restored its author to his true chronological place ahead of Wycherley. This dating, he noted, shows Etherege to precede Dryden in the use of rhymed verse, which the latter had advocated but not yet attempted.[5] He also made the important observation that Etherege was the first writer of plays of the sort we agree to call Restoration comedies of manners. The material was thus at hand upon which to restore[6] Etherege as the man who "virtually founded English comedy as it was successively understood by Congreve, Goldsmith, and Sheridan."[7] But instead of seeing this rediscovered comedy as a reflection of Restoration life or as a lineal descendant, with some mutations, of pre-Restoration Eng-

[3] Now in print. Rosenfeld, *Letterbook of Sir George Etherege.*

[4] *Cibber's Lives of the Poets* (1753), III, 33, gives 1664 as the date of the first appearance of the play. This correction of Langbaine is offered without comment. Genest (*Some Account of the English Stage,* I, 54) says, "this play ... [*Comical Revenge*] gained the company more reputation than any preceding Comedy—(Downes)—it was written by Etheredge and licensed for printing July 8, 1664." Apparently Sir Edmund had overlooked these entries. He says in *The Cornhill Magazine* article (see note 2, p. 285), "According to all the bibliographers, old and new, Etheredge's *first play* [my italics] was *She Would If She Could,* 1668, immediately followed by *The Comical Revenge,* first printed in 1669.... Oldys, however, mentions that he had heard of, but never seen, an edition of this latter play of 1664." Two years later, in the reprint in *Seventeenth Century Studies,* the words "first play" are replaced by the more conservative "earliest publication." But the tenor of the article and its logic are based on the idea that Gosse had advanced the date of Etherege's entry into Restoration comedy to an earlier date than had hitherto been held.

[5] Nicoll (*Restoration Drama,* pp. 359, 362) dates *The Rival Ladies* (c. June, 1664) after *The Comical Revenge* (March, 1664). Nicoll vitiates the discovery of Gosse by saying (pp. 96-97): "There is no doubt that Roger Boyle, Earl of Orrery, was first ... as early as Jan. 25, 1661/2, he was penning a play in heroic couplets.... [He] probably got his plays acted a trifle later than those of the future poet-laureate.... On the other hand ... his plays in manuscript may well have been circulated among the court wits in 1661 and 1662."

[6] Gosse was right in insisting that after his time, Etherege's literary reputation had undeservedly faded away.

[7] Gosse, *Seventeenth Century Studies,* p. 266. The idea is emphatically endorsed by Palmer (*Comedy of Manners,* p. 31), and has wide acceptance.

lish comedy, Gosse undertook to explain Etherege's invention as the result of an acquaintance with the plays of Molière, which he imagined Etherege possessed.

Let us inspect the foundation on which Gosse based such an important conclusion. It is of two sorts, external evidence from the known facts of Etherege's life, and internal evidence from the first play itself. No one has ever discovered any exact information about the life of Etherege before March, 1664, when *The Comical Revenge* made him famous. The time and place of his birth, the place and character of his education, his residence and associations before 1664, and similar data are not vouched for in any particularity by contemporary documents. A century later, literary gossip or tradition is recorded by Oldys in meager and uncertain words. " 'Tis thought he had some education at the University of Cambridge, but it seems he travelled into France, and perhaps Flanders also, in his younger years; and at his return, studied, for a while, the Municipal Laws, at one of the Inns of Court in London".[8] A list of the books which Etherege had in Ratisbon in 1689 showed that for each English title there were about four French, including Greek and Latin classics in French translations. Among these were listed "Oeuvres de Molière. 2 tomes." But this tells us little enough about the Etherege of more than twenty-five years earlier.

In contrast with the meagerness of our knowledge about Etherege before 1664, we can find plenty of authentic evidence that after that date he had ready access to the court group and lived as a witty connoisseur of fashionable Restoration society, keen, lazy, amiable, and dissolute. We have in the *Letterbook* an unusually clear idea of the older man,

...how and upon what topics he wrote to his friends; what his amusements were; what books he was in the habit of reading; how he

---

[8] *Biographia Britannica*, III, 1841. Oldys cites his authorities for these statements in the margin: "Thos. Coxeter's MS. notes on Langbaine and Gildon's Langbaine p. 53."

bore himself, as an English gentleman, in a difference with Lady Etherege, or with the burgher precisians of Ratisbon. Dryden is but a mythical figure beside the living personality of Etherege as revealed for us in his correspondance, and in the notes of Oldys and Gildon.[9]

Baffled in our search for external proof that Etherege knew Molière before writing *The Comical Revenge,* we turn to the play itself. As with most comedies of manners, the plot gives no real clue to its nature and spirit, and a laborious summary here would be of no avail. The principal character is Sir Frederick Frollick, whom Palmer describes as "the first of a line that culminated in Congreve's Mirabell," and whom he might also have described as neither the first nor the last of a long line that descended from Fletcher's Mirabel. We must agree with Palmer that Sir Frederick is a gay gentleman, accomplished in the fashionable arts of Restoration society. His wit is revealed in epigrammatic prose, frivolity à la mode, and airy nothings said with incomparable grace. He suggests the actions we associate with Rochester, Buckingham, Sedley, and Dorset, who were all friends of Etherege as soon as we know him in London. Mrs. Rich, the widow who captures Sir Frederick, is cast from a similar mold of current fashion. Even a mere maid rises to superb prose when talking to Sir Frederick. In addition to this genuine comedy of manners, there is a prominent but conventional romantic subplot in rhymed couplets and much incidental servant-hall comedy circling about Sir Frederick's ridiculous French valet, Dufoy, who is the butt of every one. The stage is at times crowded with low rogues intent on ill-gotten gain and ugly debauchery. Thus the play conforms to the English structure with multiple plots, a constant bustle on the stage, and a mixture of genres: comedy of manners, heroic romance, and low comedy incidents.[10]

[9] Palmer, *op cit.,* p. 32.

[10] The structure of Etherege's first play has been traditionally described as a romantic play with a realistic subplot. It seems to me that there are many reasons for reversing this and calling it a realistic play with a romantic subplot. If we think of

With this interesting play to account for, Gosse was apparently misled by an assumption that Molière was the only possible progenitor of a true comedy of manners, for he overlooked the real problem and did Restoration scholarship the disservice of associating the art of Etherege with the art of Molière. No trace of such borrowing had ever been seen in Sir George. If Gosse's judgment had not played him false, the history of scholarship on this subject might have been very different. Of course the belief in the importance of French influence on Restoration literature was commonplace in nineteenth-century scholarship, and it is not hard to imagine how Gosse was misled. If the doctrine of the paramount importance of French influence seemed unassailable, and if one had just awakened to the chronological priority and the brilliance of Etherege, the need of proving him a conscious disciple of the French comic master would seem imperative; even more, the fact of such a relation would appear as an a priori necessity. At any rate Gosse set out to find the evidence:

Gildon states that for a little while he studied law, but adds, what external and internal evidence combine to prove, that he spent much of his early manhood in France. My own impression is that from about 1658 to 1663 he was principally in Paris. His French, in prose and verse,

---

it as a realistic play, Sir Frederick Frolic becomes the chief character. Then the first title, *The Comical Revenge,* would be normalized as an allusion to his surprising loss of property, first revealed by Widow Rich in the epilogue. Dufoy, as Frolic's French valet, provides the second title by the servant-hall, low-comedy intrigue. The fully developed romantic plot need not be the main one. By all the tests of structure, Etherege made it subordinate. In a five-act play, the usual thing is for the major intrigue to dominate the first, the third, and the fifth acts. Under-plots are usually strongest in Acts II and IV. Even badly constructed plays follow this plan to some extent; surely even a badly proportioned play will allow half the time to the major plot. Apparently no one has ever noticed that Etherege, according to these standards, clearly intended the story of Sir Frederick to be the chief one. More than twice as many scenes are given to his realistic plot as are allotted to the romantic. Two and one-half times as many lines are given to the comic scenes. The realistic side dominates Act I, five lines to one; Act III and Act V, almost two lines to one. No act awards the larger share of lines to the romantic story. The play opens with the realistic plot and the mixed final scene reserves it for the very close, after the romantic figures are disposed of.

is as fluent as his English; and his plays are full of allusions that show him to be intimately at home in Parisian matters. What in the other Restoration playwrights seems a Gallic affectation seems nature in him. My reason for supposing that he did not arrive in London at the Restoration, but a year or two later, is that he appears to have been absolutely unknown in London until his *Comical Revenge* was acted; and also that he shows in this play an acquaintance with the new school of French comedy.[11]

This conjecture that Etherege did not return with Charles originated obviously enough from the need of proving his acquaintance with Molière's early plays before they were printed. Advanced as "my own impression" in the first place, it grows in the author's confidence so that he asserts it as undoubted fact five pages later:

What gave *The Comical Revenge* of Etheredge its peculiar value and novelty was that it had been written by a man who had seen and understood *L'Étourdi, Le Dépit amoureux,* and *Les Précieuses ridicules.* Etheredge loitered long enough in Paris for Molière to be revealed to him, and then he hastened back to England with a totally new idea of what comedy ought to be.[12]

For proof of this boldly precise guess, so useful to this explanation, he cites only the lack of documentary evidence of any sort. We know that Etherege read and wrote French fluently, that Oldys heard that he had been in France in his youth, and that he owned a copy of Molière in 1689. That is all we know, and that is all Gosse knew. Naturally he turned to the internal evidence of the play. But those allusions in *The Comical Revenge* that show him "intimately at home in Parisian matters" consist solely of the fact that Dufoy gave an amusing account of being taken into Sir Frederick's service.

He was lounging [wrote Gosse] on the new bridge in Paris, watching the marionettes and eating custard, when young M. de Grandville drove by in his chariot, in company with his friend Sir Fred. Frollick,

---

[11] *Seventeenth Century Studies,* pp. 261-62.　　[12] *Ibid.,* p. 267.

and recommended Dufoy as a likely fellow to be entrusted with a certain delicate business, which he carried out so well, that Sir Frederick made him his valet.[13]

This is the only specific allusion to Paris to be found in the play. It drops out of sight in comparison with the much larger amount of evidence that Etherege knew London, knew London manners, and knew English drama.[14]

Likewise Gosse's evidence that Etherege knew Molière is amazingly scanty in comparison with his confident assertions. He tells us that "The real hero of the first three comedies of Molière is Mascarille, and in like manner the farcical interest of *The Comical Revenge* centers around a valet, Dufoy."[15] It is not clear whether Gosse intends this to refer to a device of plot or, as it is commonly taken, as a declaration that Dufoy as a character is modeled after Mascarille. If the resemblance is a device of plot, the lack of identifying peculiarities nullifies his conclusion, since the device of the servant as the manipulator of plots is common to every one connected even remotely with classic comedy: Plautus, Terence, Jonson, and Molière, for example. If Gosse meant to trace Dufoy as a character to Mascarille, he should have based the relation on likenesses between the two that are not common to the type. The Mascarille of the early Molière is a clever, intriguing servant, a brilliant example of the ancient comic type. In the first two plays he directs the whole plot. He

[13] *Ibid.*, pp. 268-69. This may not seem quite fair to Gosse, who said "the plays [not the first play] . . . show him intimately," and so on, but actually he must mean the first or there is no point. In fact the two later plays contain no more evidence than the first.

[14] Hickerson traces the structure of the romantic subplot (which he calls the tragicomic plot) to Middleton's *Fair Quarrel*. The comic plot resembles Shirley's comedy of manners in many particulars, but it is closer to Fletcher's in others. Spirit, matter, and form are all in the English tradition. See Hickerson, "Significance of James Shirley's Realistic Plays," pp. 299-306.

[15] *Op. cit.*, p. 267. A friendly reader of an early draft of this chapter suggested that I give more of Gosse's evidence. There is no more. The sentence above is literally the only approximation to a detailed likeness that Gosse cites between Molière and *The Comical Revenge*.

is never a butt, not even in *Les Précieuses ridicules,* though his master often is. Dufoy on the other hand is a silly, contemptible butt. He has almost nothing in common with Mascarille except the relation of a valet to his master. As James Shirley had brought valets to the English stage long before, it is futile to call in Mascarille to explain Dufoy.

Scholarship followed Gosse's lead for a long time. Vincent Meindl, however, dismisses the identification of Dufoy with Mascarille but discovers a similarity between the plots of *Le Dépit amoureux* and the serious plot of *The Comical Revenge.* In both, two young ladies love two young men who love the same lady. During the play one man transfers his love and all are happy.[16] W. Harvey-Jellie, however, repeats as unqualified facts Gosse's conjectures concerning Etherege's Parisian residence and his use of Molière.[17] Miles conjectures that the realism of *The Comical Revenge* was inspired by Etherege's knowledge of Molière's success in "transcribing a Parisian fad" in *Les Précieuses ridicules.*[18] The existence of such knowledge of *Les Précieuses,* one must remember, depends largely on the truth of Gosse's conjecture that Etherege had seen Molière's play in Paris. Surely the mere fact that two men wrote realistic plays of current life is inadequate reason for asserting that the later must have been influenced by the earlier. Surely if we lack evidence of influence, we must assume its absence rather than its presence. Miles, however, does cite one apparent borrowing also. With Meindl he finds that the serious plot "harks back" to *Le Dépit amoureux.* But he finds a new likeness in the fact that in both plays a master and a valet woo a lady and her maid. M. Gillet also leaned heavily upon Gosse's conclusions. A few salient expressions will reveal his attitude:

[16] *Sir George Etheredge, sein Leben, seine Zeit und seine Dramen,* pp. 169-72.
[17] *Les Sources du théâtre anglais à l'époque de la restauration,* pp. 59-61.
[18] Miles, *Influence of Molière on Restoration Comedy,* pp. 61-63.

Ses [Etherege's] pièces trahissent une connaissance profonde de la vie élégante de Paris. ... De l'aveu des critiques anglais les plus autorisés [Ward, Gosse, and *Chambers's Encyclopaedia,* according to Gillet's footnote] Sheridan et ses ascendants sont issus de Molière, grâce à Etheredge ... le théâtre anglais doit à Molière l'importation du *valet* comme personnage dramatique et que ce valet paraît dans notre pièce pour la première fois. ... Ce [conversational] style léger est la deuxième dette, et non la moindre, d'Etheredge envers Molière ... c'est la première pièce imprégnée de l'esprit de Molière qui parut en Angleterre.[19]

In thus crediting Etherege's style to Molière, Gillet was following the vague implication of Gosse with unsupported affirmations of a positive sort. Miles, however, had already denied the truth of this.[20] Gosse, Meindl, Miles, and Gillet each compared Etherege's play to Molière, and each was friendly to the discovery of likenesses, if not actually eager to make Etherege's dependence seem important. Yet each one found a different point of similarity, one that none of the others accepted. That fact alone shows the unsubstantial quality of their evidence and destroys any significance one might give to their alleged parallels.

Gosse likewise declares that Etherege's second play, *She Would If She Could* (February, 1668), was "founded upon a reminiscence of Tartuffe."[21] And since this play had not been printed, he takes Etherege on an imagined trip to Paris in 1667. "The only direct similarity between the French and English play is this, that Lady Cockwood is a female Tartuffe, a woman of loud religious pretensions, who demands respect and devotion for her piety, and who is really engaged, all the time in the vain prosecution of a disgraceful intrigue."[22] This judgment of Gosse's has long since been refuted by the repeatedly observed evidence that Lady Cockwood is a lascivious old woman who pursues gallants

[19] Gillet, *Molière en Angleterre,* pp. 33-39, *passim.*
[20] *Op. cit.,* pp. 181-82.
[21] *Seventeenth Century Studies,* p. 271.
[22] *Ibid.,* p. 271.

because they will not pursue her. She is made comic by her failure to see the limitations of her faded charms. Her hypocrisy consists solely in her countrified efforts to deceive her husband and to maintain the externals of social decency. We know that her type was

introduced into the comedy of manners by James Shirley in *The Lady of Pleasure* [1635]. . . . Lady Cockwood, also, has immediate predecessors whom she resembles more closely than she does Lady Aretina, notably Lady Love-all of *The Parson's Wedding* [1664].[23]

Miles makes no attempt to relate Etherege's second play to Molière, silently following Ward and Meindl in rejecting Gosse's parallel. In his 1899 revision of *English Dramatic Literature,* A. W. Ward accepts Gosse's judgment in tracing a relationship between Dufoy and Mascarille,[24] but in a footnote he dismisses the parallel to *Le Tartuffe* as "far-fetched." Meindl also declines to accept Gosse's judgment.[25] There is, therefore, no good reason for tracing *She Would If She Could* to Molière.

Etherege's third and last play, *The Man of Mode, or Sir Fopling Flutter* (March, 1676), represents the highest point of the comedy of manners before Congreve. Not even Gosse finds any specific borrowings in the play. He quotes the passage in which Sir Fopling Flutter criticizes the ladies' clothing and then remarks, "The hand that throws in these light touches, in a key of rose-colour on pale gray, no longer reminds us of Molière, but exceedingly of Congreve." Since this passage[26] is the nearest to a demonstrable borrowing from Molière to be found in all Etherege's plays, how slight the influence must have been! Meindl believes the same passage from *The Man of Mode* is related to

[23] Hickerson, "Significance of Shirley's Realistic Plays," p. 337.
[24] Ward, *English Dramatic Literature,* III, 445-46.
[25] "Wir können ihm [Etherege] doch gewiss soviel Selbständigkeit zumuthen, ein Motiv, das ganz zeitgemäsz und ganz aus dem gesellschaftlichen Leben herausgegriffen war, zu erfinden." (*Op. cit.,* pp. 198-99.)
[26] Act III, scene 2.

Les Précieuses ridicules and he points to other similarities between Etherege and Molière; but he does not elevate any of them
to the rank of borrowings, nor does he urge any important conclusions about Molière's effect on Etherege.[27] Sir Fopling's discussion of clothes, Miles states,[28] is adopted from scene 9 of *Les
Précieuses ridicules*. His attempts at dancing[29] and singing[30]
were also suggested, he declares, by the same scene. There are so
many points of difference between the two passages and such a
possibility of coincidental development that we cannot accept the
ascription without qualification. Etherege's audiences considered
Sir Fopling a portrait and tried to identify him among the current dandies.[31] It seems clear then that dandies of the time may
have suggested Sir Fopling to Etherege. The coincidental qualities of interest in dress and the social graces, dancing and singing,
are not very surprising. English dandies copied French dandies
in actual life, and so stage portraits could be similar without
any literary borrowing. In the terms developed above, in Chapter
II, one must deny the existence of "enough points of resemblance
or such identifying peculiarities as to bar the likelihood of coincidence." It is possible that Etherege recalled Molière in these
scenes, but we cannot be certain. The total case for Molière's
influence on Etherege is now reduced to a possible but not proved
borrowing in this last play.

Since the time of Gosse's work, opinion has receded from his
positive affirmation. Felix Schelling expressed doubts about
Molière's influence on Etherege.[32] Even Gosse himself lost some

---

[27] Instead he remarks in advance, "Die Anlehnung des Restaurationsdramas an
französische Quellen war überhaupt ungemein häufig" (*Sir George Etheredge, sein
Leben, seine Zeit und seine Dramen*, p. 169).

[28] *Influence of Molière on Restoration Comedy*, p. 233.

[29] Act IV, scene 1.

[30] Act IV, scene 2.

[31] See Verity, *Works of Sir George Etheredge*, p. xiv.

[32] See *Cambridge History of English Literature*, VIII, 154-58 (which appeared in
1912).

of his positiveness.[33] Since the appearance of John Palmer's *The Comedy of Manners*, 1913, the opposite opinion has frequently been asserted. Louis Cazamian ignores all idea that Etherege can be explained through Molière.[34] Without any intention of imitating Falstaff's cautious example of administering a coup de grâce to a corpse, I hope this account will help nullify the influence of a fallen idea that has been widely disseminated and accepted.[35]

The conclusion is that no likeness between Molière and Etherege is close enough to prove that borrowing occurred. Without proof of borrowing, talk of influence is unfounded. Even if the possible borrowing in Etherege's last play is conceded, there is still no sound evidence that *The Comical Revenge* or *She Would If She Could* was derived from Molière, nor even that Etherege had witnessed or read any of his plays before 1676. Consequently there is no foundation for the more ambitious thesis that the whole school of Restoration comedy is the product of his influence working through Etherege's early and influential comedies of manners, which modern scholars have shown to be British products. Etherege secured little or nothing from Molière and hence transmitted nothing to his successors.

[33] See his article on Etherege in *Encyclopædia Britannica*, 11th ed. (1910), IX, 807.

[34] Legouis and Cazamian, *History of English Literature*, II, 43.

[35] Traces of the heresy can be found, for example, in the following works: Ward, *English Dramatic Literature*, III, 445; *Dictionary of National Biography*, XVIII, 44; Charlanne, *L'Influence française en Angleterre au xvii* siècle, p. 300. Harvey-Jellie, *Les Sources du théâtre anglais*, pp. 59-61; *Chambers Encyclopaedia*, IV, 434; Miles, *Influence of Molière on Restoration Comedy*, *passim*, especially pp. 61-68, 135-39, 175-82; and Nicoll, *Restoration Drama*, p. 178.

V: WILLIAM WYCHERLEY

WILLIAM WYCHERLEY, whose dramatic career ended simultaneously with Etherege's, took an interest in Molière that was reflected in borrowings of matter and in suggestions for artistic procedure. Our study shifts therefore from vain attempts to identify borrowings to the investigation of the nature and extent of an unquestioned influence. In the preceding chapter we observed the futile efforts to ascribe intangibilities of Etherege's art to Molière's influence when no proof exists that borrowing occurred; here we face the task of giving suitable interpretation to his influence upon Wycherley when the major facts of borrowing have been known from the beginning. What would Wycherley have been without his acquaintance with Molière's work? What use did he make of his French borrowings? Let us consider his four plays in the order in which they appeared, starting with *Love in a Wood, or St. James Park* (*c.* April, 1671),[1] his debut as a playwright.

Although the author had spent his most impressionable years in France,[2] this play indicates that he began his dramatic career after making a large acquaintance with English comic tradition. A light social satire interspersed with scenes of mere farcical intrigue, *Love in a Wood* has characteristics that stem from

[1] It seems inappropriate in this study to disturb the tangle of evidence concerning the dates of Wycherley's plays. Unfortunately the aged Wycherley undertook to tell Pope when he wrote his comedies. This dubious evidence of a forgetful old man has been the source of conflicting opinions held by many scholars, including Klette, W. C. Ward, and Perromat. I have decided to ignore all this and to accept the dates assigned by Allardyce Nicoll, as I have consistently done in all other instances.

[2] When about fifteen he was sent to live in western France, where he was admitted to good French society. He remained there until shortly before the return of Charles II.

Jonson: the submergence of satire in amusement, the shaping of farcical action from stratagems of opposed intriguers, and the use of characters whose "humors" provide only eccentric whimsy.[3] His flimsy plot of rakish gentlemen pursuing disguised ladies in a dark park recalls Dryden and Sedley, although it is not accurate to trace the play specifically to the latter's *Mulberry Garden* (May, 1668), as Klette does, inasmuch as the resemblances are commonplaces.[4] The episode of a lecherous alderman blackmailed by a bawd-mother and her whore-daughter is an essential echo of Middleton and Brome. His characters include numerous types familiar to readers of seventeenth-century comedies, for example, a fashionable gallant with taste in wit, a lecherous, hypocritical business man from the city, a bawd, a mistress capable of blackmail, a silly knight who thinks he is very clever in plotting, an amorous, husband-seeking widow pretending to be shy and virtuous, a would-be wit who deluges the world with his similitudes, and contrasting with these, two rakish gentlemen lured into marriage with discreet but gay young ladies; and a pair of very serious lovers carry on another thread of the plot. Wycherley is cynical, brutal, and brilliant in his invention of false-wit similitudes with which to garnish Dapperwit's affected conversation, but otherwise not nearly so witty as in later plays. There is no demonstrable trace of Molière in the play.[5]

Wycherley's second play, *The Gentleman Dancing Master*[6]

---

[3] For an account of the development of these elements in Jonson, see Davis, "The 'Sons of Ben' in English Realistic Comedy," I, 160-92.

[4] Klette, *William Wycherley's Leben und dramatische Werke,* pp. 41-47.

[5] This opinion coincides with many; for example, that of Perromat (*William Wycherley,* p. 122): "... de toutes les comédies de Wycherley, *Love in a Wood* est précisément la seule où l'on ne retrouve aucune trace de Molière." It seems that Klette (*op. cit.,* pp. 41-47) is the first to allege any traces of Molière. Miles (*Influence of Molière on Restoration Comedy,* p. 69) repeats the unproved assertion he made in connection with Etherege, discussed above in Chap. IV, that since *Love in a Wood* and *Les Précieuses ridicules* are both close transcripts of contemporary life, the former must have been the result of Wycherley's acquaintance with the latter.

[6] How little Wycherley depended upon Calderon's *El Maestro de Danzar* is shown by Perromat (*op. cit.,* pp. 147-57).

(January, 1672) contains a situation in the first scene that bears a resemblance to an episode in *L'École des maris.*[7] In both plays a lady uses her fiancé as an unwitting messenger to her lover. Although Wycherley here very probably copies Molière, the fact is of little importance in the history of Restoration comedy. All that trifling borrowings prove is that the borrower was acquainted with the source;[8] we know from later borrowings that Wycherley read Molière, and so a proof of the borrowing of this slight episode is of little interest. Perromat remarks about the frequent fault of exaggerating the value of such parallels:

Les critiques, partant sans doute de cette idée que Molière fut lit-téralement pillé par les auteurs dramatiques anglais après la Restaura-tion, et que Wycherley lui-même lui doit beaucoup pour ses deux dernières pièces, ont pensé qu'il avait dû s'en inspirer aussi pour son *Gentleman Dancing Master,* et ils se sont ingéniés à découvrir des points de ressemblance. On finit toujours, en cherchant bien, par découvrir quelque ressemblance entre deux oeuvres, aussi hétérogènes soient-elles: c'est un simple jeu de patience. Il ne s'ensuit pas que l'une ait inspiré l'autre.[9]

There is keen judgment in Ward's remark that *"The Gentleman Dancing Master* resembles Molière in manner more than any other of Wycherley's plays."-[10] A careful analysis of this resemblance will show that it lies in the mocking tone of spirited farce. Wycherley has momentarily replaced brutality and cynicism with lightness and high spirits and tends toward social satire without overstepping the bounds of farce. As social satire the play recalls vaguely the matter of Molière's great *comédie-ballet, Le Bourgeois Gentilhomme,* which had barely been printed long enough for Wycherley to see it. The similarity does

[7] Miles (*op. cit.,* p. 232) cites three other specific resemblances to *L'École des maris* and *L'École des femmes,* none of which has identifying peculiarities.

[8] As I have pointed out in Chap. II, borrowings that do not carry form, matter, or spirit to an appreciable degree cannot be used to demonstrate an influence.

[9] *Op. cit.,* p. 158.

[10] *English Dramatic Literature,* III, 463.

not possess identifying peculiarities, however, and there is slight reason to think he borrowed it. The ancient plot of the father's hindering the daughter's lover and trying to marry her to a man of his choice was copied repeatedly by Molière, but this social and dramatic commonplace has also been used by almost everyone else, and so means nothing in this connection.[11]

The relation of *The Gentleman Dancing Master* to the dramatic styles in England, on the other hand, is intimate and significant. Mr. Formal, a prosperous London citizen, having lived in Spain for a long time, has developed such a fancy for Spanish manners that he tries to force them on his London household. He assumes the name of Don Diego. In addition he possesses an extreme

---

[11] The need of keeping the pre-Restoration literature clearly in mind is evident in reading Perromat, *op. cit.,* pp. 362-78, in which he argues that Wycherley's great innovation was to bring realism back to the English stage to replace the dominant use of conventions. He says (pp. 375-76):

"Une des faces de l'originalité de Wycherley est, justement, d'avoir saisi, à l'instar de Molière, qu'il fallait faire désormais du théâtre avec sa seule expérience, n'écrire que ce que l'on connaissait bien ou sentait bien, laisser parler et agir la nature, et que, si l'on ne pouvait bannir tout à fait la fiction, il fallait du moins ne mettre que le minimum d'arrangement et d'atténuation nécessaire pour encadrer la réalité. Est-il téméraire de dire que, sans son expatriation, Wycherley ne se serait jamais assimilé à un aussi haut point les enseignements de Molière? Wycherley passa en France ces années de jeunesse où l'intelligence et le goût se forment; ses relations fréquentes avec la société cultivée, qui l'avait accueilli, exercèrent sur sa destinée une action décisive. S'il ne revint pas en Angleterre avec une idée absolument nette de ce que devait être désormais la comédie, puisque, en 1660, *Le Dépit amoureux, Les Précieuses ridicules,* et *Sganarelle* seuls avaient été joués, il était tout disposé par ses souvenirs, et son caractère aidant, à se rapprocher bien vite de Molière et à chercher chez lui un modèle et un appui."

Will such an attempt to trace as vague and widespread a quality as realism succeed? Miles, for example, would prove Molière's influence on Etherege by the realism of *The Comical Revenge* (March, 1664), a realism that both Gosse and Palmer find worthy of great praise. Elevating Wycherley to the initial place, Perromat denies any considerable realism to Etherege before *The Man of Mode* (March, 1676), which he thinks was learned from Monsieur Paris of *The Gentleman Dancing Master* (*c.* January, 1672). From such contradictions of judgment, I infer that abstract realism is too subjective to be followed through a maze of conflicting influences. If the likeness is not accompanied by identifying peculiarities or by external proof of the unique source, wishful thinking is probably asserting itself.

Although his work is recent (1921), Perromat had the misfortune to write just before the announcements of the findings of recent scholarship on the relations of Restoration and pre-Restoration comedy. The studies of Nicoll, Dobrée, Lynch, Wilson, Mueschke, Hickerson, and Davis have made his views prematurely old.

Jonsonian "humor" of contrariety and will always oppose everything suggested to him. He immures his daughter Hippolita at home to await her marriage with her cousin, Mr. Paris, a silly Frenchified Englishman of a type familiar to Restoration playgoers. A mere three months in Paris has given Mr. Paris all the affectations that could be loaded on any one human frame. Hippolita instinctively gulls Paris into bringing Gerrard, a young gallant, to see her. At the sudden return of Don Diego in the midst of their first interview, Gerrard is compelled to pass himself off as a dancing master. Diego resents his nephew's imitation of the French, and forces him to turn Spanish. Mrs. Caution, Formal's sister (i.e., Don Diego's), warns him of Gerrard's character, but the old man's "humor" of contrariety forces him to defend Gerrard. Thus the lovers get their chance. When the marriage of Hippolita and Gerrard is confessed to him at the close, he declares with amusing stubbornness that he has connived at the match from the first, and says to Gerrard,

...I know now you think that I will give you little or nothing with my daughter, like other fathers, since you have married her without my consent—but, I say, I'll deceive you now; for you shall have the most part of my estate in present, and the rest at my death.—There's for you: I think I have deceived you now, look you.[12]

In this farce we have a burlesque of the recent interest in Spain that, on the stage, received new impetus from Sir Samuel Tuke's *The Adventures of Five Hours* (January, 1663) and Dryden's Spanish settings; of course the vogue started in the days of John Fletcher. There is a satire on the Frenchified English that echoes James Howard's *The English Monsieur* (December, 1666) and anticipates Sir Fopling Flutter, Mrs. Fantast,[13] and a host of others. The capricious "humor" produces real fun, but lacks psychological insight. Wycherley again shows his familiarity with

---

12 Act V, scene 1: "The Mermaid Edition," p. 240. All subsequent citations will be to this edition.
13 In Shadwell's *Bury Fair* (c. April, 1689).

the oft-repeated technique of contrasting true-wits with social pretenders. He has evidently absorbed the comic tradition of England completely and integrated it into his dramatic personality. This lightest and gayest of his plays is an indigenous development, with the examples of Jonson, Fletcher, Shirley, Dryden, Sedley, and Etherege in the playwright's mind. It falls short of the true comedy of manners because, as occurred repeatedly with the Caroline playwrights, the social criticism is lost in the farce of situation and character. This failure even is in the British tradition.

The "Sons of Ben" ... Brome, Randolph, Marmion, Nabbes, Davenant, Glapthorne, Mayne, Cartwright, Cavendish, and Killigrew— ... never fully realized that excessive emphasis in their social comedies on comedy of farcical intrigue ... spoiled the artistry of these comedies and kept them from rivalling the Restoration comedy of manners at its best....[14]

When Wycherley began his third play, *The Country Wife* (January, 1675), he altered his method to a surprising degree. Instead of drawing upon the stereotyped characters and situations of native tradition, he went abroad for suggestions and brought back characters and incidents from Molière and Terence. Apparently he commenced by importing three characters from *L'École des femmes,* and then sardonically adapted them to the English stage. In addition he took many elements of dramatic matter from the play and something from *L'École des maris.* Before itemizing his borrowing, we need to recall the plays involved.

In *L'École des maris* Molière discusses the development of a girl into a suitable wife (see above, in Chapter III, for details) and points out the folly of repression. In *L'École des femmes,* it will be recalled, he shows the futility of depending upon ignorance as a guarantee of marital docility. The play centers in the

14 Davis, "The 'Sons of Ben' in English Realistic Comedy," II, 933-35.

folly of Arnolphe, the middle-aged bourgeois who reared Agnès according to his formula for insuring fidelity. Everything in it is subsidiary to the one purpose of showing the futility of crossing the natural inclinations of youth. This is why, despite the fact that Agnès has been reared in total ignorance, she loves Horace naïvely, purely, and earnestly. In Wycherley's play Horner, a wit and rake, has circulated the rumor of his surgical emasculation; this is his strange device for bringing to his bed those ladies who are careful of their reputations but eager to enjoy forbidden fruit with impunity. Sir Jasper Fidget is the first cuckold. Lady Fidget is another of the line descending from Jonson's Mrs. Otter, skilled in keeping her honor instead of her virtue. Sir Jasper's sister, Mrs. Dainty, and Mrs. Squeamish also enjoy Horner's prowess as a gallant rake in adequate disguise. Chief among the victims of the hero's skill in horning is one Pinchwife. After years of reckless debauchery, the latter has gone to the country and married Margery, a young girl too ignorant even to want to come to the city. Pinchwife, bringing her to attend the wedding of his sister, resolves to protect her from contact with the evils of the city. Lacking the background of experience common to the "honorable" ladies, Margery, even before she sees Horner, falls foolishly into that state of sensual desire that passes for love in Restoration comedy. She tricks her husband and rushes to Horner's chamber. The play ends with triumph for Horner, who leers at the closing "dance of cuckolds."

Wycherley's use of borrowed matter may now be listed. From Terence he took only the device of Horner's pretended disability. In Act I, after Horner and his plan have been introduced, Pinchwife enters to narrate his marriage and defend the policy of marrying a fool for a wife, in a free adaptation from Act I of *L'École des femmes*. This covers about five pages. Mrs. Pinchwife tells her husband, Act IV, scene 2, of her love for Horner, in a way that resembles Agnès's confession to Arnolphe in Act II, scene 5 (two pages), but Wycherley fails to use the *il m'a pris* passage, the nearest to flippant innuendo about the sex relation in all Molière. A few pages farther in the same scene,[15] Pinchwife forces Margery to write a letter to Horner. She substitutes another for the one dictated and tricks Pinchwife into delivering it. Later she writes a third letter,[16] which Pinchwife forces her to complete.[17] *L'École des maris,* Act II, scene 3, is the source for the trick of using a man to deliver a letter to a rival, but not for the other parts of the exchange of letters. Wycherley expands the comic possibilities of the letters far beyond what Molière tried to do. In Act II, scene 2, Harcourt woos Alithea in the presence of her fiancé, Sparkish, in a scene that depends for several pages on *L'École des maris,* Act II, scene 9, for the situation and plot device.[18]

In addition a few epigrams and phrases resemble expressions in *L'École des femmes;* the likelihood that such are verbal echoes is great, of course, because Molière was obviously in Wycherley's mind, but they cannot signify anything beyond that already established fact.[19]

As Molière's figures crossed the English Channel, their natures underwent changes that reflect the satiric wit of the importer. Horace, an honorable and romantic young lover, is not Molière's

[15] "Mermaid edition," pp. 317-18.

[16] Act IV, scene 4 (pp. 333-34).

[17] Act V, scene 1 (pp. 336-37).

[18] The declaration of Miles (*The Influence of Molière on Restoration Comedy,* p. 227) that the "play is an adaptation of *L'École des femmes,* modified in acts iv and v by *L'École des maris,*" exaggerates the indebtedness and neglects Wycherley's originality. As Perromat says (*op. cit.,* pp. 188-89): "Wycherley, pour sa comédie de *The Country Wife,* a fait à Molière des emprunts assez importants. Ici pas de doute... mais, à notre avis, il n'y a pas lieu de crier si fort au scandale.... En transportant dans sa pièce les prototypes de Molière, Wycherley ne les a-t-il pas 'situés' dans un milieu, dans un cadre purement anglais? Ne les a-t-il pas modifiés et transformés? Ne leur a-t-il pas ajouté des traits empruntés aux hommes de ce pays particulier auquel il appartenait? Et cette transposition et cette transformation seules ne permettent-elles pas à l'adaptateur de revendiquer une certaine part d'originalité? Il est difficile, ce me semble, de répondre par la négative."

[19] Churchill, *Country Wife and the Plain Dealer,* pp. 180-87, cites eight of these in his notes.

male lead, but he is the prototype of Horner, the chief figure in
Wycherley's play, a witty, suave rake of incredible sensuality
and diabolical effrontery in gaining ends which are a patent
mockery of a sane life. Horace is a relatively colorless young
man; Horner is a wit of the first rank. The pages sparkle with
his phrases, at times in languid cadence, "A beauty masked, like
the sun in eclipse, gathers together more gazers than if it shined
out"; at times with euphuistic balance, "The woman that marries to love better, will be as much mistaken as the wencher
that marries to live better"; at times with sardonic baldness, as
when to Pinchwife's "there will be danger in making me a
cuckold," he replies, "Why, wert thou not well cured of thy
last clap?" Horner's basic stratagem, which Wycherley took from
the *Eunuchus* of Terence, of course, characterizes him simultaneously as a wag, and, from another view, as a sensualist.
Horace's normal desire for the wife he loved is replaced by
Horner's meaningless appetite for sheer copulation, planned
without love and achieved without emotion. The closing spectacle of victorious Horner suitably rewarded with the punishment
of one more exigent wench on his hands is a triumph of irony.
Horace's reward by contrast is real and permanent.

In turn Arnolphe, a respectable bourgeois with some foolish
notions that need the castigation of purifying laughter, becomes
the wretched Pinchwife, to whom Horner remarks, "So then
you only married to keep a whore to yourself." Both characters
are alike in several ridiculous externals; both anticipate horns in
the most timorous fashion; both choose to marry an ignorant
girl, preferring a marriage free from faithlessness to one full of
domestic felicity. Both men are also ridiculous in their habit of
saying too much, although Pinchwife excels in blunders of this
sort to such an extent that we suspect the device of being "comic
decoration," a side amusement for the audience. But in basic natures they are as far apart as a French provincial town is from

the Restoration London court. Arnolphe explodes over his catastrophe; Pinchwife sighs with a certain comic fortitude. Arnolphe is much more human and normal in his emotions; Pinchwife is an unrealistic Jonsonian "humor." Arnolphe is a figure one can somehow respect, despite his deserved punishment for following a foolish course; Pinchwife is a butt for whom no one can feel a twinge of concern.

The contrast between Agnès and Margery is the most striking of the three. Molière's girl has good sense. She makes an instinctive response to Horace, loving naïvely but wholly, not with her senses merely. Wycherley's Margery is of totally different stuff. Her starved senses yearn for a handsome male—an actor, a servant, or the first Horner she meets. She is the embodiment of feminine lasciviousness; a staple in the Restoration comedy, she is made piquant and unusual by her ignorance of the way the Restoration world goes about securing the satisfaction she craves. Noble love makes Agnès defy the world to win her husband. Comically fierce carnality makes Margery defy her husband to gain an hour with her paramour.[20] Margery is ignorant because she came from the country (country life being a Restoration *bête noire*), not naïve through lack of education (problems of education could not interest Restoration audiences). She asks eagerly, "Do the town-women love the playermen too?" Agnès loves Horace on sight, but Margery is ready for Horner as soon as her husband foolishly tells her Horner has complimented her. Agnès respects Arnolphe as her guardian, but Margery boldly flatters Pinchwife with insincere terms of endearment to hide the lover she has not yet found. Horace brings innocent Agnès a great

[20] Dr. Perromat's analysis of the transformation of Arnolphe and Agnès into Pinchwife and Margery is illuminating and useful (*William Wycherley,* pp. 189-201), but in considering Margery a sympathetic character, he seems to have overlooked the peculiar social norm of Restoration life, where frankness and truthfulness, which Margery undoubtedly possessed more than any one else in the play, were proofs that she was a fool, for she admitted what social sense taught people to dissemble. Since Wycherley did not assign her any prospect of future happiness, as he did Alithea, he surely meant her to be a comic figure.

revelation; London brings the naturally vile Margery a great opportunity—there is no end to such contrasts, and they all reveal Wycherley's art and satiric purpose.

Yet this is a Restoration comedy containing wits, witty women, would-bes, cuckolds, country butts, and lecherous ladies. Wycherley offers, with great likeness to contemporary life, a picture of the gay figures interesting to Restoration audiences. While Horner, Pinchwife, and Margery alone owe any of their origin to Molière, other figures are of interest, some for their conformity to recognized types, and some for their deviations from what one expects in a Restoration comedy. Sparkish is a standard gentleman gull, descended from Shirley. His pretensions to wit and social *savoir faire* make him the butt of the true-wits. He is perfectly revealed by his response to Harcourt's request to be taken to Alithea: "I would not go near her now for her's or my own sake; but I can deny you nothing; for though I have known thee a great while, never go, if I do not love thee as well as a new acquaintance." [21] Dorilant and Harcourt are both dimmed by the brilliance of Horner, but Harcourt gains from his greater place in the plot as the successful wooer of Alithea. The latter is far from the normal witty lady of Restoration comedy, but she clearly belongs to the type. She has the sense to maintain her virtue as the *sine qua non* of a good marriage; she flirts with Harcourt with a little of the expected boldness of the type; but she has been stupid to accept a coxcomb like Sparkish. She is not given much wit. Her demand that her future husband be incapable of jealousy is her only positive sign of a right mind in the witty sense. But her acceptance of Sparkish for such a reason (and her shift to mediocre Harcourt for no better) seems ironic. Although she keeps her technical chastity, she fares little better than Mrs. Dainty and Mrs. Squeamish, who violated the basic principle of the Restoration social code for women by not preserving their

[21] "Mermaid Edition," Act III, scene 2 (p. 293).

chastity until marriage. Their admitted irregularity heightens the impression of universal depravity and may be artistically justified on that basis. The scene in which the wine loosens the tongues of the three gay women, each of whom thinks she alone knows the secret of the eunuch's virility, is ironic enough to justify any means of getting it there.

In addition, a brilliant realism and a faultless use of witty epigram for comic decoration make *The Country Wife* the most sparkling of Wycherley's comedies, giving repulsive material an astonishing verve and vitality. At the moment I do not recall another play that makes such deft and ever-changing use of one comic device, namely, the presentation of a character less acute in his perceptions than the audience. Not even the wits and Alithea get off scot-free from this form of ridicule. The most elaborate collection of double meanings ever put into one play begins with the first talk with the Fidgets [22] and lasts until Horner says to Pinchwife, with utter duplicity, "I must pronounce your wife innocent, though I blush whilst I do it." [23] The author's amazingly fertile genius sows sexual innuendo broadcast throughout the play.

With a taste for ironic cynicism that is well-nigh perfect, he depicts a society where the morals derive from the goat and the characters are all as "lecherous as sparrows." This masterpiece of malicious imagination and saturnine portraiture reveals his unexcelled genius for mordant wit, for the skillful use of popular English dramatic types, and for theatrical effects. He begins with Molière's play and ends with a brilliant reflection of the fashionably corrupt society of his own country. The merits of his work are due to his genius and not to what he took. Its effect is achieved by the masterly ordering of events so that every action is logically motivated. Instead of giving us mere mixture of satire

[22] *Ibid.*, Act I, scene 1 (p. 251).
[23] Act V, scene 4 (p. 359).

and farce, Wycherley has learned from Molière how to focus his implications so that successive situations make the same cynical revelation of the bitterness implicit in a life devoted to the pursuit of pleasure. Here one aspect of Molière's comic genius is truly influential in a significant way. Through him Wycherley has achieved a tone that is artistically superb. "Look," says he in effect, "see this thing you call love." With the subtlest irony of all, he perfected the familiar Restoration level of his play with such attention to realism that many in his audiences would unwittingly applaud their own satirization, for he inwardly felt an Olympian mockery of the social standards exemplified by the wits and the witty women: he makes them unconsciously betray the vacuity of the ends they shamelessly pursue. This comedy is what it is because Wycherley was a dramatic genius, a Restoration gentleman, and a reader of Molière. Yet Molière provided none of the wit, none of the brilliant style, only one point in the dramaturgy, only a few threads of the plot, and only the broad suggestions from which three native English characters emerged.[24] The spirit central to *The Country Wife* is a Restoration reaction to Molière, not a copy of him.

When he came to his last play, *The Plain Dealer* (December, 1676), the initial impulse for Wycherley's observation and imagination was *Le Misanthrope*. He began with a decision to naturalize the Frenchman, to re-think the whole play in terms of English character and English social background. Molière's famous masterpiece expresses a sane social philosophy by the sensitive use of irony of situation and of character. Almost devoid

---

[24] Ever since Voltaire wrote about *The Country Wife* in "Sur la comédie" (*Lettres sur les Anglais*), the use of *L'École des femmes* has been generally known. Klette (*William Wycherley's Leben und dramatische Werke*) discovered the use of *L'École des maris*. He thought he found borrowings from *Le Tartuffe* and *L'Impromptu de Versailles*, but no one else agrees.

Van Laun (*Dramatic Works of Molière Rendered into English*, II, 142) and Miles (*Influence of Molière on Restoration Comedy*, p. 227) over-emphasize the importance of Molière's matter. Ferchlandt (*Molière's Misanthrop und seine englischen Nachahmungen*, pp. 26-28) alone finds traces of *Le Misanthrope* in this play.

of plot, the play presents the conversation of Alceste and of his friends about him. The total effect is to make this ill-adjusted member of the society of the court of Louis XIV delicately and politely ridiculous, because he demands the whole truth, unflinching sincerity, and absolute justice in a milieu that has learned the art of compromise in all things social.

Alceste first protests against his friend Philinte's tolerance and lack of honest statement in every remark. He soon insults the poetaster Oronte by telling him his sonnet is no good; then he tries to woo the beautiful young widow Célimène by objecting to her complacence toward other suitors and by writhing over the gay nothings he hears in her society. Célimène, in fact, can hold her own either as a gay satirist of those absent or in a rough-and-tumble verbal battle with the hypocritical prude, Arsinoé. She is not insensible of Alceste's many good points, but her decision is not yet made. Alceste is also the object of Arsinoé's desire, and even Éliante confesses a tender feeling for him to Alceste's friend, who modestly wishes to be her second choice when she is ready to decide. On every occasion, Alceste makes a fool of himself through his quixotic egoism masquerading as a desire for truth and honesty. His dealing with Oronte in the court of honor is absurd, his belief in Arsinoé's slanders of Célimène will not stand up in a test, and his offer of marriage to the gentle Éliante compels refusal because he candidly admits he is offering himself on the rebound from Célimène. When Célimène has been softened by her sense of guilt in writing harsh "characters" of every one, even Alceste, he spoils his chance of winning her by demanding that she bury herself in rural solitude with him. The play comes to an end when Éliante offers her hand to Alceste's best friend, and they hurry away to persuade Alceste not to banish himself from all society, as he has threatened to do.

The character of Alceste has become Protean in the hands of

the critics, but his essential ridiculousness, his absurd excess of virtue, is surely central to Molière's plan.

Ridicule [says John Palmer] lies in wait for the man who runs to an extreme. Wisdom consists in a perpetual adaptation of the man to his environment. Virtue is social. The reasonable man is before all things conformable.[25]

For those in tune with the spirit of great comedy, this requires no argument, but there does exist a need for establishing Alceste's comic nature, a need created by the rationalizations of numerous romantics, who have found in him a sympathetic reflection of their own objections to the imperfect world. Too noble, too refined, too thoroughly unaware that the views of others may have some reason in them, and too certain to spoil a good case with overemphasis, Alceste, like his idealizing admirers, lacks an instinct for the middle ground of common sense. An excess of virtue makes him ridiculous from first to last. If a sensible man dislikes the amenities of a social world, he will live by himself in peace. If he dislikes the customary procedure for trying lawsuits, he will avoid litigation, or, once involved, do the necessary things in silent distaste. If he dislikes the manners of fashionable Parisian widows, he will certainly refrain from wooing one. Alceste is consistently comic because he feels that he is always right and that the rest of the world never is. His wells of egotism are bottomless.

The romantic Rousseaus are always unable to laugh with Molière precisely because they are too much like Alceste, whom they make the embodiment of noble ideals and the perfection of social virtues. They point to the fact that Alceste has much right and truth on his side, forgetting that the artistic Molière always gave his full figures the many contradictions found in real men. But the play shows that the author meant him to be steadily, though delicately, comic.[26]

[25] *Molière, His Life and Works*, p. 327.
[26] For a good recent expression of this point of view, see Palmer, *ibid.*, pp. 332-40.

What sort of play did Wycherley produce from this? Manly, a frank, courageous, blunt, unmannerly sea captain, has taken to his "sea-life only to avoid the world," for he trusts no one except his treacherous friend Vernish and Olivia, a perfidious coquette. With equal folly he is suspicious of his only sincere friend and of self-effacing Fidelia, a young lady of good family and fortune, who has loyally attached herself to him in the Viola-like guise of page.[27] When the Dutch war breaks out, he entrusts all his jewels and wealth to his coquette and his coquette to his false friend. Faithful Freeman and Fidelia sail with him. Having lost his ship in battle, he returns with the merits of his companions and the perfidy of those he trusted yet to discover. Those discoveries and his violent reactions to them constitute the major plot of a play full of vigorous action and blunt speech. Manly finds his Olivia married to Vernish and his casket apparently stolen. As though to hasten his slow understanding of her real character, Olivia falls in love and thrusts her sensual attentions upon Fidelia. Manly forces the latter to make an assignation with the faithless mistress, and then he shamelessly revenges himself by secretly taking the page's place. In a closing scuffle, he thrusts his sword through Vernish, recovers the casket, and decides to wed the page, whose real sex is this moment revealed to him. Meanwhile his true-wit lieutenant has thrust himself into the affairs of the litigious Widow Blackacre and, through his ascendancy over her simple son Jerry, has forced her into a liberal settlement.

On the side of matter, Wycherley's use of Molière was extensive and masterly. The main action of *The Plain Dealer* replaces Molière's plotless plot, but many useful and characteristic incidents are transposed to the new key. In Act I the exposition of

[27] The rôle of Fidelia, traditionally considered a borrowing from Shakespeare's *Twelfth Night,* was traced direct to Bandello by Klette (*op. cit.,* pp. 61-63). Perromat decided that Barnaby Rich's version in *Farewell to the Military Profession* is the immediate source. See Perromat, *William Wycherley,* pp. 288-91. The material seems too conventionalized for final identification.

Manly and Lord Plausible follows Molière's Act I; although Lord Plausible is not at all like Philinte, for this scene he has a similar function to perform, to draw out the principal character in conversation. Act II is comparable to Molière's Act II at innumerable points, but with important changes also in the plan, the most striking being the deferring of Manly's entrance to the end. Olivia dominates her petty drawing room full of fops in much the way that Célimène shines before her group of French courtiers, but she has the prudishness of Célimène's enemy, Arsinoé. Olivia's bold refusal of Manly has been likened to Célimène's last talk with Alceste. In this scene Wycherley also imitated Molière's example in *La Critique de l'école des femmes,* by defending *The Country Wife.* W. C. Ward says,

The scene in the second act, between Olivia, her cousin, and the two "pretty fellows," Novel and Plausible, was suggested by a dialogue between Célimène and her admirers, in the second act of *Le Misanthrope,* but the detail is almost entirely Wycherley's own, and is enlivened with such diverting antitheses and such brilliant fancy that, perhaps, few scenes more masterly are to be found in the entire range of English comedy from the time of the Restoration downwards.[28]

In Act IV, scene 2, Wycherley treats Lord Plausible and Novel in a manner that recalls vaguely Acaste and Clitandre in Act III, scene 1, and Act V, scene 4. In Act V Eliza tells Olivia of the talk about her, recalling Arsinoé of Act III, scene 4. Olivia turns aside Vernish's jealousy in Act V, scene 1, somewhat after the manner of Célimène's use of the compromising letter in Act IV, scene 3. Like Alceste, Manly has trouble over his literary criticism. Major Oldfox writes as wretchedly as Oronte.[29]

---

[28] Introduction to the play in "The Mermaid Series," p. 365.

[29] More than twenty years before Wycherley's death, Langbaine published the comment that Manly and Olivia were borrowed from *Le Misanthrope* (*Account of the English Dramatick Poets,* p. 515). Wycherley later ridiculed those writers who have an "Itch of being thought Originals" (*Posthumous Works,* Part I, p. 3). This may be a sort of admission of the fact, which everyone else admits. A detailed analysis of these borrowings may be found in Ferchlandt, *op. cit.,* pp. 28-42; or Perromat, *op. cit.,* pp. 236-76.

Reduced to general terms, the evidence is clear that Wycherley selected thoroughly English personalities fitted to the special society of Restoration England, and placed them in an action that followed Molière's general scheme. For example, Alceste, the polite, cultured gentleman of the French court, becomes Manly, the outspoken, brutal ship captain. Both of them possess a belief in the iniquity of mankind and in their own merits, and both love unresponsive women, but in their manners and actions, as well as in their speech, each man conforms to the ways of his country and his station. Coarse Manly would have been totally insensitive to the issues between Célimène and Alceste; Olivia is therefore a lying, cheating, promiscuous woman, with enough hypocrisy to make his better impression of her seem plausible. The artistic merits of this procedure are warmly defended by Perromat:

Les personnages du *Misanthrope* appartiennent à la société la plus haute et la plus raffinée. Alceste, Philinte, Clitandre, Acaste, Oronte sont gentilshommes de Cour, et quelle Cour! Célimène est une femme du meilleur monde. Leur conversation est admirablement réglée, leur language sévèrement châtié. On se dit des choses fort désagréables sans jamais choquer la bienséance.—Le monde que peint Wycherley n'est peut-être pas plus mauvais, plus méchant ou plus perverti, mais il est moins élégant, moins distingué, moins strict sur les questions d'étiquette; il est en même temps plus cynique. Et si son manque de délicatesse morale, sa grossièreté de sentiments, son fond de brutalité sont plus apparents et offensent davantage, c'est qu'il n'avait pas pour les masquer cette exquise politesse des manières extérieures, cette galan-

---

It may be useful also to reiterate that Voltaire's description of Widow Blackacre as a comtesse of Pimbesche (from Racine's *Les Plaideurs*) is based on independent observations of common elements in life in two different countries, not on borrowing. Some scholars as recent as Klette (*op. cit.,* p. 61) are somewhat misleading on the point, although W. C. Ward (*op. cit.,* p. 366) and Perromat (*op. cit.,* p. 269), among others, are clear. Voltaire said, in "Lettre sur la comédie" (*op. cit.,* V, 34), "Vous remarquerez qu'on a encore lardé cette pièce d'une comtesse de Pimbesche, vieille plaideuse, parente du capitaine, laquelle est bien la plus plaisante créature et le meilleur caractère qui soit au théâtre."

terie impeccable, qu'aucun pays, dit-on, n'a jamais mieux connues ni mieux pratiquées que la France du xvii⁰ siècle.[30]

This difference is not due, as Macaulay and Taine reiterate, to Wycherley's desire to degrade everything he touches; it arises from his artistic impulse to integrate everything into the life he saw about him, as his plain-dealing prologue bluntly tells his audience.

> But the coarse dauber of the coming scenes
> To follow life and nature only means,
> Displays you as you are, make his fine woman
> A mercenary jilt, and true to no man:
> His men of wit and pleasure of the age
> Are as dull rogues as ever cumber'd stage:
> He draws a friend only to custom just,
> And makes him naturally break his trust.

Voltaire long ago passed the classic judgment on the play in comparison with Molière's.

Les traits de la pièce de Wicherley sont plus hardis que ceux de Molière; mais aussi ils ont moins de finesse et de bienséance. L'auteur anglais a corrigé le seul défaut qui soit dans la pièce de Molière; ce défaut est le manque d'intrigue et d'intérêt. La pièce anglaise est intéressante, et l'intrigue en est ingénieuse; mais trop hardie pour nos moeurs.[31]

We see at once that the spirit and intention of the French play have been greatly altered. A delicate satire on the social folly of being too uncompromisingly truthful and sincere has been turned in places into a berserker denunciation of society for its want of honor, truth, and sincerity. But in some places an irrelevant satire of social affectations obtrudes, and in others the loud noise of farce drowns out the social and moral issues. Even Manly, who rages at the conduct of others, is capable of the gross revenge on Olivia. Actually the social folly ridiculed in Molière

---

[30] *Op. cit.,* p. 261.
[31] *Op. cit.,* V, 34.

becomes the virtue praised in Wycherley. Two explanations are possible. On the one hand, English manners, even of the Restoration, allowed so much more bluntness of speech than the French that it would be hard for the English to think of plain dealing as a folly. Wycherley's envenomed philippics against the hypocrisy of mankind emphasized an idea familiar to the race that bred Marston, Nashe, and Jonson. As a supreme compliment, Restoration England dubbed Wycherley "Plain-Dealer" for the rest of his life, and Dryden punningly called him Manly Wycherley. Molière's acute study of a delicately comic character would have left Englishmen confused; Wycherley may have altered the effect in a conscious effort to adapt to his audience. On the other hand, the misunderstanding of Molière's intention was almost instantaneous, even in France. The unsigned letter inserted in the first edition in 1667 gives an early basis for the idea that Molière used Alceste as a plain-dealing voice against the hypocrisies of the age.[32] John Palmer believes the "legend of Alceste as an embodiment of philosophic virtue" arose from Baron's interpretation of the rôle.[33] As Baron took the part of Alceste from 1673 onward, this interpretation might well have reached Wycherley as Molière's conception. A shift in the sympathy of an actor could create a new spirit in Molière's play that would be close to the spirit of Wycherley's.[34] We are therefore not in possession of the evidence to demonstrate whether Wycherley consciously altered the spirit of the French comedy to make it conform to his own standards and to the standards of British manners, or whether he endeavored to reproduce the spirit of the

[32] The "Lettre écrite sur la comédie du Misanthrope" is generally credited to Donneau de Visé. See Despois-Mesnard, *Oeuvres de Molière*, V, 368-441.

[33] *Molière, His Life and Works*, pp. 342-44.

[34] See Matthews (*Molière*, pp. 202-22) for an interpretation of *Le Misanthrope* close to the spirit of *The Plain Dealer* (which Matthews had no occasion to mention); and Palmer (*op. cit.*, pp. 327-44) for a brief account of how such misinterpretation of Molière arose. Matthews would credit the *Lettre* mentioned in the note above to Molière, instead of de Visé.

play and fell unwitting victim of the wrong interpretation. The probabilities are, however, in favor of the former, because, despite the strong French influence in his youth, Wycherley was English to the core. His acceptance of his honorary title of "Plain-Dealer" suggests his own leaning. If he had a Manly-bias in his nature, his reading of *Le Misanthrope* would probably be colored by this "humor." In either case, the influence of Molière is less than it was in the case of *The Country Wife,* and the influence of English social life is greater.[35]

In *The Plain Dealer,* then, Wycherley produced a play whose incidents and general action must carry the burden of devastating satire of the manners of the age, with its hypocrisy, duplicity, lubricity, cheating, selfishness, slander, and carnality of every sort. Wit for its own sake is largely absent. The Restoration stratification of social types is found only at lighter moments. In many ways the intention of the author seems closer to *Volpone* than to *The Way of the World.* Molière's sound morality has fused with the almost-forgotten memory of Jonson's ethical intentions. As a result, Wycherley's last play is not his best artistically, although its terrifying bludgeon blows cannot be forgotten. Only *The Country Wife* deserves to be classed with the greatest comedies of manners. It achieves this distinction because it subordinates farcical matter and ethical implications to the one end, the presentation of social satire. Aside from the needless distraction of the broadly farcical subplot of Freeman and Widow Blackacre, *The Plain Dealer* confuses ethical satire with social, and its defects arise from this confusion. The author has forgotten the experience of the Caroline dramatists, that the two types of satire do not mix well.[36]

In summarizing the evidence we have gathered, we observe

---

[35] The reader will see this as a clear example of the application of the Criterion I mentioned above in Chap. II. Here a pseudo-Molière comic spirit is at work. It lacks centrality in the source.

[36] See Davis, "The 'Sons of Ben' in English Realistic Comedy," II, 930-45.

that as Wycherley progressed from play to play, as he became, so to speak, more completely himself and likewise more distinctly British, he leaned more heavily upon Molière. As the memory of his adolescent years spent in France became dimmer, there was a steady increase in the extent and profundity of the influence Molière exerted upon him. The use of Molière is nil in the first play, negligible in the second, very important in the manner of the third, and formative of the spirit and of much of the matter of the fourth. Wycherley was too complacent in taking his own where he found it to bother to hide his borrowing. But the art and the power are clearly Wycherley's, not Molière's. As he himself wrote later,

> For tho' the Matter that a Writer treats of be not new, the Disposition, Method, or Uses of it may be new; as it is the same Ball which good and bad Gamesters play with, but one forces or places it better than another, by a different Art, Use, or Disposal of it.[37]

This influence from France, which grew in inverse ratio to the normal processes of recollection, is understandable enough if we assume that it came from reading, not from hearing, the great playwright. Our author arose from this reading with useful materials, particularly suggestions for leading characters and for good situations. In his later plays he incorporated elements that are central to the Frenchman's matter, and after a complete Anglicization, he made these elements central to his own. He thus owes a large debt for matter, but, most important of all, he seems to have learned how to achieve the effects of comic irony, and, to some extent, how to sustain these effects by the elimination of the usual irrelevant farcical incidents. But this borrowing of technique must not be confusedly called an importation of true spirit, for the benign, reflective sobriety of Molière is wholly different from the profoundly malicious cynicism of Wycherley. Yet without Molière, if one may judge by the first plays, he

[37] *Posthumous Works,* pp. 7-8.

might have been a sardonic wit who missed greatness through a confusion of ends. In the later plays an excellence arises from a change in dramaturgy, and this change may have been suggested by ideas from France. Perhaps it was the reaction of his mind to Molière's that made Wycherley great.

VI: JOHN DRYDEN AND THOMAS SHADWELL

NEITHER Dryden nor Shadwell is important enough in the history of Restoration comedy, particularly as it relates to Molière, to deserve a whole chapter by himself in this study; on the other hand, neither deserves submergence into the general group of minor writers. As a compromise, we must ask these inveterate enemies to lie down together. One can see some resemblances between them, but the similarities can provide only a specious sort of unity on which to consolidate two essentially disparate discussions. It is true that each had a habit of turning out plays he did not admire, in order to make money he could not do without. Each raised this business to a high degree of competence, and each fell short of producing examples of great comic art. Each lived and wrote during the whole span of years from the return of Charles until after the flight of James. Each enjoyed contemporary success and received the flattery of contemporary imitation. Finally, each wrote plays in the dramatic tradition that had come down from early Jacobean days; and each borrowed from Molière. But we must ignore all these likenesses as not pertinent, and put the two men side by side in this chapter merely to give them the degree of emphasis they deserve.

JOHN DRYDEN

Dryden opened his long theatrical career with *The Wild Gallant* (February, 1663), a poorly received maiden effort which possesses many elements reminiscent of Jonson, Fletcher, and Shirley, and some that were destined to find a prominent place

in later Restoration successes. Its interest for this study arises
from its intermediate place in the evolution of the comedy of
manners. For example, the two young women, Lady Constance
and Isabelle, are gay and witty, not wholly unlike Rosalura and
Lillia Bianca in Fletcher's *The Wild Goose Chase* (c. 1621), although more like Gatty and Ariana of *She Would If She Could*
(February, 1668). Isabelle forces on Sir Timorous a prenuptial
bargain that reveals the Restoration dislike of country life; in
this proviso scene she also insists, as Millamant does later, on
"the choice of my own company, my own hours, and my own
actions." She had previously resolved to capture Sir Timorous
for his money; her pursuit is gaily shameless.[1] While Sir Timorous resembles the gull of the older Jonsonian mode, he also
conforms to a common type of Restoration butt, the simple, unmannerly rural knight. The episode of pretended pregnancies,
which closes the plot, is on the level of Brome's vulgarities; the
incidental flashes of wit are anticipatory of similar qualities in
later plays. Lady Constance and Loveby are at an interesting
intermediate stage of dramatic development: too flippant for the
romantic mood, they are too obviously in love with each other
to achieve the absence of emotion characteristic of lovers of the
best Restoration style. Dryden fabricated the plot from pre-
Restoration materials, concealing his sources by removing verbal
likenesses and by recombining familiar elements. A recent analysis
of *The Wild Gallant* found character or plot resemblances to
Fletcher's *Wit at Several Weapons* (1608-9), Middleton's *Fair
Quarrel* (1616), Brome's *City Wit* (1629), and *Mad Couple Well
Matched* (1636), and Shirley's *The Witty Fair One* (1628) and
The Lady of Pleasure (1635). The last of these, in turn, is based
on an earlier pattern, reverting to Fletcher for a device that
Shirley could not provide, a witty leading man opposite the witty

---

[1] *Dramatic Works of Dryden*, ed. by Scott-Saintsbury, II, 72-76 (Act III, scene 1).
All citations to volume and page found below refer to this edition.

woman.[2] By this combination Dryden produced the Restoration town wit and "arrived at the essential pattern of the Restoration comedy of manners."[3] No trace of Molière is found here;[4] the play is important in this study because it provides us with the first piece of potent evidence that the Restoration comedy of manners might have arisen independent of Molière's comic spirit. It reveals some of the possibilities of the English dramatic resources.[5]

In *The Rival Ladies* (*c*. June, 1664) Dryden made his first adaptation of his flirtatious lovers to tragicomedy. By this time Etherege had used not dissimilar characters in *The Comical Revenge, or Love in a Tub* (March, 1664), and the pattern of true Restoration comedy was taking form. While crediting Dryden with the "heralding" of the comedy of manners, "if not with its inception," Allardyce Nicoll notes the salient points of his comic matter.

Dryden introduces a kind of spurious romance into his comedies which Congreve never knew. Sometimes he is more given to humours: and nowhere did he know the fine sparkle and zest with which the masters of the new comedy irradiated their compositions. The heroes of Etherege and of Congreve, too, are more dilettante than Dryden's are: there is a certain intensity about the wild madcap flirtations of

---

[2] Hickerson, "Significance of James Shirley's Realistic Plays," pp. 288-99, 199-237.

[3] *Ibid.*, p. 299.

[4] So far as I can learn, this opinion is held by every one except Gillet (*Molière en Angleterre*, p. 122). In the section, "Traces éparses de l'influence de Molière," he gives three commonplace parallels lacking identifying peculiarities, and says that the play "fut d'abord représentée sans succès en 1663, mais reparut sur la scène en 1669. Dryden y avait apporté certaines modifications dont quelques-unes sont inspirées de Molière." Since only the 1669 version is extant, it seems that the need of avoiding a false chronology makes him believe Dryden inserted these trivial details from Molière into the revised version. The conclusion is entirely forced. Molière has not been shown to be the source of anything in the play.

[5] See Gaw, "Tuke's *Adventure of Five Hours* in Relation to the 'Spanish Plot' and to John Dryden," for evidence that *The Wild Gallant* had no Spanish source. The conclusions are summarized on page 60. Allen (*Sources of Dryden's Comedies*, pp. 1-49) gives a detailed analysis of *The Wild Gallant* in relation to its British sources and to the comedy of manners.

Dryden's Lovebys and Fainalls that is more emotional and more real, in the ordinary sense of that word, than the cynical intellectualism of the characters, let us say, of Etherege. The world of roués did not sit very well on Dryden. He had a heart and he showed it, and, although he could be more vulgar and more indecent than the worst of them, he sets our sympathies a-trembling for his lovers, wicked, frivolous, stupid creatures though they be.[6]

Two years later, in *Secret Love, or the Maiden Queen* (March, 1667), Dryden brought his flirting lovers to their highest development in Celadon and Florimel, and thus made what has been called his greatest contribution to the comedy of manners.[7] In the same year he used Molière's *L'Étourdi* as the source of *Sir Martin Mar-All, or the Feigned Innocence* (August, 1667), which was discussed at some length above, in Chapter III.

When Dryden failed to acknowledge a moderate debt to Molière for matter in *An Evening's Love, or the Mock Astrologer* (June, 1668), he provided the opening for Langbaine's later attacks on his literary honesty. He admits in the preface and in the epilogue that the play is an alteration of *Le Feint Astrologue* of Thomas Corneille, which is, he says, a version of Calderon's *El Astrologo fingido*. He defends his adaptation, pointing to the addition of the parts of Wildblood and Jacintha as considerable, and insists that the wit and language are his own. Langbaine violently attacked Dryden as a habitual plagiarist, and specifically charged that this statement of his is deliberately false, for Wildblood and Jacintha, said he, were copied from *Le Dépit amoureux*. He also mentioned two other borrowings from Molière, which he charged Dryden with concealing.[8] Dryden's truthfulness in regard to his use of Corneille cannot be ques-

---

[6] *Restoration Drama*, p. 214.

[7] By Allen, *op. cit.*, pp. 106-10. Allen also analyses Dryden's use of material from *Le Grand Cyrus* of Madeleine de Scudéry (pp. 80-106).

[8] Langbaine, *Account of the English Dramatick Poets*, pp. 131-77.

tioned.[9] In the first two acts no borrowings from Molière are found. The chief figures of the play are Restoration English rakes pursuing two young Spanish women, who surprise the audience by proving to be as witty and as emancipated as their sisters of the contemporary English stage. By the time we reach the third act, one of the lesser figures, Aurelia, uses language that recalls Molière. She is an exponent of "spiritual and refined language," by which she means such affectations as the overuse of "furious" as an omnibus adjective, the dragging of imaginative euphemisms into common speech, and a fashionable slurring of pronunciation. This seems to be a species of English folly, but the euphemism, "the counsellor of the graces," is an exact translation of Madelon's *"le conseiller des grâces"* in *Les Précieuses ridicules.* A short passage will illustrate these points.

Aur. How am I dressed to-night, Camilla? is nothing disordered in my head?

Cam. [Aurelia's maid] Not the least hair, madam.

Aur. No! Let me see: Give me the counsellor of the graces.

Cam. The counsellor of the graces, madam!

Aur. My glass, I mean: What, will you never be so spiritual as to understand refined language?

Cam. Madam!

Aur. Madam me no madam, but learn to retrench your words; and say ma'am; as, yes ma'am, and no ma'am, as other ladies' women do. Madam! 'tis a year in pronouncing.

Cam. Pardon me, madam.

Aur. Yet again, ignorance! Par-don, madam! fie, fie, what a superfluity is there, and how much sweeter the cadence is—par'n me, ma'am! and for your ladyship, your la'ship.—Out upon't, what a furious indigence of ribbons is here upon my head! [10]

[9] Ott (*Über das Verhältnis des Lustspiel-Dichters Dryden zur ... Molière*, pp. 23-33) made a detailed study of Dryden's plot in relation to its sources. Harvey-Jellie (*Les Sources du théâtre anglais à l'époque de la restauration*, pp. 81-87) retraces the material. More recently Allen (*op. cit.*, pp. 154-70) restudied the evidence. All three agree that *Le Feint Astrologue* of Thomas Corneille is the chief source of the plot, but that the wit and the language are Dryden's.

[10] Act III, scene 1. In *Dramatic Works*, III, 296-97.

The probabilities favor the conclusion that Aurelia's affectations are sketched from life, for the enjoyment of such a satire depends upon the existence of the folly ridiculed. But Aurelia reminds the modern reader, and doubtless she also reminded Dryden, of her French cousins, Madelon and Cathos, and he made the specific borrowing of a few words from the play, nothing more.

In the same scene, Alonzo and Lopez, two Spanish nobles, produce three pages of comic conversation that Dryden obviously composed with his Molière open at *Le Dépit amoureux,* Act II, scene 6. In his play Molière brought a pedant, Métaphraste, into a conversation with Albert, an elderly gentleman. After the parade of meaningless knowledge usual with stage pedants, Métaphraste prevents Albert from talking by insistent interruptions, chiefly to say that he is listening or is silent, and to complain that Albert says nothing. Dryden drops the pedantry. He makes both Alonzo and Lopez eager to speak and both resentful of the other's insistence on speaking. Thus the spectacle of two men talking at once replaces interruption. In both plays the episodes end when one character puts the other to flight by ringing a bell in his ears. While Molière's scene is imitated from *Le Deniasé,* by Gillet de la Tessonerie (acted in 1647, printed in 1652),[11] Dryden used the more obvious source, and even translated phrases freely into his version.[12] As the passage is out of character for the Spanish gentlemen, Dryden seems to have used it for its intrinsically comic action; he did not derive these characters from Molière, nor did he use him again in the part of the plot in which they appeared.

A passage of a dozen lines reveals Camilla extracting money from Aurelia's suitor, Don Melchor de Guzman, by a trick that

---

[11] See Despois-Mesnard, *Oeuvres de Molière* I, 444, note 3.
[12] Gillet (*Molière en Angleterre,* pp. 170-77) gives the evidence in parallel columns.

follows *Le Dépit* very obviously for about a half dozen short speeches.[13]

The same method of composing, with Molière open before him, was used more extensively in Act IV, scene 3. Having promised Jacintha money that he cannot deliver, Wildblood decides to "face it out with another quarrel." The ensuing five pages are a close adaptation, at times mere translation, of a quarrel in *Le Dépit*. But the source again provided the incident, not the characters.[14] Everything before and after the passage borrowed takes a different line of action, and Dryden's characters have no general resemblance to Molière's.

Our examination of the plays involved in the controversy started by Langbaine reveals some arguments on both sides. Although Dryden did use Molière without saying so, his contention that his characters are original is also sound enough, for they satisfied the Restoration notions of gallant rakes and witty women. They possess a kind of *savoir faire* that is much more Restoration English than French. On Langbaine's side, the evidence is clear that in four disconnected passages Dryden has utilized comic devices found in Molière. None of these is so well integrated with the character that it entirely avoids the classification of "comic decoration."[15] In no case is the character or the intrigue determined by the borrowing.[16] It is much more likely

---

[13] Cf. Dryden, Act IV, scene 2, with Molière, Act I, Scene 2.

[14] Cf. Dryden, Act IV, scene 3, with Molière, Act IV, scenes 3 and 4.

[15] I am borrowing this useful phrase from Campbell (*Comedies of Holberg*, p. 108). He defines it: "In all comedy there must be many moments the humour of which depends, not upon their relation to the dramatic purpose of the whole play, but solely upon their own extraordinary and unexpected nature. They are devices for keeping the audience amused by the way, while the humour of a situation or of a character is being systematically yet gradually presented."

[16] In his zeal to prove plagiarism, Langbaine (*op. cit.*, p. 131) afforded an early example of a very common fallacy: "he borrowed incident, *ergo* he borrowed characters involved in the incident." In giving to Wildblood and Jacintha an incident from *Le Dépit amoureux*, Dryden did not borrow the characters, for their characteristics would be essentially unchanged if the borrowed matter were stricken out of the play; those characteristics are not from Molière.

that the need recalled Molière and that Dryden took what he wanted where he found it.[17]

Dryden presented no more comedies for four years, and then, in 1672, brought out two plays owing little or nothing to Molière, but deserving some discussion. The first, *Marriage à la Mode* (*c.* May, 1672), contains a typically English satire on women who aspired to be more refined than the average; such satire goes back at least to the "ladies collegiates" of *The Silent Woman* (1609). Miss Lynch has traced in detail the existence in seventeenth-century English society of a serious cult of *Astrée* and of platonism,[18] and shows that it bridged the gap of Puritan domination.[19] English women, then, with an ambition for the social ornaments of the more cultured, would naturally imitate something not totally unlike French *préciosité*. Satirists would observe these affectations and ridicule them without any debt to Molière or any acquaintance with the spirit of the Hôtel de Rambouillet. Early *préciosité,* it must be remembered, was a serious and fairly intelligent movement for the refinement of French speech and manners, which early in the seventeenth century were decidedly crude. Under the inspiration of the Marquise de Rambouillet, it established the salon and stimulated current literature and active scholarship. Naturally such a large body of people had a "lunatic fringe" that pushed attempts to refine life and language to absurd extremes. By the time Molière arrived in Paris from the provinces, the refinements had been inflated into an ethereal bubble awaiting the pin prick of comic laughter. All Paris was solemnly respectful to a silly cult whose adherents affected to abandon their real emotions, their common sense, and,

---

[17] Although developed independently, my list of borrowings above coincides exactly with that of Ott (*op. cit.,* pp. 23-64). Gillet (*op. cit.,* p. 88) would add *L'École des maris, Le Tartuffe,* and *Don Juan.* His only citation of a parallel passage to one of these (with *L'École des maris,* pp. 168-69) is far-fetched. Allen (*Sources of Dryden's Comedies,* p. 155) seems to have unlimited confidence in Gillet.

[18] *Social Mode of Restoration Comedy,* Chaps. I-IV, *passim.*

[19] *Ibid.,* pp. 107-36.

in general, all realities of human existence. The leadership had shifted from the Marquise to her daughter and to the romance-writing Mademoiselle de Scudéry. The latter had led the refined lovers to the middle of her Map of the Tender Passion—and there they were destroyed by the barbs of the savage Molière. While platonism and romance were international, the distinctly French aspects of *préciosité* were the center of Molière's attack. Thus it is easy to see that though Melantha of *Marriage à la Mode* faintly recalls the *précieuses* of Molière's satire, her absurdities have little in common with French affectations. She is in effect almost a "humor" type, for she has one master impulse, to render her manners and speech elegant with studied posture and hastily memorized French words, which she requires her maid to provide daily.[20] As French was commonly spoken in England, Restoration audiences surely knew many ludicrous pretenders to a facility in the tongue; audiences likewise knew French well enough to catch the wit of the play, much of which they would otherwise miss. Melantha, for example, speaks translated French idiom, "He mocks himself of me." [21] So there is, after all, nothing so close that a positive connection can be affirmed. It is likely that Dryden was unable to think of Melantha without recalling Molière, and some of the faint resemblances may be echoes. Probabilities are not facts; it is a possible, not a certain borrowing.

Dryden's second comedy of the year, *The Assignation, or Love in a Nunnery* (*c.* November, 1672), contains nothing that can be positively credited to Molière, although a few slight similarities can be found.[22] It needs no extended consideration here, for

[20] Act III, scene 1. *Dramatic Works*, IV, 303-5.
[21] Act V, scene 1. *Ibid.*, IV, 348.
[22] Miles (*Influence of Molière on Restoration Comedy*, p. 225), for example, says that Benito is a free adaptation of Lélie in *L'Étourdi*. Benito is a foolish servant, who persists in imagining he is a witty and gallant gentleman. All his efforts are blunders that interfere with the amours of his master. Lélie is a stupid master who hinders his clever servant in the latter's efforts to help him gain his beloved. The only resemblance is that comedy is made of blundering about a love affair.

traces of Molière are much less prominent than the evidences that the author is in the sphere of the English tradition. During the next eighteen years Dryden produced eleven plays without using anything from Molière. If the identification of a possible borrowing in *Marriage à la Mode* is rejected, the gap extends twenty-two years, from *The Mock Astrologer* to *Amphitryon, or The Two Socias* (April, 1690). As soon as one opens this latter play, one encounters in the dedicatory letter Dryden's frank admission of dependence, which deftly shifts into a modest claim to originality:

> It is true, were this comedy wholly mine, I should call it a trifle, and perhaps not think it worth your patronage; but when the names of Plautus and Molière are joined in it, that is, the two greatest names of ancient and modern comedy, I must not presume so far on their reputation, to think their best and most unquestioned productions can be termed little. I will not give you the trouble of acquainting you what I have added, or altered, in either of them, so much, it may be, for the worse; but only that the difference of our stage from the Roman and the French did so require it. But I am afraid, for my own interest, the world will too easily discover that more than half of it is mine; and that the rest is rather a lame imitation of their excellences than a just translation. It is enough, that the reader know by you, that I neither deserve nor desire any applause from it: if I have performed anything, it is the genius of my authors that inspired me; and, if it pleased in representation, let the actors share the praise amongst themselves. As for Plautus and Molière, they are dangerous people; and I am too weak a gamester to put myself into their form of play.[23]

By this last phrase Dryden seems to be offering apologies for the merit of his facile recasting of a continental play into a strictly British mold, which is the chief virtue his production possesses. The prologues and the lengthy expository speeches of Plautus and Molière are put into dialogue, in conformity with the stage tradition of England. The increase of complication over Molière is not very great, consisting chiefly of the Phaedra-

[23] *Dramatic Works,* VIII, 8-9.

Gripus material; in many instances direct dramatization is effectively substituted for indirect matter in his predecessors. The "gratuitous indelicacy" with which Scott reproaches him [24] is the normal Restoration comic idiom. The adaptation, taken all in all, is masterly, not servile. Although Molière is largely an intermediary for the influence of Plautus, he is not wholly so, for Dryden borrowed some unimportant material that originated with the second version. Miles has noticed a comic incident that is very probably borrowed from *Le Mariage forcé* [25]—an amusing challenge to fight a duel. Such a minor incident is, however, of little significance. *Amphitryon* contains Dryden's last borrowing from Molière.[26]

After a study of the three *Amphitryons*—by Plautus, by Molière, and by Dryden—I am drawn to the sensible remarks of Saintsbury:

It is probable that in point of absolute originality there is not much to choose between them, for Plautus must pretty certainly have had a model. The Roman poet is the most humorous of the three, as Molière is the most decent in treating a situation where to be decent without being dull is a proof of consummate art. But in the life and bustle proper to comedy Dryden excels both his formidable predecessors, and two particular innovations of his,—the introduction of Judge Gripus, and the separation of the parts of Sosia's wife and Alcmena's hand-

---

[24] *Ibid.*, p. 2.

[25] *Op. cit.*, p. 225.

[26] Miles has reported borrowings from Molière also in *The Kind Keeper, or Mr. Limberham* (March, 1678), *The Spanish Friar, or the Double Discovery* (March, 1680), and the tragi-comedy, *Love Triumphant, or Nature will Prevail* (1693), but a critical examination of the resemblances does not allow me to classify any of them as probable. He says, for example (*op. cit.*, p. 109), that in *Limberham* Dryden professed to write a social satire in imitation of *Le Tartuffe;* and (p. 231) that "Mrs. Saintly is a free adaptation of Tartuffe." Dryden, in reality, professed in his dedication to Lord Vaughan, (*Works*, VI, 9) that "It was intended for an honest satire against our crying sin of *keeping*," obviously a sin entirely outside the scope of *Le Tartuffe*. In discussing the removal of his play from the boards after only three performances, a removal that Saintsbury says is "certainly mysterious," Dryden remarks merely (*ibid.*, VI, 10) that the "same fortune" (apparently legal suppression) befell Molière's *Le Tartuffe*. Mrs. Saintly is a conventional Restoration stage type, a lascivious old woman hiding behind the cloak of Puritanism. Her hypocrisy is her sole likeness to Tartuffe.

maid are exceedingly happy. It should perhaps be observed that to speak of Dryden's play as a mere adaptation of Molière's, as both French and German writers not uncommonly do, is an entire mistake; and those who make it can hardly have read both pieces, or, if they have done this, can hardly have read Plautus.[27]

Over a period of thirty years then, Dryden produced eight comedies and several tragicomedies with comic plots, none of them showing the excellence to be expected from the greatest and most versatile genius of the Restoration. His deserved place as literary leader of the age was not won by his comedies, though they are far from negligible. Perhaps his loud contempt for comedy as a literary genre was the cause of his relative mediocrity in the type. Perhaps it would be more in accord with present-day modes of thought to say that it was the effect, the usual device for defending oneself by minimizing the importance of what one does not do well. In either case his materials for comedy would not be likely to influence his whole thought deeply. Dryden as lyric poet, as literary critic, as translator, as satirist, or even as writer of heroic and tragic drama would not be affected by the materials which he chose for use in his least successful genre.

In two of the eight comedies, *Sir Martin Mar-All* and *Amphitryon,* there is a heavy debt, but in both the Frenchman was an intermediary adapter of an earlier play, and, while writing each, Dryden had another version on his table at the side of Molière's text. Two more of the eight, *An Evening's Love* and *Marriage à la Mode,* contain minor borrowings, in one case probably rather than certainly. Very little that is strictly original with Molière can be found, and none of it is central to Dryden's comic material, which is composed primarily of flirtations between lovers fond of playing "amatory Battledore and Shuttlecock," to use Saintsbury's happy phrase. These lovers are nearly always entangled in flippant sexual intrigues, they talk brilliantly, and they

[27] *Dramatic Works,* VIII, 4-5.

behave in general accord with Restoration manners. With the scene of the play nominally laid in some foreign land, we have a combination that recalls the romantic Elizabethans, who almost habitually dramatized English manners and institutions with the name of another country attached. All this is far from the norm of Molière.

THOMAS SHADWELL

At the side of Dryden we place his enemy and butt, the arrogant imitator and worshiper of Jonson, Thomas Shadwell, whose plays remain to challenge Dryden's telling charges of dullness. When he opened the career that carried him in comedy above his tormentor's level, he chose the field of realistic comedy in the manner of Jonson and incurred a considerable debt to Molière. In the preface to *The Sullen Lovers, or the Impertinents* (May, 1668), Dryden, Etherege, and Sedley were all hit by the criticism of recent plays, in which "the two chief persons are most commonly a swearing, drinking, whoring ruffian for a lover, and an impudent, ill-bred Tomrig for a mistress, and these are the fine people of the play." Although admittedly written in the vein of Jonson, Shadwell avowed his debt to Molière in the preface:

The first Hint I receiv'd was from the Report of a Play of *Moliere's* of three Acts, called *Les Fascheux,* upon which I wrote a great Part of this before I read that; and after it came to my Hands, I found so little for my Use (having before upon that Hint design'd the fittest Characters I could for my Purpose) and that I have made Use of but two short Scenes which I inserted afterwards (*viz.*) the first Scene in the Second Act between *Stanford* and *Roger,* and *Moliere's* Story of Piquette, which I have translated into Back-gammon, both of them being so vary'd you would not know them.[28]

There is no reason for thinking this is other than a substantially accurate statement of the facts.

[28] *Works of Shadwell* (1720), Vol. I.

Molière's *Les Fâcheux,* his first *comédie-ballet,* from which Shadwell got his "hint," was put together in fifteen days. The plot is not important. Éraste, lover of Orphise, in his efforts to see her, is constantly interrupted by a series of bores, each a hit on a contemporary type or person. After an even dozen appear, Éraste unexpectedly wins the father's consent to marry the girl, and the play ends with his ennui over the intrusion of maskers. In *The Sullen Lovers,* Shadwell reproduces the general intention of a social satire and the same general plot, a succession of encounters with bores. He makes extensive alterations in all details, the characters becoming wholly English. All his "impertinents" possess individual "humors." Two or three times as bulky, his play amplifies and complicates, where Molière's depends upon the perfection of a single stroke. Éraste is fairly civil in his annoyance and is amused to a certain degree; he has no "humor." Shadwell replaces him by Stanford, "a morose, melancholy Man, tormented beyond Measure with the impertinence of People and resolved to leave the World to be quit of them." Shadwell adds Lovel, a friend to Stanford, who gets recreation by laughing at these same impertinents and at Stanford's misanthropic hatred of them. He also invents Emilia and Carolina, "of the same humor" as Stanford and Lovel respectively. The bores are reduced in number and given more action and greatly exaggerated "humors." They are fully Anglicized. Character types and relationships echo the witty woman and her suitors, as well as the social pretenders found in Shirley's synthesis of Jonsonian and Fletcherian materials.[29] The play centers in the same situation as Molière's, the manners are vulgarized, the speeches are occasionally obscene, but the deft imagination of Molière is missing; on the whole, however, it contains the same social criticism and develops it by the same method. Yet it owed its great success very largely to Shadwell's realism and his portrayal of recognized

---

[29] See Hickerson, *"Significance of James Shirley's Realistic Plays,"* p. 357.

types of "humors." It ranks fairly high as an adaptation of Molière.[30]

Shadwell seems to have interested himself more in the Jonsonian side of *The Sullen Lovers* than in the contribution of Molière to his plot, for in his second comedy, *The Humorists* (*c*. December, 1670), he was an entirely English writer of a realistic "humor" comedy of no inconsiderable verve. His model was the Duke of Newcastle's *The Humorous Lovers* (March, 1667). Shadwell followed the taste of the time, the speech of the court, and the precedents of the English stage in his comic portrayal of Crazy, the diseased, but not disheartened, lover of all women. The other types are the witty coxcomb, the vain fop, the verbose parson and fellow of a college, a French surgeon originally a barber, an amorous old lady, a silly city woman, a "vain Wench," and a busy bawd. Contrasted to these are "a gentleman of wit and honour" and "a witty, ayery young Lady" who win each other.[31]

After *The Miser* (January, 1672), the adaptation of Molière's *L'Avare* discussed above in Chapter III, came *Epsom Wells* (December, 1672). By this time Shadwell had shifted in the direction of the wit he had initially abominated. While *The Miser* goes halfway, *Epsom Wells* has as a "chief Subject...Bawdy and Profaneness,"[32] and Shadwell is no longer on the side of humors and decency to the exclusion of Restoration manners. *Epsom*

[30] Much unacceptable identification of slightly similar social types is found in the comments of Van Laun and Miles. Stanford hates bores and rails misanthropically; hence the easy assertion that he is a copy of Alceste. He resembles Alceste no more than he does Shakespeare's Timon or Marston's Malevole. Vague similarities between other characters in *Le Misanthrope* are called borrowings, on even less foundation. A bit of pedantry raised a debt to Pancrace of *Le Mariage forcé,* as though Molière first staged pedantry and pedantic speech.

[31] Miles (*Influence of Molière on Restoration Comedy,* p. 231) stands alone in asserting that "The courting of Theodosia by Crazy, Brisk, and Drybob is a reminiscence of *Le Misanthrope,* where Célimène is courted by Acaste, Clitandre, and Oronte." The only clear similarity is in the number of suitors.

[32] The words he applied to his competitors in the preface to *The Sullen Lovers* (*Works,* 1720, I, [10].

Wells was justly rated very high in the author's estimation. Dryden's random shot, the remark that the wit was Sedley's, must have hurt cruelly. The play is a gayly immoral, realistic expression of many of the social attitudes characteristic of the best comedies of the time. It owes nothing to Molière.[33] Instead, it shows that when he abandoned the "humors" of Jonson, Shadwell turned to the successes of Etherege, Dryden, and Sedley. Dr. Borgman has pointed out that the plot of *Epsom Wells* "bears a closer resemblance to *She Would If She Could* than to any other play." [34] The characters and the action are both in the English tradition. Selection of a watering place for a background recalls Shirley's *Hyde Park* (1632), Brome's *The Sparagus Garden* (1635), Sedley's *The Mulberry Garden* (May, 1668), and Wycherley's *St. James's Park* (c. April, 1671), and it anticipates Rawlins' *Tunbridge Wells* (c. March, 1678), and Shadwell's later *Bury Fair* (c. April, 1689). In all these the characters and the action are related in some degree to the manners and peculiarities of a background familiar to the English. In *Epsom Wells,* Raines and Bevil together with Carolina and Lucia, provide the social norm of Restoration wits of both sexes. Kick and Cuff are cowardly pretenders to the rank of gentlemanly rakes. The two subplots introduce a gulled country justice and two London citizens, who have the surprising experience of making their cuckolding the source of their dominance over their wives. As usual in English comedy after Jonson, the shams of social pretenders are contrasted with the manners of the socially secure. Thus Shadwell was still a grandson of Ben, even when "humors" were dropped.

[33] Miles (*op. cit.,* p. 230), Nicoll (*Restoration Drama,* p. 175), and others mention an episode in the closing scene of Act IV, which they say comes from *Le Médecin malgré lui.* The similarity consists of one of the oldest motifs in low comedy, a quarrel between man and wife. Miles says, "Cuff, Kick, and Clodpate are reminiscences of Acaste, Clitandre, and Alceste in *Le Misanthrope.*" Again the resemblance seems to be entirely in the number.

[34] *Thomas Shadwell,* p. 153.

Shadwell's next attempts were in opera. In the second of these, the elaborate *Psyche* (February, 1675), he undoubtedly used something from Molière's share of *Psyché,* a *tragédie-ballet* in five acts. Molière, Quinault, and Corneille had written this unimportant product in hasty collaboration at royal command. Shadwell admits only his use of the *Psyche* of the *Metamorphoses* of Apuleius. Interest in the work, such as it is, relates to its stress on elaborate scenes and advanced stage machinery, and to its place in the evolution of the opera in England. The author is duly apologetic in the prologue.

> For he [the author] this gaudy Trifle wrote so fast,
> Five Weeks begun and finish'd this Design,
> In those few he snatch'd from Friends and Wine;
> And since in better Things h'has [sic] spent his Time,
> With which he hopes ere long t'attone this Crime.
>
> . . .
>
> But none of them [his foes] yet so severe can be,
> As to condemn this Trifle more than he.[35]

Adaptation, paraphrase, or copy, *Psyche* had no measurable influence on English comedy and brought nothing distinctive of Molière to England.

The only other play of 1675 that calls up the thought of Molière is Shadwell's *The Libertine* (June, 1675), which deals with the well known Don Juan legend, of which Molière's *Le Festin de pierre* is a famous dramatic version. Scholars are now generally agreed that Shadwell drew from *Le Nouveau Festin de pierre* by Rosimond, although he probably knew Molière's play.[36] There is some indirect influence, for Rosimond came after Molière and utilized his work. Shadwell's version resembles both in having a fatal close, although his treatment is essentially comic.

During the next eighteen years Shadwell staged and published

[35] *Works,* 1720, Vol. II.
[36] See Miles, *op. cit.,* p. 231; Reihmann, *Thomas Shadwells Tragödie "The Libertine" und ihr Verhältnis zu den vorausgehenden Bearbeitungen der Don Juan-Saga,* p. 60.

nine more comedies, only two of which show any relation to Molière, even for the details of "comic decoration." Nevertheless, as in the instances of Etherege, Dryden, and Congreve, allegations of borrowings have been carried to extremes. As a matter of fact, it was only after he had turned away from a close imitation of Jonsonian "humors" and from a careful adaptation of French comedy that Shadwell reached, in *Epsom Wells,* a level of excellence above Dryden and only slightly below the accepted leaders, for in wit, *vis comica,* realism, and dramaturgy, *Epsom Wells* and *The Squire of Alsatia* (May, 1688) are as original as anything in the period. The fact that he did borrow previously seems to have led critics to assume a wholesale plagiarism where none existed. Superficial likenesses, that prove nothing, are cited, for example, by Miles, to show that Shadwell borrowed from Molière in *Epsom Wells, The Virtuoso* (May, 1676), *The Woman Captain* (*c.* September, 1679), *The Squire of Alsatia, Bury Fair* (*c.* April, 1689), *The Amorous Bigot* (*c.* March, 1690), *The Scowrers* (*c.* December, 1690), and *The Volunteers, or the Stock Jobbers* (*c.* November, 1692).[37] In only two cases is the evidence convincing. The first of these, *Bury Fair,* shows an interesting and complex relationship to Molière that needs careful analysis. The spirit of the play is extraordinary, considering its time and antecedents. Four years before the début of Congreve and nine before the attack of Jeremy Collier, the new poet laureate pointed the way to an unsalacious comedy in which clearly romantic impulses appear in the leading characters.

Mr. Oldwit, a devotee of the sort of wit heard in the days of the first Charles, and his intimate friend, Sir Humphrey Noddy, an enthusiastic perpetrator of practical jokes and absurd puns, are copies from the Duke of Newcastle's *The Triumphant Widow, or the Medley of Humours* (November, 1674). They are excellent examples of the lower order of would-bes, those who thought

[37] *Influence of Molière on Restoration Comedy,* pp. 224-43.

boisterousness the height of wit. The same types had appeared in *The Virtuoso* thirteen years earlier, and in many other plays. An important aspect of the plot seems to have been borrowed directly from Molière's *Les femmes savantes*. In this play, Bélise, Philaminte, and the latter's daughter, Armande, are devoted to a "higher life" that makes the mundane, physical side of existence too coarse for their consideration. They despise Philaminte's honest bourgeois husband, Chrysale, and are contemptuous of his daughter, Henriette, for she is a common-sense woman who aspires to such unspiritual things as a husband, children, and household duties. All these figures have general counterparts in Shadwell's play. Much more unusual than a borrowing of plot elements from Molière is the abandonment of the social norm of the conventional Restoration play. *Bury Fair* has no rakish hero; not even the ridiculed women, Lady Fantast and her daughter, are placed in any questionable situations. Although Wildish seems to have entered the play with the past of the usual Restoration gallant, he objects to the name of wit. Unlike Wycherley, who disliked the name because too many pretenders had assumed it, Wildish shows the beginning of his disgust with the loose life of the Restoration true-wit and his growing desire for an honorable, common-sense existence. Lord Bellamy's praise of rural life and sober conduct is much further from the tone of the Restoration comedy of manners and closer to the sentimental comedy of a later date. Gertrude, intelligently parrying Wildish's wooing until she believes he will be a worthy husband of a type she can trust, honor, and obey, brilliantly combines the mental agility of current wit with the good sense and decent morality of romantic comedy. This abandonment of Restoration social flippancy is central to the spirit of *Bury Fair;* such good sense is also central to Molière. It would be too much to assert that the great dramatic trend toward morality which is attached to the name of Collier is due to the influence of the French dramatist acting through

Shadwell, but there can be no doubt that Molière's incidental adherence to the standard of the *honnête homme* of seventeenth-century France is contrary to the Restoration mode. There are evidences of such a point of view in some of Shadwell's comedies before *Bury Fair*. In a way it is also implicit in his heritage from Jonson. The most natural inference would be that Shadwell's acquaintance with Molière reënforced his impulses to turn away from the norm of the Restoration comedy of manners and to produce a play with an attitude toward life much nearer the center of the great Frenchman's social attitude than a Restoration playwright had hitherto produced.

In addition to this possible borrowing of spirit, Shadwell put into *Bury Fair* several minor borrowings of matter from Molière that together constitute an important part of the play's excellence. Wildish's decision to foist off La Roch as Count de Cheveux is a very successful adaptation [38] of La Grange's hoax in *Les Précieuses ridicules*. This advantageous borrowing naturally suggests that Lady Fantast and her daughter would be imitated from Madelon and Cathos, but a careful examination of their affectations will reveal that they are of essentially different fabric. Shadwell must have consciously rejected the type of *les précieuses* in favor of figures more realistically allied to British follies. Thus he blended the empty idealism of Philaminte and Armande, of *Les Femmes savantes,* with British affectations toward a "higher life" as he knew it, perhaps recalling the group about the Duchess of Newcastle, with which he had been extensively associated in his earlier years. In any case Lady Fantast and Mrs. Fantast are different from any other affected ladies of Restoration comedy and very similar to Molière's learned ones. They have taken on a high-toned jargon of romantic compliments; for them love is a

[38] Only two years after, Langbaine said (*Account of the English Dramatick Poets,* p. 445) that Shadwell had improved Molière. Borgman (*Thomas Shadwell,* p. 227) believes that "the episode in which the two Fantasts are rendered ridiculous by the barber-count is the best handled of any comic incident in Shadwell."

platonic courtship; no idea is important to their minds unless it is expressed in ponderous polysyllables, preferably with Latin or Gallic sonority.

This borrowing from *Les Femmes savantes* produced the rather definite resemblance of Gertrude to the sensible Henriette of Molière's play.[39] Gertrude perhaps was also introduced for contrast. Molière did not invent, but he certainly exploited with conspicuous success the dramaturgic device of contrasts in character types. In *Bury Fair,* this device is used, perhaps more extensively, more effectively, and more nearly in the manner of Molière than in any other English play of the century. The intelligent, sober Lord Bellamy and the gradually reforming Mr. Wildish balance the silly old-fashioned wits, Sir Humphrey Noddy and Mr. Oldwit. Lady Fantast and Mrs. Fantast are similarly faced by the sincere Gertrude and romantic Philadelphia. Perhaps the antics of La Roch balance the follies of Trim, although, it must be admitted, in a different way. Here surely is an important influence, and a rare one, on dramatic form.

The last play of Shadwell's to contain a convincing parallel to Molière is *The Amorous Bigot, with the Second Part of Tegue O'Divelly* (c. March, 1690). Produced in the closing days of his career, it is a potboiler of little merit. It contains, as Dr. Borgman says,[40] a great many tested dramatic devices from Shadwell's own works and from others. Most of the alleged borrowings from Molière are not convincing,[41] but the resemblance of the Belliza-Elvira relationship to a minor device in *L'École des maris,* which had become common stock, is apparent. Like Sganarelle, Belliza keeps his daughter locked up. In both plays the imprisoned girl dupes the jailor into making essential communications to her lover. In both, the older man delivers proof of the younger one's love in equivocal words that the elder takes for acquiescence in

[39] Heinemann, *Shadwell-Studien,* pp. 69-72.
[40] *Op cit.,* p. 235.
[41] Cf. Miles, *op. cit.,* p. 224 with Borgman, *op. cit.,* pp. 231-32.

defeat. The incident is not important, and the debt is correspondingly slight.

Shadwell produced fourteen comedies in all. Two of these, *The Miser*[42] and *The Libertine,* are successful adaptations of French plays, the first of which is Molière's. *The Sullen Lovers, Bury Fair,* and *The Amorous Bigot* show positive use of his work. The other nine cannot be placed on the list of proved borrowings, although they contain vague resemblances called positive reminiscences by the credulous. Shadwell's best effort is not infrequently connected with Molière. Primarily a son of Ben, or rather a grandson, Shadwell felt both literary impulses and political influences pulling him toward the common-sense standards of the middle class and away from the immoralities of the court of Charles. These influences would make him more sensitive to the decency and sobriety of the Frenchman. After Wycherley, he was the only Restoration playwright to be seriously touched by ideas from the Continent. Apparently under the inspiration of Molière, he set forth social ideas contrary to the Restoration notions. Despite these influences Shadwell was sturdily British, and his best work is, viewed largely, a continuation of pre-Restoration English comedy. To this he brought a liberal admixture of carefully observed contemporary realism, which he learned from the example and precept of Jonson and his school. But Molière's influence may also have been potent, for if we may judge by *Bury Fair,* Shadwell seems to have had a fuller understanding of Molière's virtues than any of his countrymen except Wycherley; and it was possibly from Molière that he derived in part the encouragement to turn away from Restoration standards and point, however feebly, toward the decency and morality found in the drama of sensibility.

[42] See Chap. III for a discussion of this play.

VII: THE MINOR BORROWERS

B EFORE reaching the great names of Congreve, Farquhar, and Vanbrugh, with which Restoration comedy comes to a close, we must discuss the minor plays, no matter how dull or otherwise negligible, that contain borrowings from Molière, and those that need refutory mention because they have been alleged to contain matter from him. They may well fall into chronological order, which we shall break only to the extent of completing the survey of one author before proceeding to the next. D'Avenant, Sedley, Ravenscroft, Crowne, Rawlins, Otway, Behn, Wright, and Penkethman will be considered in turn.

SIR WILLIAM D'AVENANT

It is a generally accepted fact that chronological priority in an adaptation of Molière to the English stage goes to Sir William D'Avenant. Langbaine remarks about his *The Playhouse to Be Let* (*c*. August, 1663).

I know not under what Species to place this Play, it consisting of several Pieces of different Kinds handsomely tackt together, several of which the Author writ in the Times of *Oliver,* and were acted separately by stealth; as the History of Sr. *Francis Drake* exprest by Instrumental, and Vocal Musick, and by Art of Perspective in Scenes, etc. The Cruelty of the Spaniards in *Peru*. These two Pieces were first printed in quarto. They make the third and fourth Acts of this Play. The second Act consists of a French Farce, translated from *Molliere's Sganarelle, ou Le Cocu Imaginaire,* and purposely by our Author put into a sort of *Jargon* common to the French-men newly come over. The fifth Act consists of *Tragedie travestie,* or the Actions of *Caesar Antony* and *Cleopatra* in Verse Burlesque.[1]

Sganarelle, ou le cocu imaginaire is one of Molière's early plays, a brilliant one-act farce of bourgeois life. It is built about the single plan of having the four chief characters quick to put the worst interpretation on what they see; each of the four allows his suspicions to create a separate instance of unfounded jealousy. It is a marvel of construction, little marred by the wooden denouement, which ends on the simple moral that it does not pay to believe all one sees. D'Avenant's translation, which composes the second act of this miscellaneous program called *The Playhouse to Be Let,* follows the original, speech by speech, with excisions consistently made to reduce the length. This shortening allows the omission of Gros-René and the unnamed relative of Sganarelle; the action is naturally hurried. It ends with dances and an added song by Sganarelle. D'Avenant stressed the Frenchiness of his characters, a point that obliterated the significance of the original satire. Although he borrowed the matter of the act, none of the spirit or form can be ascribed to the source, and the version has no literary merit or traceable influence on later comedy.[2]

[1] *Account of the English Dramatick Poets,* pp. 109-10.

[2] Gillet (*Molière en Angleterre,* pp. 1-4) holds to the contrary. He maintains as his major assumption that humble translations and adaptations of Molière, even though they debased the original, were the essential intermediaries for the importation to England of Molière's genius. The first decade of the Restoration is, he thinks, most important, for it is the period of importation, in contrast with the succeeding periods of assimilation. This is obviously contrary to the criteria I developed in Chapter II.

Gillet finds (*op. cit.,* pp. 28-29) that D'Avenant's *Playhouse to Be Let* originated the conventional dialect for the English theatre which we know as stage French, transmitting it first to Dufoy, of Etherege's first play. This is a debt to Molière! He thinks that perhaps this gibberish was suggested by Mascarille of *L'Étourdi!* Dr. Hickerson has since pointed out the existence of an English prototype for Dufoy. Le Friske, of Shirley's *The Ball* (1632), is a dancing master with a lingo resembling Dufoy's. (See Hickerson, "Significance of Shirley's Realistic Plays," p. 304.)

Gillet's inherent eagerness to give all possible credit to Molière is revealed by his efforts to force the date of D'Avenant's play to a point after the presentation of *L'Impromptu de Versailles.* Then he conjectures that D'Avenant was abroad to see this presentation, for the printing date is too late for his use. This enables him to believe

SIR CHARLES SEDLEY

The Mulberry Garden (May, 1668), Sir Charles Sedley's first play, opens with a scene clearly based on the exposition of *L'École des maris*. The resemblance was discussed above in Chapter II, and need not be repeated here. Sedley utilizes Molière's introductory action, but reduces it to a mere device for opening a typical Restoration intrigue. The first four pages of his play contain the sole evidence that the gay rake ever glanced at the French master, for he never returns to the source for anything. He made the characters genuine Englishmen of the last days of the Commonwealth, presenting them in a major action that approaches tragicomedy. Interest can be taken in the play as another expression of the forming Restoration taste. In general the tone is reminiscent of pre-Restoration comedies like Brome's, but the plotting is closer to Shirley. Happily the denouement is made to coincide with the decision of General Monck to bring back Charles II. All the young people are clearly trying to be witty in their speech, and present an interesting example of witty dialogue, in a prenuptial scene between Olivia and Wildish, which suggests but does not approach Congreve's.[3] Four romantic marriages and a satiric one close the play.

Langbaine probably was true to Restoration taste in his judgment:

> I dare not say, that the Character of Sir *John Everyoung,* and Sir *Samuel Fore-cast,* are copies of *Sganarelle* and *Ariste,* in *Molliere's L'Escole des Maris;* but I may say, that there is some Resemblance; tho' whoever understands both Languages, will readily, and with Justice give our *English* Wit the preference: and Sir *Charles* is not to learn to Copy Nature from the *French.*[4]

---

that the use of the bare stage, as a scene in the *Playhouse,* was copied from *L'Impromptu* and then passed on to Villiers' *The Rehearsal.* (See Gillet, *op. cit.,* pp. 32-33).

[3] *Works of Sedley,* Pinto, ed., I, 177-79.

[4] *Op cit.,* p. 487.

The nature Sir Charles copied is probably English, and the praise the play received (it was reprinted three times during Sedley's life) in Restoration times was due to Sedley's ability to maneuver his characters according to English traditions, not to what he borrowed from Molière.[5]

EDWARD RAVENSCROFT

An unusual knack for achieving theatrical success without solid merit seems to have been the good fortune of Edward Ravenscroft, the most facile and most shameless plagiarist of the period. Ranking with D'Urfey and Mrs. Behn for large quantity with no quality, he deserves study as a key to the theatrical taste he was successful in satisfying. He adapted Molière freely

---

[5] Hickerson shows that there is a close resemblance in plot to *She Would If She Could*, although it leans toward Shirley more than it does toward Congreve (*op. cit.*, pp. 340-51). My opinion, given above, is substantially in accord with that of Sedley's chief student, V. de Sola Pinto (*Sir Charles Sedley*, pp. 249-67). Dr. Pinto, however, does not emphasize the fact that Sedley dropped *L'École des maris* after the opening pages.

Sedley's method with a play more to the taste of his time is interestingly revealed in *Bellamira, or the Mistress* (May, 1687), an adaptation of the *Eunuchus* of Terence. Here the plot is taken over with considerable exactness, and many of the lines are a direct translation into the idiom of Restoration English. The characters are readily recognized in comparison with the Latin source. But a spectator or reader unacquainted with classical comedy would not look for any borrowing; the play has been too completely Anglicized in every detail to disturb the unsuspecting. All references to places, all reflections of manners and morals, and the tone are Restoration. Only in Sedley's time would one find such mocking juxtaposition of ideas as

"*Lionel.* Is she very handsome?"

"*Merryman.* She is well."

"*Lionel.* Not comparable to mine."

"*Merryman.* That's your fancy: Of Children, Mistresses and Religions our own are still the best."

Act II, scene 1 (p. 31). Cf. *Eunuchus*, Act II, scene 5. Some of the wit and nearly all the interest developed out of situations are found in the original. To these, a great many witticisms of Restoration tone and a few new situations have been added. Verbal grossness takes it far below the level of Terence, but the play is a well-designed attempt to give the same sort of pleasure to a Drury Lane audience as Terence gave at the Megalensian Games more than eighteen centuries earlier. One is impelled to believe that *L'École des maris* would have been similarly treated, if Sedley had not been aware that its simple, logical plot and considerable moral seriousness were too far from the taste of Restoration England.

and often. Six of his plays enter into the discussion; to wit: (1) *Mamamouchi, or the Citizen Turned Gentleman;* (2) *The Careless Lovers;* (3) *The Wrangling Lovers, or the Invisible Mistress;* (4) *Scaramouch a Philosopher, etc.;* (5) *The London Cuckolds;* and (6) *The Canterbury Guests, or a Bargain Broken.*

(1) The amusing adaptation found in *Mamamouchi, or the Citizen Turned Gentleman* (July, 1672), while lacking the literary merit of the original, successfully reproduces Molière's theatrical skill in *comédie-ballet* and in farce. Almost too familiar to require description, *Le Bourgeois Gentilhomme* is a comedy of manners in the external guise of a musical extravaganza. The social ambition of the rich but *gauche* Philistine, M. Jourdain, is immortally satirized. Everyone recalls his attempts to direct musicians and dancers, his lessons in dancing and philosophy, his discovery that he talks prose, his costume so ridiculously fashionable that he is attended by two lackeys to keep bystanders from laughing at him, his furious quest for beauty, and his wild ambition to woo a marquise. M. Jourdain is constantly humored and mulcted by adherents willing to flatter his hopes with reassurances. But it was left to middle-class Cléante, the suitor preferred by sensible Mme. Jourdain and the Jourdain daughter, Lucile, to stage the greatest hoax of all and thus to overcome the paternal veto. The last two acts are filled with the vast show in which Cléante appears with a huge retinue as the son of the Grand Turk himself and beguiles consent from the entranced Jourdain, who is learning to jabber Turkish and disdaining a mere marquis.

M. de Pourceaugnac, a farce *ballet,* though rich in situations giving amusement, is less unified in its satiric import. Éraste may not marry Julie because her father, Oronte, has selected the unknown M. de Pourceaugnac, a pompous fool from distant Limoges. Éraste's clever valet, Sbrigani, engineers successive in-

trigues to gull the rural butt and unite the lovers. Said to be
deranged, poor Pourceaugnac is forcibly treated with innumerable
glisters. The doctor is sent to tell Oronte that the Limousin is not
physically fit to become a husband. Sbrigani then tells Pourceaugnac that Julie is a coquettish flirt of no reputation. Julie seconds
this with a pretense of amorous enthusiasm for him after her
father and her suitor are both eager to cancel the bargain. This
scene is then interrupted by women who charge the luckless
suitor with bigamy and produce a flock of children to chorus,
"Papa." After numerous other struggles with his tormentors, the
wretch escapes and Oronte is delighted to award Julie to Éraste.

In *Mamamouchi* these two plays of Molière's are woven into
a single play that retains most of the striking elements in the
former, but leaves some of the amusing situations of the latter
for future plundering. It would be a useless task to state all the
tangled borrowings, for it would clear nothing. Some typical
details will show how inextricably Ravenscroft jumbled the material and blended the characters. Jorden, the rich citizen with
social ambitions, plays the rôle of Jourdain from *Le Bourgeois
Gentilhomme,* but he is also Oronte in the episodes taken from
M. de Pourceaugnac. Like Oronte he has no wife, and like Jourdain, he woos a woman who is masquerading as a member of
the nobility. Like both he wishes to choose his daughter's husband. Of course most of Molière's fantastic satire of Jourdain
disappears in the excitement. Sir Simon Softhead, a country
knight, a conventional English stage character, is assigned the
action of M. de Pourceaugnac when facing the intrigues of Lucia,
Cleverwit, Trickmore and Cure-al; these latter also take the parts
respectively of Julie, Éraste, Sbrigani and the First Doctor in *M.
de Pourceaugnac.* Lucia and Cleverwit are also Lucile and
Cléonte. Young Jorden takes over the part of Dorante, the lover
of Dorimène, whom Ravenscroft calls Marina; thus the son and
the father are rivals. Miles first noted that this is a recollection

of *L'Avare:* [6] Marina is a verbal echo of Marianna; Maitre Jaques, who is a teacher of French to Jorden and takes the place of the Maître de Philosophie in informing him that he can speak prose, is the name of Harpagon's cook-coachman, whose silly pretense of a reconciliation also reappears.[7] Betty Trickmore uses a device or two of Frosine's. The elements from *L'Avare* are brought to the farcical level of the other material. The finale is the extravagant Turkish ballet from *Le Bourgeois Gentilhomme.* By combining two plays, Ravenscroft loses much of the satiric force of both, and produces a remarkable program of action, burlesqued "humors," and extravaganza. Molière furnished the striking situations, the theatrical effectiveness of the details, and whatever originality remains in the characters. In this play Ravenscroft started a long career of totally uninspired adaptation of others' plays. Devoid of originality or style, he had a good sense for theatrical effects, and he copied with a conscienceless mendacity too unmoral for condemnation. His popular success was due to his feeling for stage values in the work of other men. By such endeavors Ravenscroft brought a great deal of the successful Molière to England, but none of the man Boileau called "le contemplateur."

(2) *The Careless Lovers* (March, 1673) shows Ravenscroft writing a play that is essentially Restoration English in its plot and manner. Lovewell, "a well bred gentleman," loves Jacinta, the daughter of Muchworth, an old alderman. The father wishes her married into a higher class and has selected De Boastado, a silly fop with great pretensions to foreign travel. Lovewell's friend, Careless, is a Restoration rake who despises constancy. He soon falls in love with Hillaria, Muchworth's niece and ward, who is a female wit of great daring, especially in her conversation. In fact she is a fully emancipated Restoration woman, ready

---

[6] Miles, *Influence of Molière on Restoration Comedy*, pp. 104-6.
[7] Cf. *Mamamouchi*, Act III, scene 1, with *L'Avare*, Act IV, scene 4.

even to enter a tavern dressed as a man and compete with her lover for the favor of street women. De Boastado is disposed of as a suitor by the trick in *M. de Pourceaugnac*,[8] the production of alleged wives with children and the threat of execution for bigamy. By further trickery he is married to a waiting woman and takes her back to the country with him. Muchworth accepts Lovewell as a husband to his daughter, and Careless comes to terms with Hillaria in an amusing agreement, similar to Millamant and Mirabell's, though vulgar in word, adept in innuendo. The plot revolving about the stern father resembles that of *M. de Pourceaugnac,* but it has been common property too long for it to be credited to any source. The disguising of Lovewell's servant, Toby, to mock De Boastado's fantastic dress,[9] is a free imitation of Mascarille of *Les Précieuses ridicules.* Six pages of Act II are adapted, almost translated, from *Le Bourgeois Gentilhomme.*[10] The beginning of Act V, with De Boastado disguised as a doctor, recalls Molière's *Le Médecin malgré lui* or *L'Amour médecin,* but there is nothing demonstrably borrowed. Summing up, we find ten pages of the eighty-five borrowed from Molière and three more imitated.[11] This is a low score for Ravenscroft. Rather than credit him with such unprecedented originality, we would suspect him of having stolen from his English predecessors and contemporaries.

(3) *The Wrangling Lovers, or the Invisible Mistress* (c. September, 1676) is a brisk play in the style of the Spanish comedies of intrigue. It is full of disguises, jealousies, suspicions, mistaken identities, and swashbuckling quarrels. Two of the men finally win two of the ladies. Van Laun identifies some characters with some in *Le Dépit amoureux,* but his only parallel passage is far-

---

[8] Act II, scenes 7 and 8.
[9] *The Careless Lovers* (London, 1673), Act IV (pp. 38-40).
[10] Act III, scenes 8-10.
[11] Langbaine pointed out (*op. cit.,* p. 419) the copying of *M. de Pourceaugnac,* Act II, scenes 7-8. Miles (*op. cit.,* p. 226) added the imitation of Mascarille.

fetched.[12] Ward[13] and Charlanne[14] follow Van Laun. The fact is that both plots have a general resemblance which may be traced to the use of internationally conventionalized material, but there the similarity ends. Miles silently drops the attribution.

(4) *Scaramouch a Philosopher, Harlequin a Schoolboy, Bravo, Merchant, and Magician. A Comedy after the Italian Manner* (May, 1677), is based on two of Molière's farces, *Les Fourberies de Scapin* and *Le Mariage forcé*. There is a certain low form of originality, however, in the thought of binding the two into one plot. Of course nearly all characterization disappears in such an amalgamation, and Molière's revivification of Terence's ancient *Phormio* suffers the usual *mal de mer* in crossing the English Channel. The introduction of Harlequin and Scaramouch gives the printer the chance to put "after the Italian Manner" on the title page. But most of the matter of the plot came from Molière.

The combination of two of Molière's characters, noted in the case of *Mamamouchi,* leads to even worse confusion here. Demipho and Chremes of Terence become Argante and Géronte with Molière. They are Scaramouch and Pancrace with Ravenscroft, who also gives them the rôles of Marphurius and Pancrace when material is taken from *Le Mariage forcé*. Antipho of Terence, Octave of Molière, and Octave of Ravenscroft are identical,

---

[12] In Molière's play (Act I, scene 4) Mascarille, servant to Valère, is accosted by Valère's rival, Éraste, and Gros-René, and questioned about Lucile. Assured that Éraste and Gros-René have given up the pursuit, Mascarille reveals that Valère and Lucile are secretly married. (It develops later that Valère was really married to Ascagne disguised as Lucile.) Van Laun (*Dramatic Works of Molière,* I, 183-86) quotes a scene from *The Wrangling Lovers* as "a fair sample of Ravenscroft paraphrasing Molière." In this passage Orgdano, a clever servant, accosts Sanco, a stupid one, and induces the latter to betray the fact of his master's interview with Donna Elvira, while Don Diego, Orgdano's master, overhears the conversation. Van Laun is so "hypnotized with his unique source" that he declares "Gros-René betrays the secret of Lucile's marriage to Éraste and Mascarille." If true, this statement would improve a certain parallellism in characters, but Van Laun's own translation testifies that Gros-René did nothing of the sort. I cannot see any greater resemblance than would naturally occur in intrigues of lovers who have servants to help and to hinder. The resemblance is made visible only by the elimination of the dissimilar and by the distortion of what is left.

[13] Ward, *English Dramatic Literature,* III, 315 note.

[14] *L'Influence française en Angleterre au xviie siècle,* p. 266.

but by a slight addition to the plot Ravenscroft's Octave pretends to be Alcidas, a friend of Alberto's, when Spitzaferro
(Sganarelle) refuses to marry Aurelia (Dorimène in *Le Mariage
forcé* and Hyacinte in *Les Fourberies*). She and Zerbinetta, believed gypsies in *Les Fourberies,* pretend to be gypsies in *Scaramouch,* and act the part of the real gypsies in *Le Mariage.* Most
of the work of Scapin falls to Harlequin, but an added "man of
intrigue," Plautino, relieves him of some. Three different passages of a page or two are taken from fragments of *Le Bourgeois
Gentilhomme* not used in *Mamamouchi.* Langbaine's contemptuous "I believe he cannot justly challenge any Part of a Scene as
the Genuine Off-spring of his own Brain" [15] is essentially just, but
there is a passage of four pages at the opening of Act III, in which
Harlequin goes to school with children, that may be original.[16]

(5) In *The London Cuckolds* (November, 1681), Ravenscroft
produced a scandalous success that had the honor of an annual
staging on the Lord Mayor's day until 1752.[17] Its tone harks back
to the medieval *fabliaux* in its candor in dealing with sex; for its
interest it depends upon a rapid succession of attempts of three
wives to cuckold their husbands, for its surprises it relies upon
unexpected returns, and for its humor it is content with the success of the illicit intrigues. The approved characters, the wives
and their gallants, employ their wits solely in making assignations; the feeble wit of the entire play is concentrated in the jibes
which the deceived husbands hurl at each other.

Langbaine,[18] Van Laun,[19] Ward,[20] and Miles[21] have discussed

---

[15] *Op cit.,* p. 423. Langbaine mentioned the three plays used. Others have followed.
Miles is fairly accurate in his mention of details. His ascription of Act IV to the influence of *M. de Pourceaugnac* (*op. cit.,* pp. 103-7) is incredible.

[16] Bader ("Italian Commedia dell' Arte in England," p. 141) describes this scene
among the passages independent of Molière, and then adds, "I have found no exact
parallel for the school room incident, although the school teacher and the school room
were not unknown in *commedia dell' arte* pieces."

[17] Nicoll, *Restoration Drama,* p. 244.   [18] *Op cit.,* p. 421.

[19] "Les Plagiaires de Molière en Angleterre," *Le Moliériste,* II, 238.

[20] *Op cit.,* III, 451.   [21] *Op cit.,* p. 232.

the "plagiarisms" from Molière and others. The debt is not over-whelming. To dodge the proverbial horns, one of the citizens, Alderman Wiseacre, has elected, like Arnolphe (and this is his sole likeness), to marry an ignorant girl of fourteen. The three prospective cuckolds discuss their ideas as follows:

Dash [*well*]. Then let me tell you for both your comforts, a wife that has wit will out-wit her husband, and she that has not wit will be out-witted by others beside her husband, and so 'tis an equal lay, which makes the husband a Cuckold first or oftenest.

Wise [*acre*]. You are a married man, *Mr. Dashwell,* what course have you taken?

Dood [*le*]. Ay, is yours wise or foolish? tell us that.

Dash. Look you, the security lies not in the foolish wife, or in the wise, but in the godly wife, one that prays and goes often to Church, mind you me, the religious godly wife, and such a one have I.[22]

In the end Ramble gets to the bride-bed ahead of the husband and teaches ignorant Peggy the "whole Duty of a wife."[23] Like Agnès in naïveté, she tells her husband with candid joy:

Wise. To do how?

Peg. Nay but *I* can't tell you how, but *I* have learn'd a great deal of him, and if *I* were in Bed *I* could shew you.

Wise. You are a Baggage.

Peg. Indeed Uncle *I* had forgot you told me *I* must call you Hus-band, and now Uncle-Husband, it was ten times a better Duty than that you taught me.

Wise. Very pleasant.

Peg. Yes, yes, so pleasant I could do such duty all night long.[24]

The borrowing is indirect: Wycherley had used Molière's *L'École des femmes* to suggest Pinchwife and Margery in *The Country Wife*. Ravenscroft used the latter to arrive at such situations as the above, wholly unlike Molière in spirit or form and obviously very different in matter.

[22] *The London Cuckolds* (Third Quarto, 1697), p. 4.
[23] *Ibid.*, p. 57.
[24] *Ibid.*, pp. 63-64.

(6) In the next to the last comedy of his long career, *The Canterbury Guests, or a Bargain Broken* (September, 1694), Ravenscroft showed very little originality, as this is a dressing up of his own play, *The Careless Lovers,* staged twenty-one years earlier. No new borrowing from Molière is found here, but the device used in the earlier play, the entry of deserted wives, is copied with the modification that, instead of bigamy, seduction with promise of marriage is charged.

Much of the later play, including the names of six characters, was copied almost verbatim from the earlier; De Boastado, the "Conceited Lord and Traveller," was replaced by Sir Barnaby Buffler, "A Country Knight that affects to speak Proverbs." A gluttonous justice, a blunt sea captain, a sister of Lovell, two innkeepers, and a cook were added. All of these were fitted into the earlier dialogue and given characters that border on the traditional "humors." Ravenscroft apparently admired the mediocre wit and sparkle of the merry war between Hillaria and Careless and the atmosphere of his other witty characters, for the major copying was in their scenes; he added the sea captain and Lovell's sister to increase this part of the action. We thereby see how fully the author agreed with his time in stressing the war between the sexes, on which much true comedy of manners turns.

The career of Ravenscroft may now be summarized, for in his final comedy, *The Anatomist, or the Sham Doctor* (*c.* March, 1697), he took nothing from Molière. He was a shameless borrower of the Frenchman's plots in two of his nine comedies, *Mamamouchi* and *Scaramouch;* he produced nothing, however, but farce that lost the virtue of the source and failed from incapacity to earn any interest on the loan. In *The Careless Lovers,* despite its considerable borrowing of Molière matter, in *The London Cuckolds,* and in *The Canterbury Guests,* Ravenscroft is essentially English in his point of view, method, and subject matter.

JOHN CROWNE

John Crowne's *The Country Wit* (January, 1676), is a play compounded of English characters and English "humors" in an intrigue like many on the English stage, and obviously concocted for its wit and manners. Sir Thomas Rash, an impetuous, money-minded Londoner, has suddenly engaged his daughter Christina to marry a silly country knight, Sir Mannerly Shallow, entirely on the representation of the latter's aunt, Lady Faddle, an elderly, rich, affected yearner for amatory joys. Christina loves Ramble, a wild city rake, who loves her when he stops his pursuit of other women long enough to recall her image. At this time he is chasing Betty Frisque, the expensive wench of Lord Drybone, who pays high for his senile lack of pleasing ways. Sir Mannerly is an amusing dolt of amazing stupidity. He parades his country-learned manners, and, mistaking servants for gentlemen, marries a porter's daughter. His servant loses the purse and acquires an unknown bastard to support—all on their first day in London. Ramble follows the cleared track to the willing hand of Christina. His man Merry weds Lady Faddle for her fortune. One episode in Ramble's chase of Betty Frisque includes a clear adaptation from the plot of *Le Sicilien, ou l'amour peintre;* a serenading in Act II also leads to a confusion of identity similar to that in scenes 3 and 4 of the same play, so that some eight or ten pages in a hundred owe their general character to Molière.[25]

Crowne's play was popular with the king and the court. Its merits were the merits of the other applauded plays of the time, wit, realism, and ridicule of the socially unfit. The satire on out-

[25] Van Laun says "lady Faddle et sir Mannerly Shallow ... me semblent des réminis-cences de la *Comtesse d'Escarbagnas* et de M. *de Pourceaugnac,* tandis que les scènes entre Ramble (Adraste) et Merry (Hali) sont basées sur quelques scènes d'*Amphitryon*" ("Les Plagiaires de Molière en Angleterre," *Le Moliériste,* III, 58-59). Miles says (*op. cit.,* p. 228) "The main plot was suggested by *Le Tartuffe,*" and "Lady Faddle was suggested by the Comtesse d'Escarbagnas ... and by Bélise [of *Les Femmes savantes*]." None of these is more than such a slight resemblance as a microscopic examination reveals between almost any two works.

moded compliments, the rakish hero who could turn from senti-
ment to raging sensuality in a short soliloquy, or the jibes at
critics in the mouth of Sir Mannerly—such things as these brought
the play popularity. Thus we can see that Crowne's center was
far from Molière's, even the unimportant center of the *comédie-
ballet, L'Amour peintre*. Like many others, Crowne took some
things that belonged to Molière's theatrical skill. All this is marginal to Crowne's matter, the essence of which is Restoration
taste and manners.

In *Sir Courtly Nice, or It Cannot Be* (May, 1685), John Crowne
utilized a Spanish plot, Moreto's *No pued esser,* selected, as he
explained himself, by Charles II. This became the basis of an
English comedy in the general tone of the Restoration. Sir Courtly
is an interesting and original English fop whose "humor" for
physical cleanliness is developed very fully and amusingly. Sir
Courtly uses a translation of the song, "Au Voleur," which Mascarille sang in *Les Précieuses ridicules.*[26] Crowne gives a few

[26] The Maidment and Logan edition of Crowne's works (III, 251) repeats the error
first made by [Charles Gildon], *Lives and Characters of the English Dramatick Poets*
[1698 or 1699], p. 30, with the statement, "The song of 'Stop Thief!' is taken out of
Flecknoe's Demoiselle à la Mode, who in turn had it from the French of Moliere."
Molière's version is as follows:

> Oh, oh! je n'y prenois pas garde:
> Tandis que, sans songer à mal, je vous regarde,
> Votre oeil en tapinois me dérobe mon coeur.
> Au voleur, au voleur, au voleur, au voleur!
>   *Les Précieuses ridicules,* scene 9.

Flecknoe rendered it as follows:

> Ah, ha! and have I caught you (as they say,
> Mos did his Mare) stealing my heart away.
> And wo'd you run awaywith't when y' havedon;
> I'faith, i'faith, for all you'd fain be gone,
> I'le make you dearly pay for't e're you part;
> Stop Thief, Stop Thief, my heart, my heart, my heart.
>   *The Damoiselles à la Mode,* Act III, scene 3 (p. 59).

Crowne went back to the original for this version:

> Your cruel eye,
> Lay watching by
> To snap my heart,

other indications that he had Mascarille in mind. The plays are not otherwise alike, and the characters of Mascarille and Sir Courtly resemble each other at very few points. The merit of Crowne's play is in the characters: Sir Courtly; a Cavalier Hot-Head; Testimony, a hypocritical Puritan; and outspoken Surly. All these fit well into the English background and have no prototypes in Molière.

The exact relation, however, of *The English Friar, or the Town Sparks* (*c.* March, 1690) to the works of Molière is very difficult to demonstrate; perhaps it is beyond us entirely. It seems best then to determine the range of possibilities and to accept everything within those limits as a possible explanation. Van Laun said that "le personnage principal, le père Tinical [misprint for Finical] (Affété) est imité de Tartuffe." [27] Finical and Tartuffe are hypocritical, lecherous, grasping manipulators of the devout. Crowne must have known *Le Tartuffe* long before he wrote his play. Does this mean that *The English Friar* is an adaptation of *Tartuffe,* as Miles sometimes thinks, but hesitates to assert too positively? [28] Crowne might have started to give the theatre of William and Mary's time a picture of the politico-religious intrigues of the recently ended Jacobean reign. Such a character as Finical might have come to Crowne's mind from personal observation or have been constructed from current notions, for, after all, the charges of lubricity, greed, hypocrisy, and political manipulation are perennial allegations against all racial or reli-

---

> Which you did wi' such art,
> That away w'it you ran,
> Whilst I look'd on,
> To my ruin and grief—
> Stop thief!—stop thief!
>   *Works*, III, 340.

[27] "Les Plagiaires de Molière en Angleterre," *Le Moliériste*, III, 60. In *Dramatic Works of Molière*, IV, 121, he says Crowne put some of Tartuffe's words into Finical's mouth in the closing scene. I can find only vaguely similar arguments, which might naturally arise from the situation.

[28] Contrast his statement, *op. cit.*, p. 95, with pp. 131, 158, 229.

gious opponents, Protestant against Catholic, Cavalier against Puritan, or anti-Semites against Jews. On the other hand knowing Molière and wanting to satirize Catholicism, Crowne may have started from *Tartuffe* and then altered the plot and character until he arrived at *The English Friar*. These two possibilities are the farthest apart: (1) that all likenesses are accidental, or (2) that all differences are intentional. The play is not very close to *Le Tartuffe* in spirit, plot, method, or characters. Aside from the naturally similar use of concealed witnesses of an attempted seduction, and aside from the less ordinary but not unnatural solicitude of the duped for the health of the hypocrite, there appears to be little duplication of plot elements. The possibility of some indebtedness cannot be denied, however, for *The English Friar* may be an adaptation of *Le Tartuffe;* but in that case the alterations are very complete, enough to give it a place as an independent play. Between the two limits mentioned above is the more probable hypothesis that the play started independently and that during its development reminiscences of Molière's play were incorporated. A similarity to *L'Avare* has been pointed out by Miles, the likeness of Lady Pinchgut and Harpagon.[29] Comic miserliness would always have certain common qualities, it would seem, and none of the details here is sufficiently peculiar to be traced.

A passage in Crowne's later play, *The Married Beau, or the Curious Impertinent* (*c.* January, 1694), is vaguely similar to the scene in *Les Précieuses ridicules* from which Mascarille's song *"Au Voleur"* emerged. This similarity has been ascribed to Molière's influence on Crowne,[30] but the evidence is not sufficient for one to report any probability of a borrowing.

In summary, Crowne, who is in about the third class among the writers of Restoration comedy, drew a little from Molière in two or three of his comedies; there is, of course, one positive

[29] *Ibid.*, pp. 158-59, 229.   [30] Miles, *ibid.*, p. 233.

adaptation in *The Country Wit* assayed above, in which the Frenchman's action was used to enliven the action of a subplot of the usual British sort. The method of approaching the plot of *The English Friar* was probably developed under the influence of *Le Tartuffe*. On the whole, Molière was not formative to Crowne's original work; his method and spirit did not reach England through Crowne's acquaintance with him.

THOMAS RAWLINS

Matter from Molière is certainly found in *Tom Essence, or the Modish Wife* (*c.* September, 1676) by Thomas Rawlins. This is a humble specimen of the comedy of intrigue with a feeble touch of Jonsonian "humors." The ending, with its reconciliations, reforms, and readjustments, distinctly recalls the older emotional attitudes or anticipates the later sentimental comedy, according to how one wishes to view it. The major plot turns about the desire of Mrs. Theodosia to marry the honorable Mr. Courtly against the opposition of her father, a miserly dotard, and her stepmother, a scheming young woman who has married her father for his money. The low comedy element comes from a milliner, Tom Essence, and his wife, who are conventional "humors." The first two, Mrs. Theodosia and Mr. Courtly, go through those actions of *Sganarelle, ou le cocu imaginaire* that relate to the exchange of portraits and the resultant misunderstandings. Allardyce Nicoll is perhaps too generous in saying that at least half the plot comes from Molière,[31] but the borrowing is an integral part of the matter. The play depends largely upon disguises and upon mistakes of identity in the darkness, which seem to be reminiscent of Molière, but may have come from many other sources. Miles thinks Davenant's translation of Sganarelle was the basis.[32] It really does not matter: Rawlins was not a man of any importance in comedy; he did not use

---

[31] *Restoration Drama*, p. 204.   [32] *Op cit.*, p. 239.

Molière in his later *Tunbridge Wells, or a Day's Courtship* (*c.* March, 1678). The question has therefore no significance in dramatic history.

THOMAS OTWAY

Because of genuine tenderness and undoubted poetic excellence in his tragedies, Thomas Otway arrests the attention of the reader more emphatically than his comedies deserve. Among these minor plays is an effort to Anglicize *Les Fourberies de Scapin.* Late in his career Molière had reverted to his early style and compounded another intrigue from his capacious memory of classical comedy and *commedia dell' arte.* Two young men are required by their exigent and miserly fathers to marry girls they have never seen. One has secretly married the daughter of a shipwrecked widow and the other has wedded in like secrecy a supposed gypsy girl. The valets try to help out, particularly Scapin. They dupe the fathers with stories of kidnapings, and then collect the ransom while in disguise. Complications follow furiously, with Scapin more eager to play clever tricks than to win consent. Scapin even gets his master's father to hide in a sack, where he beats him unmercifully in a feigned fight with ruffians. In the end the gypsy and the daughter of the widow are found to be the very girls the boys were supposed to marry. The play closes with a feast after Scapin tricks them once more into forgiving him. Much of the comedy is in the details, haggling over the amount of ransom and the like. Characterization is nil.

Otway's *The Cheats of Scapin* (December, 1676) is a translation and adaptation of *Les Fourberies* with all the changes needed to adjust the plot and characters to a nominally British scene at Dover. In this Otway proved a competent workman. He made no attempt to complicate the action, but on the contrary removed a few incidents entirely. It is the most creditable translation

Molière had yet had. Unfortunately the play was originally too trifling, no matter how admirably presented, to bring much of the great Molière to England. It adds to the list of farces based on the French source and probably added to the impression, already strong, that Molière was a clever man of the theatre. Otway wrote three more comedies, *Friendship in Fashion* (April, 1678), *The Soldier's Fortune* (March, 1680), and *The Atheist, or the Second Part of the Soldier's Fortune* (*c.* September, 1683). Of these *The Soldier's Fortune* is the only one making unmistakable use of Molière. It contains another version of the episode of the duped messenger found in *L'École des maris.* Here the idea is expanded to an important part of the plot, for the husband becomes the stupid bearer of a verbal message, then of a letter, and finally of a ring from his wife to the man who is cuckolding him. The device is found in early Italian *novelle,* but came to Otway from Molière,[33] for there are several closely similar details, including some verbal resemblances. Some students have thought that scene 9 of *Sganarelle, ou le cocu imaginaire* has been used also. It would be more accurate to note that in his *L'École des maris* Molière repeated an effective device he had already used in *Sganarelle.* The amusement derived from this material is applied to a totally different story by Otway, the actual cuckolding of a stupid husband by a wife who has been married against her will. An astoundingly obscene old knight, Sir Jolly Jumble, serves as an enthusiastic amateur procurer, the word amateur being applicable in either sense. Molière provided Otway with the laughable situations mentioned above, nothing more. The tone, purpose, plot, and characters are totally foreign to Molière, but familiar to readers of Restoration plays. The sequel to *The Soldier's Fortune, The Atheist,* depends on Molière for nothing,

---

[33] Gildon first noted this borrowing. Van Laun overstates the case in calling it a free translation. Miles adds that Fourbin was Scapin, from *Les Fourberies de Scapin.* There is no similarity except that both are intriguing servants and that the word Fourbin seems to recall *fourberies,* which cannot matter.

except that two slight similarities might have been borrowed.[34]

On the whole, the career of Otway as a comic dramatist puts him clearly on a level below Dryden and Shadwell, more nearly with Mrs. Behn. His close adaptation of *Les Fourberies de Scapin* evidently did not affect his later dramatic form, for he seems to have learned nothing of technique through this contact. What little he picked up after the major venture fell back into the class of petty borrowings of unimportant tricks of plotting. He always treated Molière as a mere occasional source of theatrical skill in farce.

MRS. APHRA BEHN

Mrs. Aphra Behn used material from Molière in two of the fourteen comedies that came from her pen between 1670 and 1696, but she did not depend on Molière at the start. She turned to him, apparently, as a ready source of material for her customary combination of a bristling intrigue with dissolute manners. When she rose at all above the rank of a pandaress to the taste for indecency, it was merely into the level of "uncommon ingenuity in the contrivance of stage-situations."[35]

An inveterate borrower[36] of material, she made *Sir Patient Fancy* (January, 1678) a very interesting example of the manufacture of an amusing, thoroughly British farce from one of Molière's great comedies of character. In "To the Reader," the author said,

> Others to show their breeding (as *Bays* sayes) cryed it was made out of at least four *French* plays, when I had but a bare hint from one, the *Malad Imagenere,* [sic!] which was given me translated by a Gentleman infinitely to advantage; but how much of the *French* is in this, I

[34] Miles says (*op. cit.,* p. 225) "The conduct of Porcia is a reminiscence of *L'École des femmes,* probably through *The Country Wife.* The recital by Beaugard's father of his hard luck at dice (act iii, p. 42) is an alteration of *Les Fâcheux* ii, 2." Neither identification is convincing.

[35] Ward, *op. cit.,* III, 453.

[36] See Langbaine, *op. cit.,* pp. 17-18.

leave to those who do indeed understand it and have seen it at the court.

Le Malade imaginaire, from which she got the "bare hint," Molière's great satire on the typical hypochondriac, with its amusing reiteration of his contempt for physicians, she stripped of satiric import, and thus secured a skeleton for an English farce of gay cuckoldry and amorous intrigue. The common framework is as follows: An elderly man, Sir Patient (Argan), has enjoyed bad health and worse medicine for years. He has recently married a young woman (Béline), who pretends a great love but feels none. He tries to force his daughter Isabella (Angélique), to marry a silly man, Sir Credulous Easy (Thomas Diafoirus), although she loves Lodwick Knowell (Cléante). Isabella has a young sister Fanny (Louison). Sir Patient (Argan) is finally induced to test the love of his wife and his daughter by pretending to die. The daughter is found loyal and the wife appears heartless in her selfishness. Thus he is disillusioned.

Mrs. Behn's play differs from Molière's, because she has put an entirely different sort of flesh and blood on these bones. Sir Patient is not Argan; he is a testy, rich, cuckolded alderman with a "humor" for being ill; his imaginary illness is a device of the author to produce surprise turns in the farcical plot. Béline fools Argan for his money, for which she married him; Lady Fancy married Sir Patient in order to finance her amour with her gallant. Isabella and Lodwick are the usual Restoration lovers. To them Mrs. Behn added the customary second pair of lovers; although they do not show much verbal brilliance, the four represent the social norm of the Restoration stage, zealous, but not overvirtuous, lovers. Instead of a French blockhead like Thomas Diafoirus, Isabella's unwelcome suitor, Sir Credulous Easy, is a British type, the rural knight whom the others know how to gull. Some critics[37] trace him to *M. de Pourceaugnac.*

[37] E.g., Summers, ed., *Works of Aphra Behn,* IV, 4-5.

Langbaine traces him to "*Sr. Amphilus* the *Cornish* Knight, and his Man *Trebasco* in Brome's Play called *The Damoiselle*," [38] but the type has appeared so many times in English plays and with so many slight variations that no specific source for the stock figure is plausible. Certainly we need not go to France for a vaguely similar character.

Mrs. Behn's audacious invention of Fanny, a skilled bawd at the age of seven, is shocking and revelatory of existing taste. Fanny and Isabella are in the garden at night.

Isab. Well, I have no mind to let this dear mad Devil *Lodwick* in to night.

Fan. Why, Sister, this is not the first Venture you have made of this kind, at this Hour, and in this Place; these Arbours were they tell-tales, cou'd discover many pretty stories of your Loves, and do you think they'll be less faithful now? pray trust them once again. Oh, I do so love to hear Mr. *Lodwick* protest, and vow, and swear, and dissemble, and when you don't believe him, rail at you,—avads, 'tis the prettiest Man—

Isab. I have a strange apprehension of being surpriz'd to night.

Fan. I'll warrant you, I'll sit on yon Bank of Pinks, and when I hear a Noise I'll come and tell you; so *Lodwick* may slip out at the back Gate, and we may be walking up and down as if we meant no harm.

Isab. You'll grow very expert in the Arts of Love, *Fanny*.

Fan. When I am big enough I shall do my Endeavour, for I have heard you say, Women were born to no other end than to love: And 'tis fit I should learn to live and die in my calling.—Come, open the Gate, or you'll repent it. [39]

Thus Molière's innocent Louison is corrupted to fit Restoration taste.

The close of the play is another indication of the wide gulf between *Sir Patient Fancy* and *Le Malade imaginaire*. Molière was too wise to believe Argan could be reformed. Instead the great satirist boldly burlesques the medical faculties in a *ballet*

[38] *Op cit.*, p. 21.
[39] Act III, scene 5 (*Works*, IV, 51-52).

ritual, in which Argan is made his own physician as a consolation for the loss of a son-in-law trained in medicine. This gives the end a fantastic inconclusiveness which assumes that men are not subject to genuine conversion from their innate follies. Mrs. Behn is not so sincere. After Lady Fancy and Wittmore announce their immoral intentions, Sir Patient says, in closing the play:

I forgive it you, and will turn Spark, they live the merriest Lives—keep some City Mistress, go to Court, and hate all Conventicles.

> *You see what a fine City-Wife can do*
> *Of the true-breed; instruct her Husband too:*
> *I wish all civil Cuckolds in the Nation*
> *Would take example by my Reformation.*

Thus the traditional close of Ben Jonson reappears with morality inverted. Into the plot Mrs. Behn put another character, Lady Knowell, mother to Lodwick and Lucretia, an affected and amorous widow, who is amusing in her contempt for other than learned tongues and polysyllabic expression. She might have been recalled from Bélise, of *Les Femmes savantes,* but the imitation is very slight.[40] A medical consultation is also vaguely similar to a consultation in *L'Amour médecin.* Both of these are probable but not certain borrowings.

As vulgar farce of amorous assignations and lovers dodging under beds and behind curtains, the play is amusing and fitted to its time. The borrowing from Molière is initial to much of this matter; but those elements selected from the original material were far from central to the art of the great playwright.

In a later comedy, *The False Count, or a New Way to Play an Old Game* (c. September, 1682), Mrs. Behn turned to Molière for the second and last time and found in *Les Précieuses ridicules* some useful material. Wishing to make fun of a young lady, Isabella, who is comic in her belief in her excessive social importance, she recalled Molière's pretentious young ladies, and gave

---

[40] Summers (*op. cit.,* IV, 4-5) is very positive in this ascription.

her, for a lover and husband, Guiliom, a chimney sweeper disguised as a nobleman. The hoax is worked up by other characters, as a punishment for her snobbishness. While too many likenesses exist for one to believe the similarity accidental, there is no close copying. Isabella is a social snob, not a *précieuse*. Guiliom is a gay chimney sweep who enjoys his efforts at impersonation and has no such belief in his own social prowess as made Mascarille and Jodelet butts as well as tools of their master. Isabella is forced at the end to keep her husband and help him to be a false count. Molière's famous characters suggest some of the outlines of Guiliom, but his development is reasonably independent.

In all, Mrs. Behn wrote fourteen comedies between 1670 and 1696. None has any distinction on its own account, and none contributed anything to the development of the Restoration comedy of manners. The sole merit for the modern reader is their indication of the taste of a time that found them worth applauding. As we have already indicated, Molière was used in two of the plays, in one formatively, but without artistic insight.

THOMAS WRIGHT

In *The Female Vertuosoes* (April, 1693), Thomas Wright, Betterton's experienced assistant in the handling of stage machinery, brought out his own play, an adaptation of *Les Femmes savantes*. In his dedication Wright said,

> ... the Design of which, as it was drawn some Years ago from the great Original of French Comedy, by an Ingenious Friend of mine, who bears now too serious a Character in the World, not to reckon such a Trifle among his *Delicta Juventutis,* was last Winter, by my Importunities, extorted from him.

Wright made a free paraphrase of his source, adapting the names of characters and their spirit to the English scene and to the customary vulgarities of the Restoration stage, but the characters are very clearly recognizable. In general, the high comedy comes down to the level of farce, as it might have done in the hands of Mrs. Behn, but the satire of Philaminte, Armande, and Bélise as Lady Meanwell, Lovewitt, and Catchat, is still rather forceful. To this leading plot Wright added a low-comedy intrigue that centers in the perennial country gull, who arrives in the play as the suitor of Mariana, favored by her mother to replace Clerimont. This is not an inappropriate addition to Molière's plot. The style is idiomatic and occasionally spirited, but it lacks the wit to make the play important.

After Wright secured the translation of *Les Femmes savantes,* he incorporated some very amusing speeches from *Le Malade imaginaire,* perhaps from a manuscript translation such as Mrs. Behn used in writing *Sir Patient Fancy* sixteen years earlier,[41] as his "Importunities" would not have been so persistent if he could have handled the original. In Molière's comedy, Thomas Diafoirus comes to woo Angélique, Argan's daughter.[42] An academic fool, young Diafoirus discharges carefully memorized speeches of extravagant compliments and sonorous platitudes. These and some of the linking conversation are closely translated in the wooing of the gull, Timothy Witless,[43] who has studied at Cambridge and is a scholastic type of ass. A similarity to the familiar trick in *M. de Pourceaugnac* occurs:[44] a troublesome suitor is driven away by the return of his supposedly abandoned woman. This device has been too frequently copied for one to assert a direct debt when an indirect source would be more plausible. For long a frequenter of the theatres where he gained his livelihood, Wright would be more likely to use material he had seen on the boards than to depend on reading for his theatrical effects. Several clever turns of action, vaguely reminiscent of something in Molière, are probably the results of such a diffusion

[41] See above, p. 146-47.   [42] Act II, scenes 5 and 6.
[43] Act II.   [44] Act V (p. 44).

of matter. The parallels cannot be set down as positive borrowings, however, for the similarities are all conventionalized.[45]

WILLIAM PENKETHMAN

Love without Interest, or the Man too Hard For the Master
(1699), is by William Penkethman, a comic actor, who gives us
a farcical Restoration play without success, merit, or novelty. The
general action is reminiscent of dozens of previous plays, and
the tone and spirit have not advanced a bit beyond the products
of the early Ravenscroft. It attracts attention here because the
author availed himself of comic incidents from *Le Mariage forcé;*
they did not come from the version found in Ravenscroft's *Scaramouch.*

Wildman, the traditional spark, has tired of his punk, Eugenia,
and mortgaged his inheritance to Sir Fickle Cheat, a grasping,
amorous citizen. He decides to woo Sir Fickle's niece Letitia and
to "top" Eugenia on the old man. Letitia tries to be a witty
woman. Her sister, Honoraria, and Truelove have a romantic
wooing that is so filled with fustian as to be burlesque, perhaps
at the author's intention. Jonathan, acted by Penkethman, is Sir
Fickle's faithless servant and prime mover of the intrigue. When
his master foolishly entrusts him with the chest of valuable papers,
including Wildman's mortgage and the titles to the property
Sir Fickle has withheld from his nieces, Jonathan sells out to the
youngsters, and the old man is trapped. When he seeks advice [46]
of Wrangle and Sobersides, the action follows scenes 4 and 5 of
Le Mariage forcé, in a free adaptation. A little later [47] the man
is forced to accept Eugenia in a scene resembling in general conception scene 9 of Molière's little comedy. The insignificance
of the play and of the author brings the value of this rather limited borrowing of comic matter close to the vanishing point.

---

[45] Miles (*op. cit.,* pp. 230-31) lists these parallels as borrowings.
[46] Act IV, scene 2.   [47] Act V, scene 1.

SUMMARY

A summary of Molière's relation to the foregoing authors may be very brief. Not even those followers of Molière's influence in England who idolatrously credit him with creating such assets as high comedy, realism, vivid repartee, and character portrayal care to debit him with such conspicuously bad comedy as this.[48] But, as a matter of fact, I think it is clear that the minor borrowers treated Molière as did their greater confrères. They lacked respect for his views on life and did not admire his dramaturgic technique. They took from him what they could make incidental to their own conventional Restoration views and adapt to their traditional British methods of building plays. They complacently believed their work could not be improved by imitating a mere French comedian.

[48] For example, Miles, *op. cit.*, pp. 98-99, says, "The minor playwrights of the Restoration . . . seldom recognized the greatness of the Frenchman's genius. . . . The modern estimate of Molière as not only the greatest comic dramatist of France but as one of the few comic geniuses of the world, would have seemed to them the veriest nonsense."

VIII: CONGREVE, VANBRUGH, AND
FARQUHAR

ALMOST two decades elapsed between Etherege and the next comic genius;[1] but after the comedy of manners emerged from this period of mediocrity, in little more than a decade it rose to its perfect example in Congreve, receded in Vanbrugh and Farquhar, and then fell before the onslaughts of sensibility and shifting standards of morality. An entire account of this final outburst of comic excellence is beyond the scope of the present study, for the discussion of these men must be limited to their relation to Molière, inadequate as such treatment is from the broader view of dramatic history.

WILLIAM CONGREVE

"It would be interesting," says the late Sir Edmund Gosse, "to know how far, in making this advance [i.e., an advance beyond Wycherley in the distinction of characters], Congreve had wittingly gone to school with Molière."[2] The question may be widened a little. How far did he go to school with Molière, wittingly or unwittingly? How different would his comedies of manners have been if Molière had never lived? The answer should be reached by comparing the characteristics of Congreve's comedies with all possible origins, not by considering only the resemblances to the Frenchman.

Appearing eighteen years after the death of Charles II, *The*

---

[1] Thorndike (*English Comedy,* p. 341) names nine "perfect specimens of the comedy of manners," none of them between *The Man of Mode* (March, 1676) and *The Double Dealer* (October, 1693).   [2] Gosse, *Life of Congreve,* rev. ed., p. 30.

Old Bachelor (January, 1693) is a typical Restoration comedy, perhaps the most representative specimen of the genre which found support and acclaim in that earlier period. Young Congreve [3] produced a suave synthesis of dramatic stereotypes. The material is a clever pastiche of what one finds in such writers as Sedley, Dryden, Behn, Crowne, Shadwell, and even Ravenscroft. The story hinges on the dilemma of Heartwell, the "old bachelor," who shudders at the thought of marriage and yet must satisfy his sudden desire for a certain wench; she stubbornly demands a husband. Heartwell's gay friend, Bellmour, is playing with a jealous old citizen's willing young wife. The cuckold catches him in his wife's bed and is still fool enough to allow the guilty lovers to talk him into believing her innocent. In this gallant affair Bellmour's disguise as a parson is essential. As he emerges, he encounters his friend Heartwell and performs a ceremony whose invalidity is saved for the denouement. Though Bellmour and another friend, Vainlove, are wild gallants lightly enjoying every female that blooms beside their path, two spirited maids succeed in luring them into the legal rites necessary to the ladies' social standing. A rural knight is gulled by boastful Captain Bluffe and tricked into marriage to the mistress who almost captured the old bachelor. The incidents are thus seen to be standard; innumerable English plays of the seventeenth century, for example, have developed a surprise ending with some version of the hoax marriage. The characters include no new types and no new "humors." The scenes are all familiar, the street, gentlemen's lodgings, St. James Park, or a city wife's bedchamber. Here, if ever, is the utopia of gallantry: life is free of scruples, sensual pleasures do not pall, past sins do not haunt, and the future offers no fears.

While the style of the play is competent and even, it does not

---

[3] Congreve was twenty-three years old when the play was staged. He says in the dedication that it had been composed almost four years earlier.

approach Etherege's and hardly forecasts *The Way of the World*. It too seems to be a synthesis from earlier comic styles. There is little mark of genius, for example, in the similitudes which shower from almost all the characters. Sedley, Crowne, Dryden, or the early Wycherley could and did surpass Bellmour's sally at Heartwell's dilemma, "Ha, ha, how a' struggled, like an old lawyer between two fees," or they could easily match Vainlove's additional simile, "Or [like] a young wench, between pleasure and reputation." Gay Araminta is permitted to cap a scene with the banal "no; rather, courtship to marriage, as a witty prologue to a very dull play." After Heartwell knows he has been rescued from the clutches of matrimony, the play closes with four gallants all laughing,

Heartwell. —and when I wed again, may she be—ugly, as an old bawd.
Vainlove. —Ill-natur'd, as an old maid—
Bellmour. Wanton as a young widow—
Sharper. And jealous as a barren wife.

Congreve could not derive this resemblance to early plays from a fresh observation of current life, for 1693 was actually far away from 1660. Here are the old Restoration contempt for romantic love and the familiar preference for an unmoral and casual indulgence in the sex relation in which ties of affection have no place. Here the pursuit of women is the normal activity of a wit. Here the women gayly capitalize sex tantalization. Here marriage is assumed to be a black pall that threatens to come between a joyous past and a gloomy future. Obviously the author has assimilated the comic tradition of England and reproduced its matter and manner without significant change. Congreve has gone to school with a vengeance, but not with Molière.

In the interval between *The Old Bachelor* and *The Double Dealer* (October, 1693) Congreve made a great advance in literary style. In his second play he revealed much of that brilliancy of phrase which we call wit.[4] Such interest in epigram, in felicity of similitude, in boldness and aptness of imagery, had been, broadly speaking, both a dramatic and a social asset in fashionable England throughout the seventeenth century. It is the very heart of Etherege, not merely the Etherege of the plays but particularly the extraordinary gentleman of the *Letterbook*. It is reasonable to think of the mature style of Congreve as the quintessence of Restoration wit, of which such men as Etherege, Wycherley, Rochester, Sedley, Dryden, and Shadwell were zealous practitioners in conversation, as well as in letters. Coming a little later, profiting by his native genius and their experience, Congreve had the fortune to carry the mode to the highest development it was destined to receive. Serious French literature, and particularly the work of Molière, stood foursquare against such gilding of natural language. To Molière, language was a means with which to get things said; to Congreve and his innumerable British predecessors, the way things were said was one of the reasons for saying them. Verbal wit in Congreve, then, cannot be traced to the influence of Molière. George Meredith has given classic expression to the difference between them:

Contrast the wit of Congreve with Moliere's. That of the first is a Toledo blade, sharp, and wonderfully supple for steel; cast for duelling, restless in the scabbard, being so pretty when out of it. To shine, it must have an adversary. Moliere's wit is like a running brook, with

---

[4] Dobrée (*Comedies by William Congreve,* pp. xvi-xviii) gives a penetrating discussion of Congreve's style, elaborating and illustrating the idea that Congreve was a poet, "an artist who realized that his material was words, who loved words, glorying in their proper and beautiful use." Dobrée believes that Congreve developed his prose rhythms after a painstaking study of Jonson. He credits Congreve with a full mastery of sudden changes in movement, a polyphonic gamut of vowel sounds, and an artistically varied spacing of stresses. "English literature had to wait for Landor until it once more had a voice that had something of the especial quality of Congreve." English dramatic prose progressed, he thinks, steadily through Jonson, Etherege and Dryden to Congreve, and then it passed into the essays of the eighteenth century. It would hardly need argument to show that this "delicious phrase, the thrilling movement, the breath-catching swerve of tempo" is entirely too intimate a part of a language for it to be learned from a foreign idiom.

innumerable fresh lights on it at every turn of the wood through which its business is to find a way. It does not run in search of obstructions, to be noisy over them; but when dead leaves and viler substances are heaped along the course, its natural song is heightened. Without effort, and with no dazzling flashes of achievement, it is full of healing, the wit of good breeding, the wit of wisdom.[5]

Much of the success of *The Double Dealer* arose from the brilliance with which Congreve ridiculed the poses affected by characters of good social standing. Such figures had been recurring whenever the example of Jonson was influential, sometimes in the form of pseudo-literary coxcombs like Brisk or his female counterpart, Lady Froth, sometimes in the form of lady pretenders to virtue who were secretly inclined to illicit love, like Lady Plyant and Lady Touchwood. In his first play he seems to have followed the tradition of the citizen comedy, which can be traced from the days of Middleton and Brome to Shadwell and Ravenscroft; but here in his second he turns to the higher social level exploited by Shirley, Etherege, Wycherley, and Dryden. On each of these planes he placed a fitting butt. Stupid Sir Joseph Wittol and bragging Captain Bluffe are ridiculous on the level of physical fears and obviously silly pretensions. Suited to the tone of high comedy are Lord Froth, with his affected critical acumen, and Sir Paul Plyant, who is dominated by a "humor" for uxoriousness and blinded judgment about his wife. In contrast to this ridicule of the affectations of the fashionable pretenders, we find an implied approval of the true-wits, Mellefont, Cynthia, and Careless. These character types and the attitudes toward them can be found in pre-Restoration comedy and in early Restoration comedy, but not in Molière.

When Congreve insisted in his dedication that his play had a single plot, he failed to understand that the ethical seriousness of the central incidents did not harmonize with the frothy exhibition of affected wits. Despite the interlacing of one group with

[5] "Essay on the Idea of Comedy," *Works,* XXIII, 17-18.

the other, the play has the effect of a tragicomedy of thwarted villainy into which are interwoven irrelevant comic interludes of gay social satire. A lack of enthusiasm for the traditional Restoration morality has crept in. Getting more wickedness than folly into his plot, he slips from the level of absolute social comedy and comes close to the dramatic defect of mixing ethical satire with social. When he plays in Restoration style with misconduct, he reveals an undertone of morality that is totally foreign to gay Etherege but akin to the later Wycherley. Satires that deal with crimes and not with follies are apparently a temptation to good playwrights, for Jonson and Wycherley both wrote them too.[6]

Frequently the serious plot of *The Double Dealer* has been ascribed to the influence of Molière. Although Miss Lynch rejects nearly all the evidence cited by Miles in support of Molière's influence upon Congreve,[7] she concurs in finding a borrowing in *The Double Dealer*. She says:

> The resemblance between the intrigue of Congreve's Maskwell and that of Tartuffe in *Tartuffe* may well be emphasized. Maskwell has Tartuffe's gift for securing blindly devoted friends. Lord Touchwood is like Orgon in his attachment to Maskwell. As Orgon promises his daughter, Touchwood promises his niece to the villainous intriguer. And at the moment when Maskwell's treachery would have been confirmed to any one who had eyes to see, Touchwood rashly disinherits his nephew and makes Maskwell his heir (V, 1), as Orgon, at a similar crisis, disinherits his son and places his fortune at the disposal of Tartuffe (III, 7).[8]

---

[6] For detailed evidence, see Davis, "The 'Sons of Ben' in English Realistic Comedy." I think that youth alone should secure Congreve's pardon for following their mistaken example. At least he made structural advancement, for *The Double Dealer* is better planned than the very famous *Plain Dealer*. The social refinement of the Touchwood family is better adapted to high comedy than the vulgarity of Manly, Olivia, and Vernish; the men who affected wit and the women who affected virtues are suited to the setting, not dragged in like the Blackacre family to enliven an irrelevant scene. Incidentally the sexual morality is more conventional: only one true-wit amuses himself with gallantry; the witty lovers are romantically eager to marry and too earnest to flirt; and the semi-incestuous Lady Touchwood is an object of scorn.

[7] *Social Mode of Restoration Comedy*, pp. 183-88.

[8] *Ibid.*, p. 185.

Let us examine this resemblance. Congreve has elected to focus a plot about a villain. If this simple decision is not copied, and surely no one can argue that this is private property, all the parallels of the two plots that inhere in villainy or inhere in the dramatic necessity of postponing the unmasking of the villain until the denouement are developed independently. Iago, for example, had the gift of getting friends, and he also secured the attachment of the duped to himself. Miles and Miss Lynch seem too intent on likenesses to notice that Mellefont, not the "humorous" and negligible Lord Touchwood, is the real dupe of Maskwell. Likewise, Lady Touchwood, not Maskwell, is the instigating force of evil in the story, wholly unlike the calm and virtuous Elmire, who unmasked Tartuffe to her deceived husband. Thus the most likely of all the parallels cited by earlier students seems to consist in commonplaces of the theatre or of concepts of character, and therefore are not properly described as a borrowing.[9]

Let us turn to the third play, *Love for Love* (April, 1695). Having incurred his irascible father's displeasure by spending a fortune wooing the hesitating Angelica, Valentine stays in his chambers to dodge creditors. Angry Sir Sampson is trying to transfer the inheritance from Valentine to his younger son Ben, who is on the point of coming back from some years at sea. In return for ready cash for debts, Valentine signs a bargain to convey his future rights as soon as the sailor arrives. Ben comes. Valentine procrastinates by feigning madness. His conduct at last convinces Angelica that his love is sincere, and aided by Ben's tactless plain dealing, she extricates him through deft flattery of Sir Sampson. Into the story come a true-wit friend of Valentine's, a coxcomb, three comically eager women, a clever valet, and a cuckolded astrologer.

[9] Congreve was apparently in earnest when he wrote in the dedication, "[I] do not know that I have borrow'd one hint of it [i.e., the fable] anywhere." Miles says (*Influence of Molière on Restoration Comedy*, p. 195) "In *The Double Dealer*, as he avowed in the epistle dedicatory, his effort was to imitate the French." I find no such avowal there.

As the plot invited the echo of earlier Restoration flippancy, Congreve adapted his style to include broad repartee in the manner of Dryden, Sedley, or Wycherley. But, as elsewhere, he shaped the form of wit to the character who speaks it. In his "inexplicable felicity of phrase, this invariable selection of the unexpected and yet obviously the best word,"[10] much characterization is achieved; for the style regularly discloses the speaker, whether it be Angelica taunting Foresight for the infidelities of his wife, Scandal in his wild gallantries, Valentine making safety-valve speeches under the color of madness, or Sailor Ben with his fresh opinions and salty bluntness.

The satiric mood of the second play is retained, but the ridicule is directed at social follies; and so a true comedy of manners appears, a comedy free of mere farce on the one hand or of heavy ethical freight on the other. The traditions of Restoration comedy provide most of the character types, most of the dramatic situations, and the verbal flippancy. Congreve breathes into this aged body a wholly new life; he gives the characters such a realistic portrayal that he feels it necessary to disclaim an attempt at personal portraits.[11] Sir Sampson, the "humorous" angry father, is as old as Plautus and as real as a next-door neighbor. Superstitious Foresight first acted for Jonson; with a change of make-up he served Shadwell; here he finds a good rôle. Mrs. Foresight and her sister are lively members of an old stage family, women of comically robust desires and frail restraint. Miss Prue is a full sister to Margery Pinchwife and Hoyden. All these people arise from and belong in the English tradition of "humors," but each foible is fully adapted to the person who possesses it, and it exists as a mental rather than a physical trait. Despite their traditional origin, these characters are new creations; although, of course, in the more restricted sense of a copy from life rather than from letters, Sailor Ben is the only original character. His bluff sea

[10] Gosse, op. cit., p. 173.   [11] See latter part of the prologue.

speech, his hearty good sense, and his general indifference to the world of fashion, make him perhaps the best example of Congreve's ability to write from life as well as from literary sources. The fact that a man devoid of social grace is not satirized indicates a new social standard. Scarcely a situation in *Love for Love* lacks a parallel in earlier drama. Valentine turning prodigal for love of the apparently indifferent Angelica; Angelica determining to be sure of his constancy before she acknowledges her feeling for him; the angry father disinheriting the spendthrift son, who thwarts the paternal ire by feigning madness; the young second wife of Foresight cuckolding her dotard husband; the silly beau boasting of his amours, winning only the heart of an eager simpleton, and falling victim to a marriage in a mask—these are familiar enough. More novel is the Shavian boldness with which Angelica takes the masculine initiative and wins Valentine by feigning a readiness to marry his father. The freshness, the vigor, and the comic force with which Congreve recompounded familiar elements gives the play its high place as theatrical entertainment. Its realism, its satire, and its fundamental approval of decent behavior between the sexes show the further development of Congreve as an independent artist.

It should occasion no surprise to note that, in his reflective letter to John Dennis, Congreve gives ample evidence that he regularly thought in terms of the English comic tradition. He cites chiefly Jonson and his characters as examples of true "humors," which he defines as Ben himself might: "A singular and unavoidable manner of doing, or saying anything, Peculiar and Natural to one Man only; by which his Speech and Actions are distinguished from those of other Men." He reveals his developing taste as an independent artist by differing, in one respect, with the practice of the English stage, which he had himself followed in his earliest play. He does not care to laugh at characters who make him think the worse of his own human species. He thus deplores the classification of the absurdities, the impertinencies, and the noise of grotesque "Farce Fools" as "humor." He denies the term also to personal defects or natural deformities, to external habit of body such as dress or manners, and to affectations. *"Humour* is from Nature, *Habit* from Custom; and *Affectation* from Industry."￼ Instead he gives his approval to the presentation of natural "humors" as the right technique of character portrayal for the stage. He is therefore explicit in his insistence upon a distinction between affected and innate characteristics, only the latter, as elements in a true individuality, deserving the term "humor." We can see that he made Sailor Ben, Foresight, and Sampson "humorous" in this sense. English letters and life were in his mind when he wrote:

> ... there is more of Humour in our English Comick writers than in any others. ... I look upon Humour to be almost of English Growth ... the reason of it, is the great Freedom, Privilege, and Liberty which the Common People of *England* enjoy. Any man that has a Humour is under no restraint, or fear of giving it Vent.[12]

Five years later he had changed his mind and decided that true "humors" were not amusing. He felt that they deserved pity rather than laughter. Thus he arrived by a logical progression at the method he employed in this last play. The doctrine is made explicit in the dedication of *The Way of the World* (March, 1700):

> Those characters which are meant to be ridiculed in most of our comedies ... are rather objects of charity than contempt; and instead of moving our mirth, they ought very often to excite our compassion.
> This reflection moved me to design some characters which should appear ridiculous, not so much through a natural folly (which is incorrigible, and therefore not proper for the stage) as through an affected wit; a wit which at the same time it is affected, is also false.

---

[12] "Mr. Congreve to Mr. Dennis Concerning Humour in Comedy" (dated July 10, 1695), *Works of Congreve*, ed. by Summers, III, 161-68.

Congreve's mastery of comic art was definitively demonstrated in his last great contribution. One might even suspect that he never undertook another play of the type because he had a feeling that few artistic problems were left unsolved, for within the limits of the genre, as it existed in his day, it would be hard to better *The Way of the World,* except in the plot, for which no English dramatist had Molière's instinct. The plan provides that semblance of bustle and activity which the British stage had long demanded, but it possesses a closer unity than *The Double Dealer,* in which he thought he had accomplished that end. The story turns about the usual marriage of a true-wit gallant to a young lady of infinite poise and ample wealth. Mirabell, once the adulterous lover of his friend's wife, Mrs. Fainall, is wooing the lovely Millamant, half of whose fortune is left to the whim of her aunt, Lady Wishfort, Mrs. Fainall's mother. Fainall wishes Mirabell to wed Millamant at the expense of her aunt's ire, so that the fortune will be diverted to his wife and thence to himself. The game is further complicated by his mistress, Mrs. Marwood, who is in his confidence, but who has an undisclosed and unrequited love for Mirabell and is a very uncertain factor. Mirabell leads the assault by pretending a gallant's interest in the old lady, and he comes as close as he can bear to winning her easily bestowed but faded charms. The stages of the struggle between these contending forces compose the plot. The denouement is effected by the revelation of an unknown document, but this dusty device has a fresh plausibility in the characters and in their past relations. Sir Wilfull Witwoud conforms to the tradition of the rural knight and provides the comic decoration of perennially amusing crudity, though he is not quite a butt, and he has enough intelligence to aid in bringing about the union of the lovers. Painted old Lady Wishfort, who is amusing because she is, as Mirabell remarks, all that her name implies, has been conceived in a far more human form than Lady Cockwood or any of her other prototypes. Witwoud and Petulant, among the more amusing fops of the Restoration stage, are also foils for Millamant. After we glimpse her charmingly intelligent and mannered frivolity in their presence, we are prepared to understand her careless earnestness and flippant good sense when she appears with Mirabell. In such deft manipulation of traditional material lies the peculiar charm of Congreve for the literary historian. He gives conventional material a wholly new vitality. Doing nearly all the typical things, typical characters are still so individual that they step off the boards into a world of reality. Standard situations take on the verve of wholly new ones. The cadence of Congreve's prose belongs to the speech of such inimitable people. Keen-minded characters are the natural sources of the freely flowing wit. Congreve's study of artistic ends has manipulated the conventions with a finish that anyone can feel. The plot also furnishes an outlet for the author's interest in the ethics of Restoration conduct, but this concern is not allowed to outweigh the social comedy, as it did in his second play. Although a gallant true-wit, Mirabell is a rather serious young man who finds his pursuit of the languidly coquettish Millamant unhappily complicated by the trammels of his former conquests. Satiety and disillusionment lurk in the shadows behind him. He knows that beneath her superficial affectations Millamant is loyal, wise, and infinitely desirable for her own sake. His marriage will not be just a cure for a sick purse; happily it will bring an end to his days as a wild gallant, days he is eager to put behind him, for they have almost destroyed this chance for happiness and he knows that there is no health in them.[13] In place of crass villainy we find the unrepentant but sadly punished couple, Mrs. Marwood and Fainall. On the title-page Congreve appropriately quotes from the second satire of Horace:

[13] I am indebted to Miss Miriam Gabriel for first pointing out the ethical implications of *The Way of the World*. She has presented cogent argument in an article, as yet unpublished, which I have been permitted to read.

Audire est Operae pretium, procedere recte
Qui maechis non vultis . . .
. . . Metuat doti deprensa.

Thus in this acknowledged masterpiece of the English comedy
of manners, almost every element has been produced by making
artistic modifications to traditional material. Abrupt mutations
are wholly absent. *The Way of the World* contains as many resemblances to earlier successes, in all probability, as any play
ever written. Herein lies its supremacy; each detail is the end of
an evolutionary series. It is placed at the head of every list of
plays of its kind, because its genre and its materials had spent a
century growing up together. Its harmony of plot, of characters,
of atmosphere, of wit, of ethical intention, and of literary style,
is the result of happy modifications within a tradition—a touch
here, a heightening there, new combinations, and added polish
to familiar materials. Congreve the man, Congreve the artist, the
contemporary milieu, and the English comedy of manners had
all somehow grown up with an understanding that left no unre-
solved conflicts. Although he read Molière and the classics, he
schooled himself in seventeenth-century English comedy from
Jonson and Fletcher onward. He knew its successes and its fail-
ures, its aims and its needs, the manners it reflected, and the
reactions of audiences to these manners. To this knowledge he
added artistic taste and unusual critical judgment; he thought
when he wrote. None of the dramatists after Jonson has left the
clear evidence of high respect for the comic poet's calling that we
find in his incidental writings. His strength was more than wit,
more than style; it was comic genius. But it is a matter of significant fact that I can find no demonstrable borrowing from
Molière in any of his comedies.[14]

[14] I can see no gain whatever in recounting my labors on this point. A detailed refuta-
tion of all the allegations would make a book in itself, a book whose dullness would
be matched only by its futility. Parallels of incident, of phrase, of character, of tone, of
dialogue, of method, have been reported in greater numbers than one can count. I have

The creative influence on Congreve, then, was English comedy before and after 1660. For that truth there are a thousand substantial data. In electing to depict a society of gallantry, flirtation, and looseness in sexual relations; in reflecting the philosophy of life of such a social order; in approving the witty speech of true-wits and in laughing at the pseudo-wit of social imitators; in ridiculing the gulls, fops, and social pretenders of both sexes; in writing dialogue redolent of wit for wit's sake; in mixing ethical satire with social; in selecting conventional dramatic situations; in following dramatic customs and adhering to traditional dramatic structure, Congreve exploited English prototypes. He developed them to their highest expression because he was a comic genius, but on none of these things did his acquaintance with Molière's plays have a discernible effect.

SIR JOHN VANBRUGH

Although the recorded dates make Sir John Vanbrugh indubitably a contemporary of Congreve, in his careless heart Sir John was unknowingly looking beyond the coming school of morality and sensibility toward the problem play of the nineteenth century. Not a sentimentalist, as so often charged, he glanced carelessly at some of the social injustices of his times and saw them clearly. In *The Relapse, or Virtue in Danger* (December, 1696), the plight of the poverty-stricken younger brother is presented in Tom Fashion, brother of Lord Foppington, with a sympathy unique in seventeenth-century plays. This treatment is incidental to a plot that makes Tom assume the place of the traditional true-wit and win the approval of the audience by his ability to outdo his highly affected brother; thus plot motiva-

gone through this evidence, judging it by the criteria set up above in Chapter II. (For a bibliography of the works so examined, see Chapter I above, particularly notes 23, 24, 30-33, and 40-42). To my surprise, no sound grain survived the winnowing. Palmer (*Comedy of Manners*) and Dobrée (*Restoration Comedy*) make no reference at all to Molière in their extended discussions of Congreve.

tion aided and abetted the innovation. Repeatedly Vanbrugh looks behind the conventional marriage, to present the lot of those unhappily mated. His treatment is realistic, rather than comic or sentimental. He recognizes that marriage is a relationship whose inherent intimacy loads it with possibility for great suffering, if there is lack of sympathy, forbearance, and courtesy. He proposes no more radical solution than better mating, with something besides money or social position in mind.[15] Thus Vanbrugh's plays, although they are amusingly licentious at times, possess a tinge of morality not wholly unlike Wycherley's or Congreve's. The busy soldier-author-architect made his plays hastily, and therefore adapted several of them from the French, but the social observation is distinctly his own.

It would be impossible to prove by a comparison of the texts that in *The Relapse* Vanbrugh had M. Jourdain of *Le Bourgeois Gentilhomme* in mind when he wrote Lord Foppington's dressing scene,[16] but the number of minor similarities suggests that this was the case. The two scenes are totally different in their chief effect, however, and the confident beau of Vanbrugh's conception did not originate from the timid, but socially ambitious, *bourgeois* that Molière created. Lord Foppington is a splendid example of the stage dandy, some say the finest. His immediate prototype was Sir Novelty Fashion, of Colley Cibber's *Love's Last Shift* (January, 1696), of which *The Relapse* is, as every one knows, a mocking sequel. All resemblance of Foppington to Mascarille, of *Les Précieuses ridicules,* is of the superficial sort found in independent portrayals of a common social type. The play is, in general, Restoration in tone and morality. The author's prefatory insistence on his decency is typical of his flippant attitude. In all this Molière has no place.

Miles thinks that Sir Tunbelly and Hoyden are "a reflection

---

[15] For the original development of this general view, see Mueschke and Fleisher, "A Re-Evaluation of Vanbrugh," *PMLA,* XLIX (1934) 848-89.

[16] Cf. Act I, scene 3, with Molière's play, Act II, scene 5.

of Sganarelle and Isabelle in *L'École des maris,* probably through
The Country Wife." [17] Although of trifling importance, the point
is not one that can be absolutely settled. Like Miss Prue, of *Love
for Love,* Hoyden seems to be something of a Margery Pinchwife,
the comically eager country girl whom Wycherley developed, as
was shown above in Chapter V, from Molière's *L'École des
femmes.* The characteristics common to Margery, Prue, and Hoyden arise from Wycherley's chief addition to the character of
the pure Isabelle, an unrestrained sexual eagerness. It is barely
possible that some of Molière's invention filtered through, but
certainly very little. Sir Tunbelly is another specimen of the type
of rural knight who appeared on the stage regularly from Jonson's time onward; he is not like either Pinchwife or Sganarelle.
If Vanbrugh found Hoyden in *The Country Wife,* there is perhaps an almost perceptible debt to Molière. Even Miles thinks the
debt little enough, for he says elsewhere:

> It is unnecessary to remark that he [Vanbrugh] did not study
> Molière, for it is clear that he paid little attention to the structure of
> anybody's plays.... Vanbrugh's presentation of manners... is com-
> pletely lacking in the sympathy with life and the insight into character
> that distinguished Molière.[18]

Aside from these trifling possibilities, the three original plays
of Vanbrugh, *The Relapse, The Provoked Wife* (May, 1697),
and the unfinished *Journey to London* (completed and staged
by Colley Cibber under the title of *The Provoked Husband,*
1728), show no sign of Molière's influence. His plays are in
the English comic tradition. Where they depart from it, the de-
parture can be explained by reference to current attitudes in
England or to Vanbrugh's personal contribution.

We must not overlook the fact that *The Mistake* (December,
1705) is a translation of *Le Dépit amoureux.* Vanbrugh gives
Molière's play a scene-by-scene and incident-by-incident reproduc-

---

[17] *Influence of Molière on Restoration Comedy,* p. 236.
[18] *Ibid.,* pp. 212-14.

tion; he pays the compliment of a closer rendering than he has given any previous translation. On the whole, Molière's gaiety is reproduced by the masterly paraphrasing of the sense of each speech into the colloquial prose of which Vanbrugh had a ready command. The dignity imposed upon Molière by his rhymed hexameter verse prevented him from using the low-comedy incidents he employed freely enough in prose farces. Vanbrugh's version is not so hampered, and his injection of low-comedy additions, like his realistic style, is more natural to the original plot than Molière's. Vigor often replaces languor, and concrete imagery replaces vague generalizations. Compare Marinette's speech with its English version:

> *Mar.* En effet, tu dis bien, voilà comme il faut être:
> Jamais de ces soupçons qu'un jaloux fait paroître!
> Tout le fruit qu'on en cueille est de se mettre mal,
> Et d'avancer par là les desseins d'un rival:
> Au mérite souvent de qui l'éclat vous blesse
> Vos chagrins font ouvrir les yeux d'une maîtresse;
> Et j'en sais tel qui doit son destin le plus doux
> Aux soins trop inquiets de son rival jaloux;
> Enfin, quoi qu'il en soit, témoigner de l'ombrage,
> C'est jouer en amour un mauvais personnage,
> Et se rendre, après tout, misérable à crédit:
> Cela, seigneur Éraste, en passant vous soit dit.[19]

Jacin [*ta*]. That's the Way to prosper, however so far I'll confess the Truth to thee, at least if that don't do, nothing else will. Men are mighty simple in Love-Matters, Sir: When you suspect a Woman's falling off, you fall a plaguing her to bring her on again, attack her with Reason, and a sour Face; udslife, Sir, attack her with a Fiddle, double your good Humour,—give her a Ball,—powder your Perriwig at her,—let her cheat you at Cards a little, and I'll warrant all's right again. But to come upon a poor Woman with the gloomy Face of Jealousie, before she gives the least Occasion for't, is to set a complaisant Rival in

---

[19] *Le Dépit,* Act I, scene 2.

too favourable a Light. Sir, Sir, I must tell you, I have seen those have ow'd their Success to nothing else.[20]

Generally condensation is used to improve prolix passages. Compare Albert's soliloquy in Act II, scene 5, with Don Alvarez' sprightly equivalent:

> En quel gouffre de soins et de perplexité
> Nous jette une action faite sans équité!
> D'un enfant supposé par mon trop d'avarice
> Mon coeur depuis longtemps souffre bien le supplice,
> Et quand je vois les maux où je me suis plongé,
> Je voudrois à ce bien n'avoir jamais songé.
> Tantôt je crains de voir par la fourbe éventée
> Ma famille en opprobre et misère jetée;
> Tantôt pour ce fils-là, qu'il me faut conserver,
> Je crains cent accidents qui peuvent arriver.
> S'il advient que dehors quelque affaire m'appelle,
> J'appréhende au retour cette triste nouvelle:
> 'Las! vous ne savez pas? vous l'a-ton annoncé?
> Votre fils a la fièvre, ou jambe, ou bras cassé.'
> Enfin, à tous moments, sur quoi que je m'arrête,
> Cent sortes de chagrins me roulent par la tête.
> Ha!

I'll try if I can discover, by his Tutor, what 'tis that seems so much to work his Brain of late, for something more than common there plainly does appear, yet nothing sure that can disturb his Soul, like what I have to torture mine on his Account. Sure nothing in this World is worth a troubled Mind: What Racks has Avarice stretch'd me on; I wanted nothing, kind Heav'n had given me a plenteous Lot, and seated me in great Abundance; why then approve I of this Imposture? What have I gain'd by it? Wealth and Misery; I have barter'd peaceful Days for restless Nights; a wretched Bargain! and he that Merchandizes thus, must be undone at last.[21]

For the fourth act Vanbrugh successfully prolongs and elaborates the best comic scenes of the original play.[22] An examination of

---

[20] *The Mistake,* Act I, scene 1 (Dobrée, ed., *Complete Works of Vanbrugh,* III, 89).
[21] *The Mistake,* Act II, scene 1 (Dobrée ed., III, 99).
[22] "*Le Dépit amoureux* se compose de deux pièces soudées ensemble, mais que l'on

the two versions side by side is very interesting because of the additions that were made in the speeches and in the stage business. While the total length is increased to a moderate degree, the addition comes in the new business. Molière's lovers feel hurt and angry. Urged on by their servants, who are also lovers, they decide to break. Éraste declares his love cannot endure such haughty treatment. Lucile listens coldly and asks him to return no more. Agreeing to part forever, they return all gifts; he a portrait of her, she some jewels. Then they happen to read the sentiments written at the time the gifts were made. The servants urge them to go away from each other, but Éraste once more declares his love, and, after Lucile scolds him for his jealousy, they exclaim:

> *Éraste.* Mais cruelle, c'est vous qui l'avez bien voulu.
> *Lucille.* Moi? Point du tout; c'est vous qui l'avez résolu.[23]

The difference soon dissolves and he takes her home. Then the servants both express contempt for the weakness of their mistress and master. They descend to abuse, and return each other's paltry gifts of lace, ribbon, pins, knives, and scissors. The comedy gets broad:

> *Gros-René.* J'oubliois d'avant-hier ton morceau de fromage:
> Tiens! Je voudrois pouvoir rejeter le potage
> Que tu me fis manger, pour n'avoir rien à toi.
> *Marinette.* Je n'ai point maintenant de tes lettres sur moi;

---

peut séparer. L'une, la plus considérable par le nombre des scènes, est une imitation d'un *imbroglio* italien, et c'est la partie la plus faible. L'autre, plus courte, n'appartient qu'à Molière; et Molière y est déjà tout entier. C'est la seule que représente depuis bien longtemps le Théâtre français. Elle se compose de ces scènes de brouille et de raccommodement dont Molière a depuis reproduit l'idée dans plusieurs de ses comédies; mais jamais il n'a déployé une sensibilité plus vraie, une plus franche et plus naïve gaieté. Ces scènes ainsi détachées forment une petite pièce, assez complète dans son cadre restreint. ... Molière lui-même semble presque avoir autorisé cette séparation, en donnant à sa comédie un titre qui ne convient nullement au fond de la pièce et ne s'applique qu'à ces scènes de *dépit amoureux*" (Despois-Mesnard, ed., *Oeuvres de Molière*, I, [381]).

[23] *Ibid.,* Act IV, scene 3 (Despois-Mesnard ed., I, 493).

Mais j'en ferai du feu jusques à la dernière.
Gros-René. Et des tiennes tu sais ce que j'en saurai faire? [24]

In a moment laughter brings reconciliation.

In Vanbrugh's version, the servants take a more active part in the first quarrel, busily seconding the causes of their principals. Leonora throws a "Tablebook" of Don Carlos' verses at his feet.

There, Sir, take your Poetry again, 'tis not much the worse for my wearing; 'twill serve again upon a fresh Occasion.

He tosses a handful of letters at her feet,

. . . a Pocketful of your Prose. There.

Then she flings his letters in his face. The servants engage in instant battle too. Sancho exclaims:

'Cods my Life, we want Ammunition; but for a shift— There, and there, you saucy Slut, you.
[Sancho *pulls a Pack of dirty Cards out of his Pocket, and throws 'em at her; then they close; he pulls off her Head-cloaths, and she his Wigg, and then part, running she to her Mistress, he to his Master.*[25]

Though both women are determined to hold the field, the storm is soon over. Don Carlos "Carries her [Leonora] off, embracing her, and kissing her Hand." The servants then resume the quarrel, calling names and returning gifts. He returns a handkerchief he has cherished, first blowing his nose in it. She takes off the garters he gave and "slaps 'em about his Face." Just as he lifts his cudgel, she leaps about his neck in an amorous frenzy, and the storm blows over.

Molière's scene is unmistakably broadened, but not to such an extent as to alter the psychology of *Le Dépit*. It might even be defended as more natural and more amusing than the original. Vanbrugh has merely developed the low comedy inherent in the

[24] *Ibid.,* Act IV, scene 4.
[25] Act IV, scene 1 (*Dobrée* ed., III, 117).

original. Perry finds an explanation of these alterations in Vanbrugh's limited interest in romance. He says:

It is interesting to note how much more at home Sir John seems to be in the low-life passages from Molière than with the high flown romantic sentiments in which the main plot of *Dépit Amoureux* abounds, and the same tendency may be observed in his other adaptations. It is curious that again and again he should choose a romantic play on which to exercise his talents: *Aesop, The Pilgrim, The False Friend,* and *The Mistake* are all taken from dramas (most of them in verse) filled with noble emotions and even nobler sentiments. Perhaps Vanbrugh kept on good terms with his conscience by devoting his energies to such elevated material and then pleased himself by the prosaic and ribald way in which he treated it. At any rate, each time that he had any real success with his second-hand work, it was in the coarser passages, where he could stick to mundane concerns and did not need to soar with his original into the higher levels of romantic fancy. Such passages are generally those in which the servants are concerned, and in every case Vanbrugh has added to and developed their rôles.[26]

It might be argued that Vanbrugh was, instead, meeting the expectations of his audiences with a tone used in comedy for a hundred years before him. He does not debase Molière's play, although he necessarily changes the tone, but really carries out what its spirit ought to have been. *The Mistake* is the first good acting translation of Molière into English.

There remains one unimportant, but baffling, question. In February, 1704, Vanbrugh, Congreve, and Walsh translated or adapted *Monsieur de Pourceaugnac* under the title of *Squire Trelooby,* Molière's Limousine gull becoming a Cornish squire. The play was staged that spring with great success. An anonymous quarto volume, entitled *Monsieur de Pourceaugnac, or Squire Trelooby,* was published in April. The preface declares it to be independent work, and elsewhere Congreve declared this was "none of ours." In 1734, when all three of the original au-

---

[26] *Comic Spirit in Restoration Drama,* pp. 103-4.

thors had died, Ralph produced *The Cornish Squire,* which he said came from the manuscript of the original three men and which he had altered somewhat. One cannot even say that the original text is not extant in one of these versions.[27] But no matter who wrote the versions we have, and no matter how many or how few translations there were, someone adapted Molière; but since Ozell and others were soon to set about the translation of all Molière's work, this version, which had a short stage life, is not very important. There is none of the matter nor spirit of Molière in Vanbrugh's remaining original plays, *The Provoked Wife,* and *The Journey to London,* and none crept into his translations from Le Sage, Boursault, and Dancourt. Obviously Molière was not a vital influence in Vanbrugh's art, especially if we concede Palmer's extreme praise that "In every case his adaptations from Dancourt, Boursault, even Molière, are better than their originals." [28]

GEORGE FARQUHAR

When George Farquhar went to his untimely grave, amidst the plaudits of *The Beaux' Stratagem,* in 1707, a prophetic Thalia might have foreseen that the great comedy of manners had died. It is the last of its kind. Some go further, John Palmer, for example, in insisting that "Farquhar killed the comedy to which he contributed the last brilliant examples," [29] because he introduced moral problems where they did not belong. Others, like William Archer, defend him for the same essential facts; viz., that he

[27] Genest (*Some Account of the English Stage,* III, 409) gives some of the documentary evidence. Sir Edmund Gosse (*Life of Congreve,* pp. 135-38) gives a clear account of the known facts.

[28] *Comedy of Manners,* p. 225. Dametz (*John Vanbrughs Leben und Werke,* p. 192) pays the same tribute in a more restricted form: "Man vergleiche z.B. die Scene zwischen dem Vater Leonoras, Don Alvarez, und Don Lorenzos Vater, Don Felix, mitt der betreffenden Scene im Molièreschen Stück, oder die Scene, wo das einander schmollende Liebespaar auftritt, so wird man jedenfalls dem Vanbrughischen Stück den Vorzug geben."

[29] *Op. cit.,* p. 242.

had no "wit" as Wycherley or Congreve would define it, and that he manifested some interest in "moral sensibility" where it had been too long lacking.[30] Wit was surely replaced by Irish impudence in Sir Harry Wildair, who is, under various names, the hero of every play. But all agree that a felicitous mastery of theatrically effective comic incident gives life to Farquhar's plays. This is the more remarkable because he was manipulating stock characters and conventional situations with the verve of wholly new material. But all this has little enough to do with Molière. Moreover the record is so free of false hopes of finding an influence that there is little even to refute. Schmid gives no space to Molière, and Miles admits that he "hardly belongs in a discussion of Molière's influence."[31] This is not surprising, for Farquhar holds his secure place in literature because of his fertile genius for originating comic figures in the Irish-British manner.

SUMMARY

Congreve, Vanbrugh, and Farquhar close the history of Restoration comedy. The first of these carried the true comedy of manners to its highest level in England without leaving evidence that Molière was, in an important way, formative of his genius or of any detail of his art. What is there in Congreve that cannot be fully explained without allusion to the Frenchman? In con-

---

[30] See Archer's introduction to *George Farquhar* ("The Mermaid Series"), pp. 15-29, especially p. 16.

[31] Schmid, *George Farquhar, sein Leben und seine Original-Dramen*. Van Laun called a conventionalized similarity between Farquhar's first play, *Love and a Bottle* (1699) and *Le Bourgeois Gentilhomme* a positive borrowing ("Les Plagiaires de Molière en Angleterre," *Le Moliériste*, III, 139). On about the same sort of evidence, Miles says Squire Mockmode is copied from M. de Pourceaugnac. The sole resemblance is that both are country gulls. The likeness of Mockmode to Jourdain of *Le Bourgeois Gentilhomme* lies merely in the fact that both had tutors. Shirley also employed a gull with a tutor; the likenesses are accidents. In *The Constant Couple, or a Trip to the Jubilee*, Farquhar took nothing from Molière. Miles thinks Act II, scene 5, was suggested by *Le Médecin malgré lui*, Act I, scene 5. (See Miles, *op. cit.*, p. 227.) The resemblance consists in the fact that Smuggler and Sganarelle are beaten by men who are not angry with them. Miles also finds a passage in *The Beaux' Stratagem* which he thinks is "freely adapted" from *Le Tartuffe;* I see nothing distinctive about the resemblance.

trast Vanbrugh was a liberal and assimilating borrower. No matter what he found in his sources, he absorbed it into his own gay and superficial self, gave it a dash of Elizabethan verve, and turned it out. Molière contributed heavily, and while this may have been of importance in the subsequent history of Molière in eighteenth-century England, it did not materially affect the original comedy of Vanbrugh. Farquhar bears many resemblances to Vanbrugh: he showed even more vitality and animal exuberance, he seemed to be a more positive echo of long-forgotten Jacobean energy of action, and his gaiety was more intense and more dashing. He did not use a thing from Molière, who was not, we must conclude from the evidence, a contributor to the spirit of these three men. Even though we hold Vanbrugh's insouciant borrowings of matter before us, we must close with a minimizing gesture against all assertions of Molière's influence upon them.

IX: THE BORROWINGS AGAINST THE BACKGROUND

ONE OF the principles of this study is that influence upon a larger mass of literature, such as the comic drama of a period, must be considered in the light of the whole of that literature, not in the light merely of those examples in which borrowings occur. In order that the reader might understand the relation of Molière to authors who did borrow from him, the preceding chapters have largely ignored the nature and product of those Restoration playwrights who did not. In this chapter the readers must again traverse the same forty years[1] of dramatic history, as swiftly perhaps as tourists through an art gallery. Plays whose authors borrowed from Molière are put into their chronological place, and the much larger number free from his influence are now brought into the focus of this study. The approach is strictly chronological, so that time, the first guide to cause and effect, may make its valuable contribution to a sense of proportion.

The Restoration comedies found in the earlier chapters to contain certain or possible borrowings from Molière are listed in their order on pages 180-81.

Let us lay this table beside the chronological list given in Appendix B. The average rate of production of comedies over

[1] I am restricting the subject matter of Chapter IX strictly to the years 1660-1700. In Chapter VIII I ran over the latter limit to include the works of Vanbrugh and Farquhar, because existing interest in them as Restoration comedies extends to their relation to Molière. But this exception does not make it desirable to go beyond 1700 for a survey of Molière's relation to comedies of the Restoration.

the forty years, 1660-1700, was five plays a year. Not quite one in twelve (sixteen plays in all) contains enough material from Molière to be described as adaptation, under which heading are included all borrowings that were substantially formative. Fourteen other plays unmistakably contain borrowings that are not extensive enough to be very influential in shaping results. Eight remaining plays contain resemblances that cannot be positively affirmed or certainly denied as resulting from the English authors' acquaintance with the Frenchman. Altogether thirty-eight Restoration plays, nearly one in five, have some connection with Molière.

1660–1670

Mention was made in Chapter III of the turning of the early Restoration theatre to pre-Restoration materials. It was there shown that much of the manner and tone of the comedy arose from the influence of Jonson, Fletcher, Shirley, and their satellites. Some of this influence came through reading, some was acquired through the presence of old successes as living drama on the stage, and some may be explained by the fact that several writers, Abraham Cowley, Sir Robert Stapylton, Thomas Killigrew, the Duke and the Duchess of Newcastle, John Tatham, and William D'Avenant bridged the dark years as dramatists in both periods. Surely the imitation of former giants by later pygmies is most natural. But new comedies came slowly; only six were staged during the years 1660, 1661, and 1662. Of these Cowley's *Cutter of Colman Street* (a rewriting of his pre-Restoration *The Guardian*) and Robert Howard's *The Committee* are the best known.[2] Like Tatham's *The Rump,* Howard's play belongs to

[2] Ward (*English Dramatic Literature,* III, 394 n.) speaks of the hypocritical Mr. Day of this play as "a vile kind of Tartuffe." This is an example of a likeness that cannot be a borrowing, for *Le Tartuffe* was still unwritten. The observation of such examples provides a wholesome corrective to undue credulity in such matters. With Shakespeare's Timon, Marston's Malevole. Middleton's Hoard, and Massinger's Overreach in mind, one will hesitate before saying any misanthrope or any miser is painted after Alceste or Harpagon. Ward, of course, makes no such mistake.

RESTORATION COMEDIES CONTAINING CERTAIN OR POSSIBLE BORROWINGS FROM MOLIÈRE

Comedy	Adapted from:	Borrowed from:	Possibly Borrowed from:
D'Avenant's Playhouse to Be Let, 1663	Sganarelle, 1660		
Dryden's Sir Martin Mar-All, 1667	L'Étourdi, 1658		
Sedley's Mulberry Garden, 1668		L'École des maris, 1661	
Shadwell's Sullen Lovers, 1668		Les Précieuses ridicules, 1659 / Dépit amoureux, 1658	
Dryden's Evening's Love, 1668	Les Fâcheux, 1661	L'École des femmes, 1662	
Flecknoe's Damoiselles à la Mode, 1668	L'École des maris, 1661 / Les Précieuses ridicules, 1659		
Lacy's Dumb Lady, 1669	Le Médecin malgré lui, 1666		
Caryl's Sir Salomon, 1669	L'École des femmes, 1662		
Betterton's Amorous Widow, c. 1670	George Dandin, 1668		L'École des maris, 1661
Medbourne's Tartuffe, 1670	Tartuffe, 1669		
Wycherley's Gentleman Dancing Master, 1672			Bourgeois Gentilhomme, 1670 / Précieuses ridicules, 1659
Shadwell's Miser, 1672	L'Avare, 1668		
Dryden's Marriage à la Mode, 1672		L'Avare, 1668	
Ravenscroft's Mamamouchi, 1672	Bourgeois Gentilhomme, 1670 / M. de Pourceaugnac, 1669		
Ravenscroft's Careless Lovers, 1673		M. de Pourceaugnac, 1669	
Wycherley's Country Wife, 1675	L'École des femmes, 1662	L'École des maris, 1661	
Shadwell's Psyche, 1675			Psyché, 1671
Shadwell's Libertine, 1675			Don Juan, 1665

Précieuses ridicules, 1659

Critique de l'école des femmes, 1663

Femmes savantes, 1672
L'Amour médecin, 1665

L'École des femmes, 1662
Les Fâcheux, 1661

Mariage forcé, 1664
Tartuffe, 1669
M. de Pourceaugnac, 1669

Bourgeois Gentilhomme, 1670

Le Sicilien, 1667

Sganarelle, 1660

Bourgeois Gentilhomme, 1670

L'École des maris, 1661
L'École des femmes, 1662

Précieuses ridicules, 1659

Précieuses ridicules, 1659
Précieuses ridicules, 1659
Femmes savantes, 1672
L'École des maris, 1661
Amphitryon, 1668

Malade imaginaire, 1673
M. de Pourceaugnac, 1669

Mariage forcé, 1664

Fourberies de Scapin, 1671
Misanthrope, 1666

Fourberies de Scapin, 1671
Mariage forcé, 1664
Malade imaginaire, 1673

Femmes savantes, 1672

Crowne's Country Wit, 1676
Etherege's Man of Mode, 1676
Rawlins' Tom Essence, 1676
Otway's Cheats of Scapin, 1676
Wycherley's Plain Dealer, 1676

Ravenscroft's Scaramouch, 1677

Behn's Sir Patient Fancy, 1678

Otway's Soldier's Fortune, 1680
Ravenscroft's London Cuckolds, 1681

Behn's False Count, 1682
Otway's Atheist, 1683
Crowne's Sir Courtly Nice, 1685
Shadwell's Bury Fair, 1689

Shadwell's Amorous Bigot, 1690
Dryden's Amphitryon, 1690
Crowne's English Friar, 1690
Wright's Female Vertuosoes, 1693
Ravenscroft's Canterbury Guests, 1694
Vanbrugh's Relapse, 1696
Penkethman's Love without Interest, 1699

the early group of political comedies described by Allardyce Nicoll.[3] In its method of characterization it combines the Jonsonian tradition of "humors" with contemporary realism. Among these six examples of comedy during the earliest years of the period, we find no use of Molière. But in the summer of 1663 came Sir William D'Avenant's *Playhouse to Be Let* (*c.* August, 1663),[4] which is the first to borrow from him. In the same year John Dryden staged *The Wild Gallant,* the first play of Restoration times to suggest the later comedy of manners; it owes nothing to Molière. Like *The Wild Gallant* in its combination of traditional material with contemporary realism is *The Cheats* (March, 1663). With this play was launched the career of John Wilson, who made a reputation as a Restoration follower of Jonson and a builder of plays on the pattern of the pre-Restoration successes seen in revival.[5] In all, this fourth year gave the theatre eight comedies. Borrowing from Molière makes its first appearance on the Restoration stage, but his influence is microscopic.

During the next three and one-half years a dozen more new comedies were produced before Dryden's *Sir Martin Mar-All* (August, 1667), the second Restoration adaptation of Molière. Several of the intervening plays had distinct successes at the time, and Sir George Etherege's *The Comical Revenge* (March, 1664) is one of the more notable plays of the whole period. Killigrew's

---

[3] "Political Plays of the Restoration."

[4] The staging of this play has long been assigned to 1662, which date will be found in nearly all references. The second edition of Nicoll's *Restoration Drama* gives the date found above.

[5] His second comedy, *The Projectors* (probably unacted, printed 1665), has been needlessly referred to *L'Avare,* when the common source, the *Aulularia* of Plautus, is an adequate explanation of the resemblance. Charlanne (*L'Influence française en Angleterre au xviie siècle,* pp. 287-88) is the most notable defender of the *possibility* that Wilson knew *L'Avare.* To believe this, one must accept the heresy, started by a probable slip of Grimarest, that *L'Avare* had an unrecorded presentation *years* before 1668, the date which the accurate La Grange recorded. Then one must believe further that Wilson made an unknown visit to Paris and attended this obscure performance. I hold with Ward and Nicoll that the likeness is not a borrowing. See Despois-Mesnard, ed., *Oeuvres de Molière,* VII, 1-11, for details of date of *L'Avare.*

The Parson's Wedding (October, 1664) is a revival, with alterations, of his own pre-Restoration play acted in 1640. Its satiric ribaldry makes an interesting and convincing link between the indecency of Brome's time and that of the days of Ravenscroft and Mrs. Behn. John Lacy's *The Old Troup, or Monsieur Raggou* (*c.* 1665) recalls with rough comic effect the sickening memories of soldiering during the days of the Civil Wars.

One might easily believe that the great profit of Dryden with *Sir Martin Mar-All* created a momentary confidence in Molière as the source of success, for half the comedies of the next year, 1668, followed Dryden's example. The year was otherwise a notable one in the advance of Restoration comedy. In February Etherege's second play, *She Would If She Could,* was mangled by bad acting and suffered a failure that was undeserved, for later history accords it the rank of the most distinguished comedy of the year, or of the decade. It is the only good play of the year that does not owe something to Molière. In May Sir Charles Sedley scored with *The Mulberry Garden,* and Thomas Shadwell made his début with *The Sullen Lovers, or the Impertinents.* In June Dryden presented *An Evening's Love, or the Mock Astrologer.* Then in September Richard Flecknoe secured a hearing for *The Damoiselles à la Mode,* which he had printed the year before. All four of these levied upon Molière. Flecknoe drew most heavily and gained the least, simply because he was incompetent. Shadwell owed much of his success to Molière; Dryden and Sedley, very little. Four negligible minor plays took nothing from him. The movement to plunder him, if it can be called such, continued through the next two years, 1669 and 1670, for every important play that appeared, except Shadwell's *The Humorists,* depended upon Molière for the main plot and the bulk of the matter. The three adaptations, Caryl's *Sir Salomon,* Lacy's *The Dumb Lady,* and Medbourne's *Tartuffe,* would be nothing at all without the borrowings, and Betterton's *The Amorous Widow* borrowed all of the subplot. Medbourne's *Tartuffe* is, moreover, the first attempt to grasp the serious side of Molière and import it to England entire.

Perhaps we are now in a position to survey the influence of Molière on the first decade. In so far as they used him, the actor playwrights, D'Avenant, Lacy, Betterton, and Medbourne, complete their careers at this time. The history of Restoration comedy puts them in the class of unimportant writers; although the first one named has a larger place in dramatic history, his borrowing in *The Playhouse to Be Let* had no discernible influence on any one. Flecknoe, Caryl, and Sedley, who also come before us for parting consideration, were men of wide acquaintance and influence in higher social circles, especially Sedley. Flecknoe tended to familiarize London with matter from Molière; and some echoes of intrigue and comic incident from *L'École des maris* and *Les Précieuses ridicules* may derive from him, although the success of *The Damoiselles à la Mode* must have been slight, for Langbaine thought it had never been acted.[6] It would not be a stimulating example, therefore, for others. John Caryl joined Dryden, Shadwell, and Lacy, in the use of Molière's theatrical effectiveness to make a successful play. Whatever skill he seemed to show in plotting a comedy, and whatever influence that appearance of skill exerted, really belongs to Molière. The most prominent of this group socially—and in Restoration life this could easily mean theatrically—was Sir Charles Sedley. His reputation for wit was peerless. His play, *The Mulberry Garden,* was a great success and very influential in establishing the taste for a comedy of manners, but his debt to Molière was too slight, a mere detail of plot structure, for any of his influence to be credited to the latter.

Since the careers of Dryden and Shadwell continue through the next two decades, an attempt to consider their whole influ-

---

[6] *Account of the English Dramatick Poets,* pp. 199-201.

ence would be premature at this stage, but their example so far would indicate that Molière was a good source of plot material; it would show little more. Both of these Englishmen were far more influential through their example of combining pre-Restoration dramatic modes with post-Restoration social attitudes. They were thus very important in setting the pattern for an indigenous comedy in which foreign elements were so thoroughly assimilated as to be inconspicuous even when visible.

A list of significant plays of the first decade, aside from Etherege's masterly contribution to the comedy of manners, would contain a fair number of plays with a touch of Molière in them. Aside from Medbourne's *Tartuffe* and *The Sullen Lovers* of Shadwell, which caught something of the spirit and much of the external form of what is a peculiarly structureless play without later influence—aside from these, Molière did not affect the spirit of his borrowers. The spirit of the age in England demanded a witty, gay, anti-moral comedy of manners. This started in *The Wild Gallant*, gained tremendous impetus from *The Comical Revenge*, and reached its finest expression in *She Would If She Could*. *Sir Martin Mar-All*, *The Sullen Lovers*, *The Mulberry Garden*, *An Evening's Love*, and *The Humorists* are approximately alike in drawing toward the same dramatic genre.[7] There are no discernible borrowings from Molière in this comic spirit.[8] On the contrary, Dryden's *The Wild Gallant*,

---

[7] I do not mean to imply that they drew exclusively toward the comedy of manners, for they were all of mixed character. The intrigue of *An Evening's Love* is outside the type of play we call a comedy of manners, and of course *The Humorists* is not entirely in this vein, for the influence of Jonson, usually potent with Shadwell, brought a certain satire, a moral earnestness, foreign to the tone of a comedy of manners.

[8] As it is usually defined, the comedy of manners of England is something remote from Molière's art. For example, observe how applicable this description of the comedy of manners is to Congreve and how inapplicable to Molière: "In the main, we may say, the invariable elements of the comedy of manners are the presence of at least one pair of witty lovers, the woman as emancipated as the man, their dialogue free and graceful, an air of refined cynicism over the whole production, the plot of less consequence than the wit, an absence of crude realism, a total lack of any emotion whatsoever" (Nicoll, *Restoration Drama*, p. 185).

Etherege's *The Comical Revenge* and *She Would If She Could,* Killigrew's *The Parson's Wedding,* Howard's *The English Monsieur* and *All Mistaken, or the Mad Couple,* Newcastle's *The Humorous Lovers,* and Shadwell's *The Humorists* would form a contemporary list about which one could truthfully say the following: (1) they are based upon Elizabethan, Jacobean, and Caroline elements in spirit, matter, and form; (2) they anticipate later Restoration comedy of manners better than the plays containing borrowings from Molière; and (3) they contain nothing from Molière, directly or indirectly.

About forty new comedies were staged in England during this decade, 1660-1670. Of these, ten show borrowings from Molière. Six of the ten may be described as servile adaptations by negligible playwrights, *The Playhouse to Be Let, The Damoiselles à la Mode, The Dumb Lady, Sir Salomon, The Amorous Widow,* and *Tartuffe.* Two others, *The Mulberry Garden* and *An Evening's Love,* borrowed a few details only. The remaining two, *Sir Martin Mar-All* and *The Sullen Lovers,* are more important. Molière provided the basic idea of their plots and some of the incidents. This might have been more influential on dramatic form, if the two plays used had not been his poorest structurally, so poor that Dryden and Shadwell were both able to bind their plots more firmly than he had done.

So far, then, Englishmen have turned readily to Molière for help in their dramatic problems, but the results cannot be said to have brought an appreciable amount of his spirit or of his form to England. Meanwhile English plays are showing a constant trend in the direction of the artificial comedy of manners.

1670–1676

In sharp contrast with the year 1670, whose three comedies were all based on Molière, was the year 1671, which saw the birth of seven new comedies, not one of which drew on him for anything. Three of them deserve brief mention here, because of their oblique relation to the present problem. Mrs. Aphra Behn brought out her first comedy,[9] *The Amorous Prince, or the Curious Husband* (*c.* May, 1671), without using the works of the French master, although she borrowed from him later in her career. The greatest success of the year, *The Rehearsal* (December, 1671),[10] by George Villiers, Duke of Buckingham, shows how completely independent the English stage could be from Molière, even in its most satiric moments. Its superficial similarity to *L'Impromptu de Versailles,* in employing a stage as the scene and dramatic criticism as its subject matter, has prompted only the most idolatrous discoverers of "influence" to trace its origin to France.[11]

The seven new plays of 1672 include several that bear a considerable relation to Molière. Edward Ravenscroft produced the first in his long series of dramatic thefts, which had great popularity and little lasting merit. His *Mamamouchi, or the Citizen Turned Gentleman* (July, 1672) mangles two of Molière's masterpieces. Shadwell, likewise, drew heavily for *The Miser,* but the result is adapted to the tone of the Restoration. The important plays of the year are Shadwell's *Epsom Wells,* Dryden's *Marriage à la Mode,* and Wycherley's *The Gentleman Dancing Master.* Aside from two possible borrowings, these owe nothing to Molière.

[9] Her one previous play, *The Forced Marriage, or the Jealous Bridegroom* (December, 1670), is a tragicomedy (Nicoll, *op. cit.,* p. 352).

[10] It was also in great demand in printed form. Nicoll (*ibid.,* p. 375) mentions six printings before 1700 and six more by 1775.

[11] Gillet (*Molière en Angleterre,* p. 30) speculates as follows: "Mais pourquoi songer à Shakespeare, alors qu'il est possible que Davenant connût *l'Impromptu de Versailles* (11 october 1663), qui présente avec le premier acte de *The Playhouse to be let* une analogie technique frappante? *L'Impromptu,* qui, lui aussi, montre un théâtre vu des coulisses, pourrait très bien servir aux mêmes fins que l'introduction de la pièce de Davenant. Plus tard, en 1671, nous retrouvons le même procédé dans *The Rehearsal* du duc de Buckingham qui, vraisemblablement l'emprunta à Davenant." The logical principle seems to be, "if it is possible to believe, it is true." Note that D'Avenant's play appeared before Molière's.

Dramatic productivity fell off in 1673 and 1674 in quantity, in quality, and in the proportion of borrowing from Molière. The Duke of Newcastle's *The Triumphant Widow, or The Medley of Humours* (November, 1674) is the only one to win even one sentence of mention in Ward's *English Dramatic Literature*. Ravenscroft's *The Careless Lovers* (March, 1673) alone borrows from the Frenchman, and it is derived largely from other sources. Most of the half dozen plays of 1675 are no better; but a year that produces *The Country Wife* is a great year. Shadwell's *The Libertine* is the only other play to have even an oblique relation to Molière.

The year 1676 was a notable one for the theatre. Eleven new plays were staged, two of which, Etherege's *The Man of Mode, or Sir Fopling Flutter* (March, 1676) and Wycherley's *The Plain Dealer* (December, 1676) are among the greatest comedies of the entire Restoration period. Thomas D'Urfey entered the field of comedy for the first time, placing three of his twenty popular comedies on the stage in six months. On the whole Molière played an important, but not dominating, rôle, being employed in several of these eleven plays. In one of them, *The Man of Mode,* the debt is not certain. In two of them, *The Country Wit* and *Tom Essence,* there is definite borrowing without dependence; in *The Cheats of Scapin* there is complete dependence without excellence, but in *The Plain Dealer* there is as important an influence of Molière as in almost any Restoration play.

Since this is the time when Wycherley brought his dilettante career as a playwright to an untimely close and when easy Etherege made an equally needless end to another brilliant record, it is a good time to summarize once more. In his three plays, Etherege did not depend on Molière for more than one comic incident, and this he may have invented for himself. Of the men less important in comedy, Shadwell, Dryden, and Crowne, the first used Molière as the basis of one play, but this is outweighed

by several better ones, notably *Epsom Wells* and *The Virtuoso,*
in which Molière had no part. Dryden made much less use of
him than during the first decade. Crowne likewise was much
more British than French in the choice of material. As these
three, together with Ravenscroft and Otway, extended their careers into the next period, we may well postpone a summary of
their works until they may be considered in their entirety. Rawlins' one feeble effort to adapt a farce was too slight for serious
evaluation. Ravenscroft showed that Molière is a good source for
uninspired hacks to copy. Otway demonstrated the possibility of
a careful and close adaptation. In the six years, 1671-76, thirty-
eight new comedies were staged. Several important writers appeared for the first time, Aphra Behn, John Crowne, Thomas
D'Urfey, Thomas Otway, Edward Ravenscroft, George Villiers,
and William Wycherley. John Dryden, Sir George Etherege, and
Thomas Shadwell continued from the preceding decade. Of the
thirty-eight plays, twelve show some degree of borrowing from
Molière. Among these twelve, one great play derives its spirit
from him, and a second one can be so described, with reserva-
tions, Wycherley's *Country Wife* and *Plain Dealer* respectively.
Two of them, Otway's *Cheats of Scapin* and Ravenscroft's
Mamamouchi, are wholesale adaptations of his materials, made
unimportant only by the low degree of competence of the adapters. One, Shadwell's *Miser,* is an interesting and extensive borrowing of matter by an influential playwright. Two more,
Crowne's *Country Wit* and Rawlins' *Tom Essence,* show considerable borrowing by lesser men of farcical matter for secondary
plots. The remaining plays, Dryden's *Marriage à la Mode* and
The Assignation, Etherege's *The Man of Mode,* Ravenscroft's
The Careless Lovers, and Wycherley's *The Gentleman Dancing
Master,* contain, at the most, some possible traces of the French-
man's matter. At least four of the twenty-six plays unrelated to
Molière belong on any list of the outstanding comedies of the

period, Shadwell's *Epsom Wells* and *The Virtuoso*, Villiers' *The Rehearsal*, and Wycherley's *Love in a Wood*. With the very memorable exception of Wycherley's last two plays, the use of Molière was less significant than during the first decade, and less frequent attempts were made to naturalize him in England.

1677–1700

After the year 1676 there was a steady decline in the proportion of borrowings and in their significance in the stream of English comic production. As we have just noted, in the ten years from *Sir Martin Mar-All* to *The Plain Dealer,* twelve adaptations were made, some by as important men as Dryden, Sedley, Shadwell, and Wycherley. Five other plays definitely borrowed from Molière, and an additional five may have done so. By contrast, in the quarter century from *The Plain Dealer* to *The Way of the World,* the number of adaptations fell to three, all made by the minor writers, Ravenscroft, Mrs. Behn, and Thomas Wright. Nine other plays show borrowing and three more are on the doubtful list.[12] From Wycherley to Congreve the stream of plays flowed at less than the average rate and lacked superiority, for none rose above the usual level of Dryden and Shadwell. The plays of Ravenscroft, Mrs. Behn, and Thomas D'Urfey appear oftenest in the list. The borrowings from Molière, which turn up in scattered comedies, are nearly always in the form of incidental passages taken out of plays that had been plundered before. Lacking formative character, such passages indicate not a great influence by Molière, but a wide acquaintance of Restoration

[12] This gives us in tabular form:

	Total Number of Comedies in List	Number Adapting Molière	Number .Borrowing. from Molière	Number Possibly Borrowing
1660-1666	24	1	0	0
1667-1676	61	12	5	5
1676-1700	115	3	9	3
Total	199	16	14	8

playwrights with his works and a readiness to use what came handy. About one play in ten bears some trace of him, but only one in forty can be called an adaptation. The year-by-year consideration is no longer of any use, for these few generalizations cover all the pertinent facts. With the appearance of Congreve in 1693, of Vanbrugh in 1696, and of Farquhar in 1698, great comedy came back to the English stage, but a traceable factor of influence from Molière had disappeared.

X: CONCLUSION

IN SUMMING UP the case of the relation of Molière to Restoration comedy, we need to remind ourselves again that sound conclusions about influences must be based upon established borrowings, i.e., resemblances which can be explained best by the later author's acquaintance with the earlier. Anything less rigid may turn out to be merely conjecture, or even wishful thinking. We need to recall once more the cautious consideration that vague analogues between the work of Molière and Restoration playwrights must not be credited to the Frenchman when native dramatic tradition or the original genius of the English author is fully adequate to account for what we find.[1]

Prototypes of the comedy of manners appeared in England before the end of the sixteenth century. For the last hundred years the yeast of Renaissance ideas of social life had worked steadily and had given the upper classes a commonly accepted mass of social doctrine. By 1600 manners had crystallized sufficiently for intelligent people to find amusement in the contrasts between the social elect and the ridiculous aspirants and pretenders to social acceptance. Realistic social comedy probably received an early impetus from the decision of James Burbage to open a theatre in Blackfriars in 1596, for here, at the center of fashionable life, troops of boys and, after 1608, the King's Men, most regularly found a public receptive to the comic treatment of manners. A realistic social comedy will arise when playwrights with a bent for realism and a flair for ridicule have audiences

---

[1] For an early insistence on adherence to the principle implied, see Lanson, "Etudes sur les rapports de la littérature française," p. 47.

that, with a contented sense of their own social or intellectual superiority, can laugh together at the sorry efforts of their inferiors to clamber up the social scale.

Of course the primary force in the comedy of manners in England was the nature and genius of Ben Jonson, whose sturdy intellectuality pulled him steadily away from the romantic fashion, with its emotional and verbal exuberances, into the ways of social common sense. The influence of the selected audience was doubtless exerted through support, for it is not hard to believe that without a favorable reception the social comedy of Jonson would have been stillborn; whereas, obviously, it grew up with Fletcher's. Both children lived to have numerous progeny, not a few of whom resulted from crossbreeding between the two strains.[2] The growth of interest in social satire was fortuitously aided by the gathering storms of civil war, for all theatres naturally became more completely Cavalier in spirit as the soberer citizens withdrew their support in a Puritanical huff. This defection left an audience glad to ridicule the manners of those who had so emphatically excluded themselves. Most playwrights are ready to flatter the prejudices of the consistent playgoers and to be callous about the feelings of those who never enter a theatre.

When Charles II was restored in 1660, the theatres hastily opened their doors under royal encouragement, after eighteen years of darkness or intermittent furtiveness. More than ever before were audiences composed of the courtier group; the middle class ceased to attend as a recognized constituency. Pepys, for example, had the theatrical taste and interests of Sedley and Rochester, although he was thoroughly middle-class in origin. The managers found almost instantly that romantic comedy, like *Twelfth Night* or a *Midsummer Night's Dream,* did not

---

[2] The eclecticism of the "Sons of Ben" has been treated in detail by Davis, "The 'Sons of Ben' in English Realistic Comedy." See pp. 783-93 for summary.

appeal, but that the satiric comedies of Jonson and his numerous prewar followers were readily applauded.[3] For three years the Restoration stage thrived on comedies selected from the old repertoire, none of the six new plays presented having any notable success. Applause came readily to the plays of Middleton, Shirley, Brome, Jonson, Fletcher, and lesser men of the Cavalier days. Such circumstances would constitute an overwhelming influence on coming playwrights; thus it is not a matter for surprise that Restoration comedy is a continuation of pre-Restoration. The surprising thing is that the world has so lately observed this patent fact.

To a Victorian mind, Restoration comedy is notable primarily for its indecency.[4] A chronological reading of the important realistic comedies from 1600 to 1642 would show a steady trend toward verbal bluntness, sexual innuendo for the fun of it, wit and rakishness as the essence of a gentleman's career, and witty daring in approved young ladies. Contempt grows for all sorts of pretenders, for country life with its antiquated manners, and for middle-class life with its peculiar virtues and defects. The association without disapproval of gallants with whores, the final seeking of marriage as a bitter remedy for a sick purse, the assumption that all business men were deservedly cuckolds, the presentation of old women ridiculous because they could not capture the lovers they pursued,—all these elements of comedy after 1660 can be found in comedies before 1642.

To a mind free from moral concerns and congenial to the comic spirit, Restoration comedy is notable primarily for its unemotional observation of the ludicrous in life. Its point of view is that of the sensual, witty, fashionable, disillusioned courtiers, who repress nothing except impulses to be sober, continent, or useful. According to their code, nonchalance is the chief virtue;

[3] Nicoll, *Restoration Drama*, pp. 168-70.

[4] For example, Macaulay, in his review of Hunt's edition of Wycherley, Congreve, Vanbrugh, and Farquhar, *Miscellaneous Works of Lord Macaulay*, Vol. V.

unconsciously it is their chief affectation. But even this absurd code and this affectation are clearly outlined in Fletcher's *The Wild Goose Chase* (*c.* 1621). Jonson, Shirley, and Brome also revealed, at times, a similar unmoral objectivity in portraying the follies and foibles of social pretenders, rakish gallants, and witty women; and so we find anticipation of the comic spirit of the Restoration comedy in English plays any time after 1600.

Now, everyone agrees, Molière's work exhibits an entirely different spirit. His attitude toward life is readily explained by a simple re-listing of those well-known details of his life that fitted him to write and produce his plays. Born fairly high in the Parisian *bourgeoisie,* with access to the court of the king as a family right, he had a sound classical education, some schooling in law, and private lessons in philosophy. As a young actor, he spent twelve years trouping to all corners of France, developing his ability as a comic actor, creating a personal company to write for, studying drama in the theatre, testing his own writings in the alembic of provincial audiences, making those acute observations of his fellow men that lie at the heart of his best comedy, and probably passing many lonely hours in wide but unpedantic reading. Thus he freed himself from the extreme provincialism of Paris, of the court, of the theatre, and of the pedants. His return to Paris during his thirty-sixth year found him ready for success and intelligently confident of his powers.

Nothing ever turned Molière entirely away from the general point of view of the middle-class Parisian. His indifference to religion, his acceptance of the common judgment of men as his standard, his lack of impractical idealism in art, morals, or things intellectual, and his attacks on extremes of any sort—all reflect his origin and his experience, and are the basis of his greatness as well as his lasting popularity. He never advances any other reason for doing a good thing than practical advantage in a social world. To him good social sense is virtue. He counsels no higher morality than prudence in the light of general experience. He feels a real vocation to preach the gospel of good sense, and attacks eccentricities, rather than vices. Like Jonson, he would "sport with human follies, not with crimes," and like all true satirists, he is impelled by a sardonic cruelty toward the foolish and the mischievous.

Like Shakespeare, Molière was always the showman. As such, he accepted the pragmatic doctrine that the purpose of a play was to please and that the test of its virtue was the money it earned. Here was no art for art's sake; here was no writing to please a coterie of esoteric critics. Senecan models and Aristotelian rules were passed over for practical issues. No *mélange des genres,* for example, could be more absurd than the *comédie-ballets,* which he uncomplainingly developed to please the king, and which are but bastard mixtures of opera, ballet, and play; but his genius fused the mixtures into a new artistic form, in which he burlesqued follies and satirized them on gayer and more extravagant heights of absurdity than any one had ever reached before. Follies he could pursue relentlessly, even his own. His highest art developed out of his instinct for all aspects of a play, the prejudices of the audience, the personalities of his actors, the effects of actions as well as words in drama. His willingness to make himself a motley to the view brought him no regrets, for he apparently arranged to make his own exit from life with the ironic paint of the *malade imaginaire* still on his face.

His dramatic matter is compounded of classic materials, French domestic farces, *commedia dell' arte,* and current successes in Spain or Italy. In general his young men are sincere lovers seeking happy marriage, his young ladies desire virtuous love in marriage, his wives, except Angélique in *George Dandin,* are faithful, and his husbands are too busy fearing cuckoldom to be disloyal. Sex morality is conventional, and it is not subject to the dramatist's ridicule. About one-fourth of his plays show a man ridiculously fearful of discovering that his wife is unfaithful. Aside from passing remarks about doctors, he makes four or five different plays turn directly on the ridicule of the medical profession. Social ambition is touched several times; avarice, social hypocrisy in the court, blunt speaking, piety as a cloak for selfishness, repression as a way to develop virtue—all meet his attacks; types of bores, and literary and philosophical pedants are victims of his mordant satire. How different all this is from the seventeenth-century English comedy of manners, in form, in spirit, in matter!

From Molière's dramatic form, according to the data accumulated in foregoing chapters, Restoration playwrights made almost no recognizable borrowings. Dryden, D'Avenant, Shadwell, and Langbaine all expressed adverse opinions of the French methods; there is no reason to believe that the prevailing Restoration opinion of comic drama included the idea that Molière was a better judge of dramatic form than his English contemporaries, or that English form was in need of improvement. Self-complacence is written all over the Restoration period. In the observation of form, many parallels in method of exposition, of plotting, and of the management of dialogue can be cited, of course, between Molière's plays and Restoration drama; but when one undertakes to prove that they must have come from the French master, the whole structure crumbles away. Only one plausible example was found in this entire study, a detail in *Bury Fair* that seems to be an instance of borrowing the method of balance of characters. Restoration London was not converted to the ways of the French theatre enough to destroy the continuity from pre-Restoration to post-Restoration plays. Neither the Elizabethan standard of a five-act play, for example, nor the Jonsonian-Fletcherian custom of a complicated intrigue showed signs of disintegration before 1700. If Molière affected form in the Restoration, it must have been only in such close combination with Elizabethan practices that his influence cannot be distinguished. Even farcical effects, at which Molière was a master, are largely developed in English plays from the convenient presence of "humor" characters, whose individual idiosyncrasies motivate any desired absurdity.

On the side of spirit, Molière's influence is very considerable in Wycherley's last two plays and clearly evident in Shadwell's *Bury Fair*. But these plays cease to be typically Restoration in spirit at the point where this influence turns them back toward ethical satire, the one important aspect of Jonson's comedies which later experience taught the seventeenth century to avoid.[5] Thus Molière's social wisdom and great common sense were very generally ignored by Restoration playwrights. Wycherley, Shadwell, and Congreve alone wrote with even a tinge of ethical satire. All three were familiar with Jonson's call to preach the gospel of good sense—and with Molière's. One of them, Congreve, probably learned much more from Wycherley than from either Molière or Jonson. But all the seriousness found in Restoration comedies, if it had come entirely from Molière, would constitute an almost negligible aspect. Within the limits of comedy, the spirit of the Restoration could hardly have been further from the essential Molière.

Under the heading of matter, then, come most of the English borrowings from Molière during the Restoration. He was a frequent source of farcical action, amusing character, or comic incident, being so used in about one new play out of ten during the forty years under consideration. The material borrowed is so disproportionately farcical, in comparison with Molière's total production, that we may be sure it was this unimportant expression of his genius that the Restoration envied. Not one of his

---

[5] See Davis (*op. cit.*, pp. 923-40) for a summarized account of the decline of ethical satire. Caroline experience proved Jonsonian ethical matter essentially undramatic and, salvaging the use of psychological bias as an adjunct to farce, dropped the rest of it for social satire and farce-intrigue. Davis finds that, until the end of the century, this experience was one of the most potent influences in shaping the course of comedy.

serious comedies of character or of manners was given good translation and adequate staging during this time. The common practice was to distort Molière's high comedies in the direction of low. The natural inference is that the Restoration was so greatly impressed by the career in the theatre of the living Molière that it had not yet been sufficiently impressed with the greatness of his works. The evidence of the chronology of borrowing leads to this general conclusion. During the early years of the Restoration period, when Molière's career was still in progress or a very vivid memory, 1667 to 1676, the attempts to transfer his success to the English stage were more numerous and were made by more important men. As time passed, the proportion of borrowings to the total production of the Restoration rapidly diminished. Aside from *Bury Fair,* all important use of Molière was made by 1676, three years after his death. For his contemporaries in England, Molière was a rich mine of theatrical tricks to which they were entitled by the immemorial custom that a theatrical effect, once exposed to the public gaze, becomes an addition to the raw material of every succeeding dramatist who is acquainted with it. The demand among playwrights for such elements of novelty with which to dress all the staples of the theatre never flags, because conditions make innovations difficult.[6] To these very fac-

---

[6] Shaw points out the restraints as follows: "I do not select my methods: they are imposed upon me by a hundred considerations: by the physical conditions of theatrical representation, by the laws devised by the municipality to guard against fires and other accidents to which theaters are liable, by the economics of theatrical commerce, by the nature and limits of the art of acting, by the capacity of the spectators for understanding what they see and hear, and by the accidental circumstances of the particular production in hand.

"I have to think of my pocket, of the manager's pocket, of the actors' pockets, of the spectators' pockets, of how long people can be kept sitting in a theater without relief or refreshments, of the range of the performer's voice, and of the hearing and vision of the boy at the back of the gallery, whose right to be put in full possession of the play is as sacred as that of the millionaire in the stalls or boxes.

"I have to consider theatrical rents, the rate of interest needed to tempt capitalists to face the risks of financing theaters, the extent to which the magic of art can break through commercial prudence, the limits set by honor and humanity to the tasks I may set to my fellow-artist, the actor: in short, all the factors that must be allowed

tors Molière's long theatrical training brought him a natural, almost instinctive consideration, just as a similar experience brought Shakespeare to a comparable integration of his literary art with theatrical necessities. None of the important playwrights of the Restoration had this professional experience. It is not surprising, therefore, that they should see Molière as the source of practical effectiveness, that they should sift his plays for devices which promised to please audiences. They borrowed at will, generally grabbing detailed bits of situation, episodes, or piquant novelties of characterization, only occasionally picking up larger units or taking over plots entire. The results of that facile adapter and plagiarist, Edward Ravenscroft, are illustrative, though extreme. Making as extensive use of matter from Molière as any of his fellows, Ravenscroft never reproduced any important aspect of his spirit, matter, or form. Molière was a convenient source of good plots, nothing more.

Playwrights of the Restoration, then, turned often to Molière, and, whenever it might advantageously be done, borrowed from him freely; there is, however, no contradiction in the final decision that, though his plays were often used, he made no significant contribution to the type of comedy we associate with the Restoration. This species of play grew in the rich soil of British social and dramatic conventions from seeds sown by Ben Jonson, who first in English dramatic history satirized the whimsies and caprices, the affectations and pretensions, of social incompetents. Concurrently, Beaumont and Fletcher brought to excellence a type of play characterized by playful antagonism between the

for before the representation of a play on the stage becomes practicable or justifiable: factors which some never comprehend and which others integrate almost as unconsciously as they breathe, or digest their food.

"It is these factors that dictate the playwright's methods, leaving him so little room for selection that there is not a pennyworth of difference between the methods of Sophocles or Shakespeare and those of the maker of the most ephemeral farce."

From a letter written in 1902. A facsimile of this letter was printed in *The New York Times,* June 2, 1912. It is reprinted by Clark, *European Theories of the Drama,* p. 475.

sexes expressed in amorous intrigue and enlivened by wit. The first comedy of manners appeared when James Shirley combined the comedy of Jonson with the comedy of Beaumont and Fletcher. Nearly all the minor dramatists of the Caroline period helped establish its dominance. With the opening of the theatres after the interval of the War and the Commonwealth, the same comedy found ready and eager applause. The moral for playwrights was obvious. There was little need to experiment with importations of the strange form and the stranger spirit of foreigners, even of the successful contemporary, Molière. To benefit by his superior skill and experience in things theatrical, they waylaid him, and turned out his pockets to steal all his rare tricks of the stage; but they ignored his ideas and spirit as coin not readily current in the land of Charles and Nell.

APPENDICES

A: THE CHRONOLOGY OF MOLIÈRE

THE following tabulation is compiled primarily from the *Chronologie Moliéresque*, by Monval and from the *Catalogue of the Molière Collection in the Harvard College Library*, by Currier and Gay. The "number of editions before 1700" is based solely on the above *Catalogue*, and consists mostly of collections containing the play under consideration.

Title of Play	Kind of Play	First Acted in or Near Paris	First Printing	No. of Editions before 1700
La Jalousie du Barbouillé	farce	?	1819	0
Le Médecin volant	farce	?	1819	0
L'Étourdi (l^{re} at Lyon, 1653)	comedy of intrigue	Nov. 1658	1663	12
Le Dépit amoureux (l^{re} at Béziers, 1656)	comedy of intrigue	Dec. 1658	1663	12
Les Précieuses ridicules	comedy of manners	Nov. 1659	1660	13
Sganarelle ou le cocu imaginaire	farce	May 1660	1660	13
Don Garcie de Navarre ou le prince jaloux	heroic comedy	Feb. 1661	1682	5
L'École des maris	comedy of manners	June 1661	1661	13
Les Fâcheux	comedy of manners (ballet)	Aug. 1661	1662	12
L'École des femmes	comedy of manners	Dec. 1662	1663	13
La Critique de l'école des femmes	comedy of manners and literary criticism	June 1663	1663	14

Title of Play	Kind of Play	First Acted in or Near Paris	First Printing	No. of Editions before 1700
L'Impromptu de Versailles	social satire and dramatic criticism	Oct. 1663	1675	6
Le Mariage forcé	farce (ballet)	Jan. 1664	1668	12
La Princesse d'Élide	romance (ballet)	May 1664	1665	12
Le Tartuffe (first 3 acts given once)	comedy of character	May 1664	1669	12
Don Juan ou le festin de pierre	comedy of character	Feb. 1665	1682	5
L'Amour médecin	farce (ballet)	Sept. 1665	1666	12
Le Misanthrope	comedy of character	June 1666	1667	13
Le Médecin malgré lui	farce	Aug. 1666	1667	12
Mélicerte (fragment)	heroic pastoral (ballet)	Dec. 1666	1674-5	10
Pastorale comique (replaced Mélicerte)	pastoral (ballet)	Jan. 1667	1734	0
Le Sicilien ou l'amour peintre	comedy (ballet)	Feb. 1667	1668	12
L'Imposteur (le Tartuffe) (once)		Aug. 1667	1669	12
Amphitryon	comedy of intrigue	Feb. 1668	1668	11
George Dandin ou le mari confondu	comedy of manners	June 1668	1669	12
L'Avare	comedy of character	Aug. 1668	1669	12
Tartuffe (freed from restraints and given repeatedly)	comedy of character	Feb. 1669	1669	12
Monsieur de Pourceaugnac	farce (ballet)	Oct. 1669	1670	12

Title of Play	Kind of Play	First Acted in or Near Paris	First Printing	No. of Editions before 1700
Les Amants magnifiques	romance (ballet)	Feb. 1670	1675	12
Le Bourgeois Gentilhomme	comedy of manners (ballet)	Oct. 1670	1671	12
Psyché	tragi-comedy (ballet)	Jan. 1671	1671	11
Les Fourberies de Scapin	comedy of intrigue	May 1671	1671	12
La Comtesse d'Escarbagnas	comedy of manners	Dec. 1671	1675	7
Les Femmes savantes	comedy of manners	Feb. 1672	1672	11
Le Malade imaginaire	comedy of character (ballet)	Feb. 1673	1675	12

B: CHRONOLOGICAL LIST OF RESTORATION COMEDIES

THE plays in this list follow the valuable hand-list printed by Professor Allardyce Nicoll in his *Restoration Drama, 1660-1700* (Second Edition, Cambridge, 1928.) The form of the titles and the dates in parentheses, which indicate the time of first performance, are based solely upon his authority. One play has been added which was unmentioned in the above source.

1660

Tatham, John, *The Rump: or The Mirrour of The late Times, A New Comedy* (June, 1660)

Thomson, Thomas, *The Life of Mother Shipton. A New Comedy. As it was Acted Nineteen dayes together with great Applause....* [1660?]

1661

Cowley, Abraham, *Cutter of Coleman-Street* (Dec., 1661)
Fountain, John, *The Revvards of Vertue*. (Not acted.) Printed 1661

1662

Codrington, Robert, *Ignoramus* (Nov., 1662)
Howard, Sir Robert, *The Committee* (before Nov., 1662)
—— *The Surprisal* (Nov., 1662)

1663

D'Avenant, Sir William, *The Play-House to be Lett* (*c*. Aug., 1663)
Digby, George, Earl of Bristol, *Elvira: or, The worst not always true* (*c*. 1663)
Dryden, John, *The Wild Gallant* (Feb., 1663)
Porter, Thomas, *The Carnival* (*c*. 1663)
Rhodes, Richard, *Flora's Vagaries* (Nov., 1663)
Southland, Thomas, *Love a la Mode* (1663)
Stapylton, Sir Robert, *The Slighted Maid* (Feb., 1663)
Wilson, John, *The Cheats* (March, 1663)

1664

Anon., *Knavery in all Trades: or, the Coffee-House. A Comedy As it was Acted in the Christmas Holidays by several Apprentices*. Printed 1664
Cary, Henry, Viscount Falkland, *The Mariage Night* (1664)
D'Avenant, Sir William, *The Rivals* (before Sept., 1664)
Etherege, Sir George, *The Comical Revenge: or, Love in a Tub* (March, 1664)
Killigrew, Thomas, *The Parson's Wedding* (Oct., 1664)

1665

Bulteel, J., *Amorous Orontus: or the Love in Fashion. Printed* 1665
Lacy, John, *The Old Troop: or, Monsieur Raggou* (*c*. 1665)
Wilson, John, *The Projectors*. (Probably unacted.) Printed 1665

1666

Howard, Hon. James, *The English Mounsieur* (Dec., 1666)

1667

Bailey, Abraham, *The Spightful Sister. A New Comedy*. (Not acted.) Printed 1667

Cavendish, William, Duke of Newcastle, *The Humorous Lovers* (March, 1667)

D'Avenant, Sir William, and John Dryden, *The Tempest, or, The Enchanted Island* (Nov., 1667)

Dryden, John, *Sr Martin Mar-all, or the Feign'd Innocence* (Aug., 1667)

Howard, Hon. James, *All Mistaken, or the Mad Couple* (Sept., 1667)

Lacy, John, *Sauny the Scott: or, The Taming of the Shrew* (April, 1667)

St Serfe, Sir Thomas, *Tarugo's Wiles, or, the Coffee-House* (Oct., 1667)

Villiers, George, Duke of Buckingham, *The Chances* (Feb., 1667)

1668

Anon., *The Feign'd Astrologer*. (Acting uncertain.) Printed 1668

D'Avenant, Sir William, *The Man's the Master* (March, 1668)

Dryden, John, *An Evening's Love, or the Mock Astrologer* (June, 1668)

Etherege, Sir George, *She wou'd if she cou'd* (Feb., 1668)

Flecknoe, Richard, *The Damoiselles a la Mode* (Sept., 1668)

Jordan, Thomas, *Money is an Asse*. (Place of acting not known). Printed 1668

Sedley, Sir Charles, *The Mulberry-Garden* (May, 1668)

Shadwell, Thomas, *The Sullen Lovers: Or, the Impertinents* (May, 1668)

Thomson, Thomas, *The English Rogue ... As it was acted before several Persons of Honour with Great Applause*. Printed 1668

1669

Boyle, Roger, Earl of Orrery, *Guzman* (April, 1669)

Caryl, John, *Sir Salomon; or, The Cautious Coxcomb* (c. 1669)

Lacy, John, *The Dumb Lady, or, The Farrier Made Physician* (1669)

1670

Betterton, Thomas, *The Amorous Widow; or, the Wanton Wife* (c. 1670)

Medbourne, Matthew, *Tartuffe; or, The French Puritan* (*c.* April, 1670)

Shadwell, Thomas, *The Humorists* (*c.* Dec., 1670)

1671

Behn, Mrs. Aphra, *The Amorous Prince, or, The Curious Husband* (*c.* May, 1671)

Boyle, Roger, Earl of Orrery, *Mr. Anthony. A Comedy* (*c.* 1671)

Corye, John, *The Generous Enemies or The Ridiculous Lovers* (*c.* Aug., 1671)

Howard, Hon. Edward, *The Six days Adventure, or the New Utopia* (*c.* March, 1671)

Revet, Edward, *The Town-Shifts, or, the Suburb-Justice* (*c.* April, 1671)

Villiers, George, Duke of Buckingham, *The Rehearsal* (Dec., 1671)

Wycherley, William, *Love in a Wood, or, St. James's Park* (*c.* April, 1671)

1672

Dryden, John, *Marriage A-la-Mode* (*c.* May, 1672)

—— *The Assignation: or, Love in a Nunnery* (*c.* Nov., 1672)

Payne, Nevil, *The Morning Ramble, or, The Town-Humours* (Nov., 1672)

Ravenscroft, Edward, [*Mamamouchi; or,*] *The Citizen turn'd Gentleman* (July, 1672)

Shadwell, Thomas, *The Miser* (Jan., 1672)

—— *Epsom Wells* (Dec., 1672)

Wycherley, William, *The Gentleman Dancing-Master* (*c.* Jan., 1672)

1673

Arrowsmith, *The Reformation* (*c.* Sept., 1673). "Attributed to Arrowsmith by Langbaine."—Nicoll

Behn, Mrs. Aphra, *The Dutch Lover* (Feb., 1673)

Duffett, Thomas, *The Spanish Rogue* (*c.* June, 1673)

Ravenscroft, Edward, *The Careless Lovers* (March, 1673)

1674

Anon., *The Mall: or the Modish Lovers* (*c.* Jan., 1674) "Sometimes attributed to Dryden."—Nicoll

Anon., *The Amorous Old-vvoman: or, 'Tis Well if it Take. A Comedy*

...*By a Person of Honour* (*c*. March, 1674) Reissued as *The Fond Lady,* 1684. "Sometimes attributed to Duffett."—Nicoll

Cavendish, William, Duke of Newcastle, *The Triumphant VVidow, or The Medley of Humours* (Nov., 1674)

1675

Anon., *The Woman turn'd Bully* (*c*. July, 1675)

Anon., *The Mistaken Husband* (*c*. Sept., 1675). "Attributed sometimes to Dryden; he was certainly responsible for one scene."—Nicoll

Belon, Peter, *The Mock-Duellist, or, The French Vallet* (*c*. May, 1675). "Attributed to Belon by Langbaine."—Nicoll

Fane, Sir Francis, *Love in the Dark, or The Man of Bus'ness* (May, 1675)

Shadwell, Thomas, *The Libertine* (June, 1675)

Wycherley, William, *The Country-Wife* (Jan., 1675)

1676

Behn, Mrs. Aphra, *The Town-Fopp: or Sir Timothy Tawdrey* (*c*. Sept., 1676)

Crowne, John, *The Countrey Wit* (Jan., 1676)

D'Urfey, Thomas, *A Fond Husband: or, The Plotting Sisters* (May, 1676)

—— *Madam Fickle: or the Witty False One* (Nov., 1676)

—— *The Fool Turn'd Critick* (Nov., 1676)

Etherege, Sir George, *The Man of Mode, or, Sr Fopling Flutter* (March, 1676)

Otway, Thomas, *Titus and Berenice.... With a Farce call'd the Cheats of Scapin* (*c*. Dec., 1676)

Ravenscroft, Edward, *The Wrangling Lovers: or, The Invisible Mistress* (*c*. Sept., 1676)

Rawlins, Thomas, *Tom Essence: or, The Modish Wife* (*c*. Sept., 1676)

Shadwell, Thomas, *The Virtuoso* (May, 1676)

Wycherley, William, *The Plain-Dealer* (Dec., 1676)

1677

Anon., *The Counterfeit Bridegroom: or the Defeated Widow* (*c*. Sept., 1677). "Sometimes attributed to Betterton; an adaptation of Middleton's *No Wit like a Woman's*."—Nicoll

Behn, Mrs. Aphra, *The Debauchee: or, The Credulous Cuckold* (*c.* Feb., 1677)

—— *The Rover: Or, The Banish't Cavaliers* (March, 1677)

Leanerd, John, *The Country Innocence: or, The Chamber-Maid turn'd Quaker* (*c.* April, 1677)

Porter, Thomas, *The French Conjurer* (*c.* July, 1677)

Ravenscroft, Edward, *Scaramouch a Philosopher, Harlequin A School-Boy, Bravo, Merchant, and Magician. A Comedy After the Italian Manner* (May, 1677)

—— *The English Lawyer* (*c.* Dec., 1677)

La Roche-Guilhen, Madame, *Rare en Tout* (May, 1677)

1678

Behn, Mrs. Aphra, *Sir Patient Fancy* (Jan., 1678)

Dryden, John, *The Kind Keeper; or, Mr. Limberham* (March, 1678)

D'Urfey, Thomas, *Trick for Trick: or, The Debauch'd Hypocrite* (*c.* March, 1678)

—— *Squire Oldsapp: or, The Night-Adventurers* (*c.* June, 1678)

Howard, Hon. Edward, *The Man of Newmarket* (*c.* April, 1678)

Leanerd, John, *The Rambling Justice, or the Jealous Husbands* (*c.* March, 1678)

—— *The Counterfeits* (May, 1678)

Otway, Thomas, *Friendship in Fashion* (Apr., 1678)

Rawlins, Thomas, *Tunbridge-Wells: or, A Day's Courtship* (*c.* March, 1678)

Shadwell, Thomas, *A True Widow* (*c.* March, 1678)

1679

Behn, Mrs. Aphra, *The Feign'd Curtizans, or, A Nights Intrigue* (*c.* March, 1679)

D'Urfey, Thomas, *The Virtuous Wife; or, Good Luck at last* (*c.* Sept., 1679)

Maidwell, Laurence, *The Loving Enemies* (*c.* Oct., 1679)

Shadwell, Thomas, *The Woman-Captain* (*c.* Sept., 1679)

1680

Anon., *The Muse of New Market: or, Mirth and Drollery Being Three Farces Acted before the King and Court at New-Market; Viz. The*

Merry Milkmaid of Islington, or the Rambling Gallants defeated.
Love lost in the Dark, or the Drunken Couple. The Politick Whore
or The Conceited Cuckhold. 1680. "The second play is a 'droll' made
from Massinger's *The Guardian,* and the third is condensed from
Davenport's *The City Night-Cap.*"—Nicoll

Behn, Mrs. Aphra, *The Second Part of The Rover* (Feb. or April, 1680)

Betterton, Thomas, *The Revenge: or, A Match in Newgate* (*c.* Aug.,
1680)

Dryden, John, *The Spanish Fryar or, The Double Discovery* (March,
1680)

Otway, Thomas, *The Souldiers Fortune* (March, 1680)

1681

Behn, Mrs. Aphra, *The Roundheads or, The Good Old Cause* (*c.* Dec.,
1681)

D'Urfey, Thomas, *Sir Barnaby Whigg: or, No Wit like a Womans*
(*c.* Sept., 1681)

Ravenscroft, Edward, *The London Cuckolds* (Nov., 1681)

Shadwell, Thomas, *The Lancashire VVitches, and Tegue o Divelly The
Irish Priest* (*c.* Sept., 1681)

1682

Anon., *Mr Turbulent: or, The Melanchollicks* (*c.* Jan., 1682). Reissued
as *The Factious Citizen, or, The Melancholy Visioner,* 1685

Behn, Mrs. Aphra, *The City-Heiress: or, Sir Timothy Treat-all* (*c.*
March, 1682)

—— *The False Count, or, A New Way to play an Old Game* (*c.*
Sept., 1682)

D'Urfey, Thomas, *The Royalist* (Jan., 1682)

1683

Crowne, John, *City Politiques* (Jan., 1683)

Otway, Thomas, *The Atheist. Or, the Second Part of The Souldiers
Fortune* (*c.* Sept., 1683)

Ravenscroft, Edward, *Dame Dobson: or, The Cunning Woman* (*c.*
Sept., 1683)

1684

Anon., *The Mistaken Beauty, or the Lyar* (*c.* Sept., 1684). "Contemporary chroniclers note an earlier edition of *The Lyar* in 1661; this Pepys had seen on Nov. 28, 1667."—Nicoll

Lacy, John, *Sir Hercules Buffoon, or, The Poetical Squire* (*c.* Sept., 1684)

Tate, Nahum, *A Duke and No Duke* (Nov., 1684)

1685

Anon., *The Rampant Alderman, or News from the Exchange, A Farce* (Probably not acted.) Printed, 1685

Crowne, John, *Sir Courtly Nice: or, It Cannot Be* (May, 1685)

Tate, Nahum, *Cuckolds-Haven: or, an Alderman No Conjurer, A Farce* (*c.* May, 1685)

1686

Behn, Mrs. Aphra, *The Luckey Chance, or An Alderman's Bargain* (*c.* April, 1686)

Jevon, Thomas, *The Devil of a Wife, or A Comical Transformation* (March, 1686)

Mountfort, William, *The Life and Death of Doctor Faustus. Made into a Farce.... With the Humours of Harlequin and Scaramouche* (*c.* 1686)

1687

Behn, Mrs. Aphra, *The Emperor of the Moon* (*c.* March, 1687)

Sedley, Sir Charles, *Bellamira, or the Mistress* (May, 1687)

1688

D'Urfey, Thomas, *A Fool's Preferment, or, The Three Dukes of Dunstable* (*c.* April, 1688)

Shadwell, Thomas, *The Squire of Alsatia* (May, 1688)

1689

Carlisle, James, *The Fortune-Hunters: or, Two Fools well met* (*c.* March, 1689)

D'Urfey, Thomas, *Love for Money: or, the Boarding School* (c. Dec., 1689)

Shadwell, Thomas, *Bury Fair* (c. April, 1689)

1690

Crowne, John, *The English Frier: or, The Town Sparks* (c. March, 1690)

Dryden, John, *Amphitryon; or, The Two Socia's* (April, 1690)

Shadwell, Thomas, *The Amorous Bigotte: with the Second Part of Tegue O Divelly* (c. March, 1690)

—— *The Scowrers* (c. Dec., 1690)

Southerne, Thomas, *Sir Anthony Love: or, The Rambling Lady* (c. Dec., 1690)

1691

Mountfort, William, *Greenwich Park* (c. June, 1691)

Smyth, John, *Win her and Take her, or, Old Fools Will be Medling* (1691). "It is possible that the play is by Underhill, who published it."—Nicoll

Southerne, Thomas, *The Wives Excuse: or, Cuckolds make themselves* (Dec., 1691)

1692

Bourne, Reuben, *The Contented Cuckold, or the Womans Advocate.* (Not acted.) Printed, 1692

D'Urfey, Thomas, *The Marriage-Hater Match'd* (Jan., 1692)

Shadwell, Thomas, *The Volunteers: or The Stock Jobbers* (Nov., 1692)

1693

Congreve, William, *The Old Batchelour* (Jan., 1693)

—— *The Double Dealer* (Oct., 1693)

D'Urfey, Thomas, *The Richmond Heiress: or, A Woman Once in the Right* (c. Feb., 1693)

Higden, Henry, *The Wary Widdow: or, Sir Noisy Parrat* (Feb., 1693)

Powell, George, *A Very Good Wife* (March, 1693)

Southerne, Thomas, *The Maid's Last Prayer: or, Any, rather than Fail* (Jan., 1693)

Wright, Thomas, *The Female Vertuoso's* (April, 1693)

1694

Crowne, John, *The Married Beau: or, The Curious Impertinent* (*c.* Jan., 1694)

D'Urfey, Thomas, *The Comical History of Don Quixote* (*c.* May, 1694)

—— *The Comical History of Don Quixote...Part the Second* (*c.* May, 1694)

Ravenscroft, Edward, *The Canterbury Guests; or, A Bargain Broken* (Sept., 1694)

1695

Congreve, William, *Love for Love* (April, 1695)

Dilke, Thomas, *The Lover's Luck* (*c.* Dec., 1695)

Dryden, John Jnr., *The Husband his Own Cuckold* (1695)

D'Urfey, Thomas, *The Comical History of Don Quixote. The Third Part. With the Marriage of Mary the Buxome* (*c.* Nov., 1695)

Granville, George, Lord Lansdowne, *The She-Gallants* (*c.* Dec., 1695)

Scott, Thomas, *The Mock-Marriage* (*c.* Oct., 1695)

1696

Anon., *She Ventures, and He Wins. A Comedy* (*c.* 1696). "The dedication is signed Ariadne."—Nicoll

Behn, Mrs. Aphra, *The Younger Brother: or, The Amorous Jilt* (*c.* Dec., 1696)

Cibber, Colley, *Love's Last Shift; or, The Fool in Fashion* (Jan., 1696)

—— *Woman's Wit: or, The Lady in Fashion* (*c.* Dec., 1696)

Doggett, Thomas, *The Country-Wake* (*c.* May, 1696)

Drake, Dr. James, *The Sham Lawyer: or the Lucky Extravagant* (*c.* Sept., 1696)

Harris, Joseph, *The City Bride: or, The Merry Cuckold* (*c.* Jan., 1696)

Manley, Mrs., *The Lost Lover; or the Jealous Husband* (*c.* April, 1696)

Motteux, Peter Anthony, *Love's a Jest* (*c.* Sept., 1696)

Pix, Mrs. Mary, *The Spanish Wives* (*c.* Sept., 1696)

Powell, George, *The Cornish Comedy* (1696)

Vanbrugh, Sir John, *The Relapse: or, Virtue in Danger* (Dec., 1696)

—— *Aesop* (Part I, *c.* Dec., 1696)

1697

Dennis, John, *A Plot, and No Plot* (May, 1697)

Dilke, Thomas, *The City Lady: or, Folly Reclaim'd* (*c.* Jan., 1697)

D'Urfey, Thomas, *The Intrigues at Versailles: or, A Jilt in all Humours* (*c.* Feb., 1697)

Motteux, Peter Anthony, *The Novelty. Every Act a Play.* (*c.* June, 1697)

Pix, Mrs. Mary, *The Innocent Mistress* (*c.* Sept., 1697)

—— *The Deceiver Deceived* (*c.* Dec., 1697)

Powell, George, *The Imposture Defeated: or, A Trick to Cheat the Devil* (*c.* Sept., 1697)

Ravenscroft, Edward, *The Anatomist: or, the Sham Doctor* (*c.* March, 1697)

Vanbrugh, Sir John, *The Provok'd Wife* (May, 1697)

—— *Aesop* (Part II, c. Dec., 1696)

1698

Anon., *Feign'd Friendship: or The Mad Reformer* (*c.* 1698)

Dilke, Thomas, *The Pretenders: or, The Town Unmaskt* (*c.* May, 1698)

D'Urfey, Thomas, *The Campaigners: or, The Pleasant Adventures at Brussels* (*c.* Nov., 1698)

1699

Farquhar, George, *Love and a Bottle* (1699)

—— *The Constant Couple or a Trip to the Jubilee* (Nov., 1699)

Gildon, Charles, *Measure for Measure, or Beauty the Best Advocate* (*c.* 1699)

Harris, Joseph, *Love's a Lottery, and a Woman the Prize. With a New Masque, call'd Love and Riches Reconcil'd.* (*c.* March, 1699)

Penkethman, William, *Love without Interest: or, The Man Too hard for the Master.* Printed 1699. [Not in Nicoll.]

1700

Congreve, William, *The Way of the World* (March, 1700)

Vanbrugh, Sir John, *The Pilgrim* (*c.* April, 1700)

BIBLIOGRAPHY

A: DRAMATIC TEXTS

IN MAKING this study, I have regularly used the valuable collection of early editions preserved in the Rare Book Room of the Library of the University of Michigan. When citing specific passages, however, I have tried to use a sound modern edition likely to be available to the reader. A good many Restoration comedies have not been printed since their original vogue in the seventeenth and eighteenth centuries. Among the authors without modern editions, except for an occasional reprint in a collection, are Betterton, Cibber, Cowley, Dilke, Duffet, D'Urfey, Gildon, Harris, the Howards, Lansdowne, Leanerd, Mrs. Manley, Motteux, Orrery, the Newcastles, Payne, Mrs. Pix, Porter, Powell, Ravenscroft, Rawlins, Southerne, Stapylton, Thomson, and Wright. Mention of the early editions is found in Allardyce Nicoll, *A History of Restoration Comedy, 1660-1700,* pp. 348-76. A selected list of modern editions follows.

[Behn, Aphra], *The Plays, Histories, and Novels of the Ingenious Mrs. Aphra Behn. With Life and Memoirs.* 6 vols., London, J. Pearson, 1871.

——— *The Works of Aphra Behn.* Ed. by Montague Summers. 6 vols., London, W. Heinemann, 1915.

Bristol, George Digby, earl of, *Elvira: or, The Worst Not Always True.* In *A Select Collection of Old English Plays.* Ed. by Robert Dodsley. 4th ed., by W. C. Hazlitt, XV, 1-107. London, 1874-76.

Buckingham, George Villiers, second duke of, *The Rehearsal.* "Arber's English Reprints," London, 1868.

[Congreve, William], *Comedies by William Congreve.* Ed. with Introduction and Notes by Bonamy Dobrée. London, Oxford University Press, 1925.

——— *William Congreve.* Ed. by A. C. Ewald. "The Mermaid Series," London, 1887.

——— *The Works of William Congreve.* Ed. by Montague Summers. 4 vols., Soho, The Nonesuch Press, 1923.

[Crowne, John], *The Dramatic Works of John Crowne.* Ed. by [James Maidment and W. H. Logan]. 4 vols., Edinburgh and London, 1873.

[D'Avenant, Sir William], *The Dramatic Works of Sir William D'Avenant.* Ed. by [James Maidment and W. H. Logan]. 5 vols., Edinburgh, 1872-74.

[Dryden, John], *Dryden: The Dramatic Works.* Ed. by Montague Summers. 6 vols., London, The Nonesuch Press, 1931-32.

—— *John Dryden.* Ed. by George Saintsbury. "The Mermaid Series," 2 vols., London, [1904].

—— *The Dramatic Works of John Dryden. With a Life of the Author by Sir Walter Scott.* Ed. by George Saintsbury. 8 vols., Edinburgh, 1882.

[Etherege, Sir George], *The Dramatic Works of Sir George Etherege.* Ed. by H. F. Brett-Smith. 2 vols., Boston and Oxford, 1927.

—— *The Works of Sir George Etheredge. Plays and Poems.* Ed. by A. Wilson Verity. London, 1888.

Falkland, Henry Cary, fourth viscount, *The Marriage Night.* In *A Select Collection of Old English Plays.* Ed. by Robert Dodsley. 4th ed., by W. C. Hazlitt, XV, 109-83. London, 1874-76.

[Farquhar, George], *The Complete Works of George Farquhar.* Ed. by Charles Stonehill. 2 vols., Bloomsbury, The Nonesuch Press, 1930.

—— *George Farquhar.* Ed. by William Archer. "The Mermaid Series," London, [1907].

Howard, Hon. James, *All Mistaken, or the Mad Couple.* In *A Select Collection of Old English Plays.* Ed. by Robert Dodsley. 4th ed., by W. C. Hazlitt, XV, 321-97. London, 1874-76.

[Howard, Sir Robert], *Sir Robert Howard's Comedy, "The Committee."* Ed. with Introduction and Notes by Carryl Nelson Thurber. [Urbana], The University of Illinois, 1921.

Killigrew, Thomas, *The Parson's Wedding.* In *A Select Collection of Old English Plays.* Ed. by Robert Dodsley. 4th ed., by W. C. Hazlitt, XIV, 369-535. London, 1874-76.

[Lacy, John], *The Dramatic Works of John Lacy, Comedian, with Prefatory Memoir and Notes.* Ed. by [James Maidment and W. H. Logan]. Edinburgh, 1875.

[Molière], *Oeuvres de Molière.* Ed. by Eugène Despois and Paul Mesnard. "Les Grands Écrivains de la France," 14 vols., Paris, Hachette, 1873-1922.

[Otway, Thomas], *Thomas Otway.* Ed. with Introduction and Notes by Hon. Roden Noel. "The Mermaid Series," London, 1888.

Otway, Thomas, *The Works of Thomas Otway. Plays, Poems, and Love-Letters*. Ed. by J. C. Ghosh. 2 vols., Oxford, At the Clarendon Press, 1932.

Quinault, Philippe, *L'Amant indiscret*. In Victor Fournel's *Les Contemporains de Molière*, I, 1-58. Paris, 1863.

Ravenscroft, Edward, *The London Cuckolds*. In *Restoration Comedies*. Ed. by Montague Summers. Boston, Small Maynard and Co., 1922.

[Sedley, Sir Charles], *The Poetical and Dramatic Works of Sir Charles Sedley*. Ed. by V. de Sola Pinto. London, Constable and Company, Ltd., 1928.

[Shadwell, Thomas], *The Complete Works of Thomas Shadwell*. Ed. by Montague Summers. 5 vols., London, The Fortune Press, 1927.

Tuke, Sir Samuel, *The Adventure of Five Hours*. In *A Select Collection of Old English Plays*. Ed. by Robert Dodsley. 4th ed., by W. C. Hazlitt, XV, 185-320. London, 1874-76.

[Vanbrugh, Sir John], *The Complete Works of Sir John Vanbrugh*. Ed. by Bonamy Dobrée. 4 vols., Bloomsbury, The Nonesuch Press, 1927-28.

——— *Sir John Vanbrugh*. Ed. by A. E. H. Swaen. "The Mermaid Series," London, 1896.

[Wilson, John], *The Dramatic Works of John Wilson: with Prefatory Memoir, Introduction and Notes*. Ed. by [James Maidment and W. H. Logan]. Edinburgh, 1874.

[Wycherley, William], *William Wycherley*. Ed. by W. C. Ward. "The Mermaid Series," London, 1893.

——— *The Complete Works of William Wycherley*. Ed. by Montague Summers. 4 vols., Soho, The Nonesuch Press, 1924.

B: WORKS ON RESTORATION COMEDY

THE borderline between comedy and other forms of dramatic and non-dramatic literature is crossed many times in some of the works listed below. A few relate to the life of the time, and some to dramatic and literary history. All touch on comedy of the Restoration at some point.

Albrecht, L., *Dryden's Sir Martin Mar-all in Bezug auf seine Quellen*. Dissertation, Rostock, 1906.

Allen, Ned Bliss, *The Sources of Dryden's Comedies*. Ann Arbor, The University of Michigan Press, 1935.

Bader, Arno L., "The Italian Comedia dell' Arte in England, 1660-1700." Unpublished dissertation, The University of Michigan, 1932.

Baker, David Erskine, *Companion to the Playhouse*. 2 vols., London, 1764.

Beljame, Alexandre, *Le Public et les hommes de lettres en Angleterre au dix-huitième siècle*. Paris, 1883.

Bennewitz, Alex., *Molière's Einfluss auf Congreve*. Leipzig, 1889.

Bernbaum, Ernest, *The Drama of Sensibility*. Cambridge, Harvard University Press, 1925.

Biographica Britannica, 6 vols. in 7. London, 1747-66.

Borgman, A. S., *Thomas Shadwell, His Life and Comedies*. New York, The New York University Press, 1928.

Cambridge History of English Literature, the. 14 vols., New York, Putnam, 1907-17.

Charlanne, Louis, *L'Influence française en Angleterre au xvii° siècle*. Paris, 1906.

Churchill, George B., *The Country Wife and the Plain Dealer*. "Belles Lettres Series," Boston, 1924.

[Cibber, Colly], *An Apology for the Life of Colley Cibber, Written by Himself*. 2 vols., London, 1756.

Cibber, Mr. [Theophilus], and Other Hands, *The Lives of the Poets*. 5 vols., London, 1753.

Clark, A. F. B., *Boileau and the French Classical Critics in England (1660-1830)*. "Bibliotèque de la revue de littérature comparée," tome XIX. Paris, 1925.

Collier, Jeremy, *A Short View of the Immorality and Profaneness of the English Stage*. London, 1698.

Dametz, Max, *John Vanbrughs Leben und Werke*. "Wiener Beiträge zur Englischen Philologie," Band VII. Wien und Leipzig, 1892.

Davis, Joe Lee, "The 'Sons of Ben' in English Realistic Comedy, 1625-1642." Unpublished dissertation, The University of Michigan, 1934.

Dibdin, Charles A., *Complete History of the English Stage*. London, 1800.

Dictionary of National Biography. Ed. by Leslie Stephen and Sidney Lee. 66 vols., London, 1885-1901.

Dobrée, Bonamy, *Restoration Comedy, 1660-1720*. Oxford, At the Clarendon Press, 1924.

Downes, John, *Roscius Anglicanus*. London, 1708.

[Evelyn, John], *Diary and Correspondence of John Evelyn, F.R.S.* Ed. by William Bray. 4 vols., London, 1862-63.

Ferchlandt, Hans, *Molière's Misanthrop und seine englischen Nachahmungen.* Halle a.S., 1907.

[Fisher], Dorothea Frances Canfield, *Corneille and Racine in England.* New York, 1904.

Gardiner, Samuel R., *History of England from the Accession of James I to the Outbreak of the Civil War, 1603-1642.* 10 vols., London, 1884-86.

—— *History of the Great Civil War, 1642-49.* 3 vols., London, 1886-91.

Garnett, Richard, and Edmund Gosse, *An Illustrated History of English Literature.* 4 vols., New York, 1906.

Gaw, Allison, "Tuke's *Adventure of Five Hours* in Relation to the 'Spanish Plot' and to John Dryden." *Studies in English Drama,* University of Pennsylvania, 1917.

Genest, John, *Some Account of the English Stage from the Restoration in 1660 to 1830.* 10 vols., Bath, 1832.

Gildon, Charles, *The Lives and Characters of the English Dramatic Poets. . . First begun by Mr. Langbain.* London, [1698 or 1699].

Gillet, J. E., *Molière en Angleterre, 1660-1670.* "Mémoires de l'Académie Royale de Belgique," deuxième série, tome IX. Bruxelles, 1913.

Gosse, Sir Edmund, *Life of William Congreve.* Rev. ed., New York, 1924.

—— *Seventeenth Century Studies.* London, 1883.

—— "Sir George Etheredge. A Neglected Chapter of English Literature." *The Cornhill Magazine,* XLIII (1881), 284-304.

Hallam, Henry, *Introduction to the Literature of Europe.* 4 vols., London, 1837-39.

Hartmann, Carl, *Einfluss Molière's auf Dryden's komisch-dramatische Dichtungen.* Leipzig, 1885.

Harvey-Jellie, W., *Les Sources du théâtre anglais a l'époque de la restauration.* Paris, 1906.

Hazlitt, William, *Lectures on the English Comic Writers.* London, 1919.

Heinemann, Georg, *Shadwell-Studien.* Kiel, 1907.

Hickerson, William H., "The Significance of James Shirley's Realistic Plays in the History of English Comedy." Unpublished dissertation, The University of Michigan, 1932.

Humbert, Claas, *Englands Urtheil über Molière*. Bielefeld u. Leipzig, 1878.

—— *Molière in England*. Bielefeld, 1874.

Hunt, Leigh, *The Dramatic Works of Wycherley, Congreve, Vanbrugh and Farquhar*. London, 1840.

[Jacob, Giles], *The Poetical Register, etc.* 2 vols., London, 1723.

Johnson, Samuel, *Lives of the Poets*. Ed. by Birkbeck Hill. 3 vols., Oxford, 1905.

Kerby, W. Moseley, *Molière and the Restoration Comedy in England*. Rennes dissertation, privately printed, 1907.

Klette, Johannes, *William Wycherley's Leben und dramatische Werke*. Münster, 1883.

Krause, Hugo, *Wycherley und seine französischen Quellen*. Halle a.S., 1883.

Krutch, Joseph Wood, *Comedy and Conscience after the Restoration*. New York, Columbia University Press, 1924.

Langbaine, Gerard, *An Account of the English Dramatick Poets*. Oxford, 1691.

Legouis, Émile H., and Louis Cazamian, *A History of English Literature*. 2 vols., London, J. M. Dent and Sons, Ltd., 1926.

Lohr, Anton, *Richard Flecknoe: Eine literarhistorische Untersuchung*. Leipzig, 1905.

Lowe, Robert W., *Thomas Betterton*. New York, 1891.

Lynch, Kathleen M., *The Social Mode of Restoration Comedy*. "University of Michigan Publications, Language and Literature," Vol. III, 1926.

Macaulay, T. B., *The History of England from the Accession of James the Second*. 5 vols., London, 1849-61.

—— "Leigh Hunt." In *The Miscellaneous Works of Lord Macaulay*, Vol. V. Philadelphia, 1910.

Meindl, Vincenz, *Sir George Etheredge, sein Leben, seine Zeit und seine Dramen*. "Wiener Beiträge zur Englischen Philologie," Band XIV. Wien und Leipzig, 1901.

Miles, D. H., *The Influence of Molière on Restoration Comedy*. New York, 1910.

Mueschke, Paul, "Prototypes of Restoration Wits and Would-Bes in Ben Jonson's Realistic Comedy." Unpublished dissertation, The University of Michigan, 1929.

Mueschke, Paul, and Jeanette Fleischer, "A Re-Evaluation of Vanbrugh." *Publications of the Modern Language Association of America,* XLIX (1934), 848-89.

Nicoll, Allardyce, *A History of Restoration Drama, 1660-1700.* 2d ed.,
Cambridge, 1928.

——— "Political Plays of the Restoration." *Modern Language Review,*
XVI (1921), 224-42.

Noyes, Robert Gale, *Ben Jonson on the English Stage, 1660-1776.* Cambridge, Harvard University Press, 1935.

Ott, Philipp, *Über das Verhältniss des Lustspiel-Dichters Dryden zur
...Molière.* Landshut, 1887-88.

Palmer, John, *The Comedy of Manners.* London, 1913.

[Pepys, Samuel], *The Diary of Samuel Pepys.* Ed., with additions, by
H. B. Wheatley. 10 vols., London, 1893-99.

Perromat, Charles, *William Wycherley, sa vie, son oeuvre.* Paris,
1921.

Perry, Henry Ten Eyck, *The Comic Spirit in Restoration Drama.* New
Haven, Yale University Press, 1925.

Pinto, V. de Sola, *Sir Charles Sedley.* London, Constable and Company,
1927.

Quaas, Curt, *William Wycherley als Mensch und Dichter.* Rostock,
1907.

Reihmann, Oskar, *Thomas Shadwells Tragödie "The Libertine" und
ihr Verhältnis zu den vorausgehenden Bearbeitungen der Don Juan-
Saga.* Leipzig, 1904.

Rosenfeld, Sybil, *The Letterbook of Sir George Etherege.* Oxford and
London, 1928.

Sandmann, Paul, "Molière's *École des femmes* u. *Wycherley's Country
Wife." Archiv für das Studium der neuren Sprachen und Literaturen,*
LXXII (1884), 153-82.

——— "Molière, Wycherley u. Garrick." *Archiv für das Studium der
neuren Sprachen und Literaturen,* LXXVII (1887), 47-84.

Schmid, David, *George Farquhar, sein Leben und seine Original-
Dramen.* "Wiener Beiträge zur Englischen Philologie," Band XVIII.
Wien und Leipzig, 1904.

——— *William Congreve, sein Leben und seine Lustspiele.* "Wiener
Beiträge zur Englischen Philologie," Band VI. Wien und Leipzig,
1897.

[Shadwell, Thomas], *The Works of Thomas Shadwell, Esq.* 3 vols., London, 1720.

Taine, H., *Histoire de la littérature anglaise.* 8ᵉ ed. Paris, 1892.

Thackeray, W. M., "Congreve and Addison." In *The English Humourists of the Eighteenth Century.* New York, 1853.

Thorndike, A. H., *English Comedy.* New York, 1929.

Van Laun, Henri, "Les Plagiaires de Molière en Angleterre." *Le Moliériste,* II (1880-81); III (1881-82).

—— *The Dramatic Works of Molière Rendered into English.* 6 vols., Edinburgh, 1875-76.

Voltaire, François Marie Arouet de, *Lettres sur les Anglais.* In *Oeuvres complètes de Voltaire,* Vol. V. Paris, Chez Firmin Didot Frères, 1869.

Ward, A. W., *A History of English Dramatic Literature.* New and rev. ed., 3 vols., London, 1899.

Wernicke, Arth., *Das Verhältnis von John Lacy's The Dumb Lady ...zu Molière's Le Médecin malgré lui und L'Amour médecin.* Halle, 1903.

Wilson, John Harold, *The Influence of Beaumont and Fletcher on Restoration Drama.* "Ohio State University Studies in Languages and Literatures," No. IV. Columbus, The Ohio State University Press, 1928.

Wood, Paul Spencer, "Native Elements in English Neo-Classicism." *Modern Philology,* XXIV (1926), 201-8.

Wright, James, *Historia Histrionica: An Historical Account of the English Stage.* London, 1699.

[Wycherley, William], *The Posthumous Works of William Wycherley Esq.; in Prose and Verse.* London, 1728.

C: OTHER REFERENCES

Works not classified under the two previous heads are listed here if I have cited them in the text or if I feel any vague obligation to them for a suggestion or a point of view. The titles referring to Molière and those dealing with the principles of literary study are not presumed to be a bibliography of those subjects.

Addison, Joseph, and Richard Steele, *The Spectator.* 4 vols., London, 1853.

Arnold, Thomas, *A Manual of English Literature*. American ed., Boston, 1876.

Ashton, H., *A Preface to Molière*. New York, 1927.

Baldensperger, F., "Littérature comparée—le mot et la chose." *Revue de littérature comparée*, 1ʳᵉ année (Paris, 1921), pp. 1-29.

Bock, Nathan, *Molière's Amphitryon in Verhältnis zu seinen Vorgängern*. Marburg, 1887.

Campbell, Oscar James, *The Comedies of Holberg*. "Harvard Studies in Comparative Literature," No. III. Cambridge, 1914.

——— "Love's Labour's Lost Restudied." In *Studies in Shakespeare, Milton, and Donne*. "University of Michigan Publications, Language and Literature," Vol. I, 1925.

Chambers, E. K., *The Elizabethan Stage*. 4 vols., Oxford, 1923.

Chatfield-Taylor, Hobart, *Molière, a Biography*. New York, 1906.

Clark, Barrett H., *European Theories of the Drama*. Cincinnati, 1918.

Currier, T. F., and E. L. Gay, *Catalogue of the Molière Collection in Harvard College Library*. "Bibliographical Contributions. Library of Harvard University," No. 57. Cambridge, 1906.

Dodge, R. E. Neil, "A Sermon on Source-Hunting." *Modern Philology*, IX (1911-12), 211-23.

Doumic, René, *Histoire de la littérature française*. Paris, 1917.

Egan, M. F., "The Comparative Method in Literature." *Catholic University Bulletin*, IX (1903), 332-46.

Erdmann, H., *Molière's Psyché: Tragédie Ballet im Vergleich zu den ihr vorangehenden Bearbeitungen der Psyche-Saga*. Insterburg, 1892.

Faguet, E., *En lisant Molière*. Paris, 1914.

——— *Les Grandes Maîtres du 17ᵉ siècle, études littéraires et dramatiques*. Rev. ed., Paris, 1892.

Fleay, Frederick Gard, *A Chronicle History of the London Stage, 1559-1642*. London, 1890.

Fournel, Victor, *Les Contemporains de Molière*. 3 vols., Paris, 1863-75.

Gayley, C. M., "What Is Comparative Literature?" *Atlantic Monthly*, XCII (1903), 56-68.

Gendarme de Bévotte, Geo., *Le Festin de pierre avant Molière*. Textes publiés avec introduction, etc. Paris, 1907.

Gundelfinger [*pseud.* Gundolf], F., *Shakespeare und der deutsche Geist*. Berlin, 1920.

Humbert, Claas, *Molière, Shakespeare und die deutsche Kritik*. Leipzig, 1869.

Hurd, Richard, "Dissertation III, On Poetical Imitation." In *The Works of Richard Hurd* (8 vols., London, 1811), II, 109.

—— "Dissertation IV, On the Marks of Imitation." In *The Works of Richard Hurd* (8 vols., London, 1811), II, 245.

Jourdain, Eleanor F., *An Introduction to the French Classical Drama*. Oxford, Clarendon Press, 1912.

Kohler, Pierre, *Autour de Molière*. Paris, Payot, 1925.

Lancaster, Henry C., *A History of French Dramatic Literature in the Seventeenth Century*. 6 vols., Baltimore, The Johns Hopkins Press, 1929-36.

Lang, Andrew, "Molière." In *Encyclopaedia Britannica*, 11th ed., 1911.

Lanson, G., "Études sur les rapports de la littérature française...." *Revue d'histoire littéraire*, III (1896), 45-70.

Lucas, F. E., *Seneca and Elizabethan Tragedy*. Cambridge, 1922.

Manzius, Karl, *Molière, les théâtres, le public et les comédiens de son temps*. Traduit du danois par M. Pellison. Paris, 1908.

Marsh, A. R., "The Comparative Study of Literature." *Publications of the Modern Language Association of America*, XI (1906), 151-70.

Mather, F. J., "Aspects of Comparative Literature." *The Nation*, LXXXII (1906), 256-57.

Matthews, Brander, *Molière, His Life and His Works*. New York, Scribners, 1926.

Meredith, George, "Essay on the Idea of Comedy and of the Uses of the Comic Spirit." In *The Works of George Meredith*, Vol. XXIII. Memorial Edition. London, 1910.

Moland, Louis, *Molière, sa vie et ses ouvrages*. Paris, 1887.

—— *Molière et la comédie italienne*. Paris, 1867.

Moliériste, Le. Revue mensuelle. Paris, 1879-88.

Monval, Georges, *Chronologie Moliéresque*. Paris, 1897.

Morize, André, *Problems and Methods of Literary History*. Boston, 1922.

Morley, Henry, *A Manual of English Literature*. Rev. by Moses Coit Taylor. New York, 1879.

Oliphant, E. H. C., "How Not to Play the Game of Parallels." *Journal of English and Germanic Philology*, XXVIII (1929), 1-15.

Palmer, John, *Molière, His Life and Works*. London, G. Bell and Sons Ltd., 1930.

Plautus with an English Translation by Paul Nixon. "The Loeb Classical Library," 5 vols., New York and London, 1916.

Posnett, H. M., "The Science of Comparative Literature." *Contemporary Review*, LXXIX (1901), 855-72.

Price, L. M., *English-German Literary Influences. Bibliography and Survey*. Berkeley, 1919-20.

Renard, Georges, *La Methode scientifique de l'histoire littéraire*. Paris, 1900.

Routh, H. V., "The Future of Comparative Literature." *Modern Language Review*, VIII (1913), 1-14.

[Scott, *Sir* Walter], *the Prose Works of Sir Walter Scott*. 28 vols., Edinburgh, 1834.

Smith, Winifred, "Italian and Elizabethan Comedy." *Modern Philology*, V (1908), 555-67.

—— *The Commedia dell' Arte*. New York, 1912.

Stoll, E. E., "Certain Fallacies and Irrelevancies in Literary Scholarship." *Studies in Philology*, XXIV (1927), 485-508.

Terence with an English Translation by John Sargeaunt. "The Loeb Classical Library," 2 vols., London, 1912.

Tilley, Arthur, *Molière*. Cambridge, University Press, 1921.

Toldo, Pietro, *L'Oeuvre de Molière et sa fortune en Italie*. Turin, 1910.

Van Tieghem, Paul, *La Littérature comparée*. Paris, Librarie Armand Colin, 1931.

INDEX